THE THIRD WORLD

OPPOSING
VIEWPOINTS

Other Books of Related Interest in the Opposing Viewpoints Series:

American Foreign Policy
Central America
China
The Environmental Crisis
Israel
Japan
Latin America & U.S. Foreign Policy
The Middle East
Problems of Africa
The Soviet Union
The Superpowers: A New Detente
Terrorism
The Vietnam War

Additional Books in the Opposing Viewpoints Series:

Abortion
AIDS
American Government
American Values
America's Elections
America's Prisons
Animal Rights
Biomedical Ethics
Censorship
Chemical Dependency
Civil Liberties
Constructing a Life Philosophy
Crime and Criminals
Criminal Justice
Death and Dying
The Death Penalty
Drug Abuse
Economics in America
Euthanasia
The Health Crisis
Male/Female Roles
The Mass Media
Nuclear War
The Political Spectrum
Poverty
Religion in America
Science & Religion
Sexual Values
Social Justice
Teenage Sexuality
War and Human Nature

THE THIRD WORLD

OPPOSING VIEWPOINTS

David L. Bender & Bruno Leone, *Series Editors*

Janelle Rohr, *Book Editor*

OPPOSING VIEWPOINTS SERIES ®

Greenhaven Press, Inc.   PO Box 289009   San Diego, CA 92128-9009

330.9172
Thi

Library of Congress Cataloging-in-Publication Data

The Third World : opposing viewpoints / Janelle Rohr, book editor.
   p.   cm. — (Opposing viewpoints series)
   Includes bibliographical references.
   Summary: Presents opposing viewpoints on various economic, social, and humanitarian issues involving the developing countries of the Third World.
   ISBN 0-89908-422-2 (pbk.). — ISBN 0-89908-447-8 (lib. bdg.)
   1. Developing countries—Economic conditions. 2. Developing countries—Economic policy 3. Human rights—Developing countries. 4. Economic assistance—Developing countries. 5. Debt relief—Developing countries. [1. Developing countries.] I. Rohr, Janelle, 1963-   . II. Series.
HC59.7.T4547 1989
330.9172'4—dc20   89-36524

1. Underdeveloped areas - Economic conditions,   CIP
2. Underdeveloped areas - Economic policy .   AC
3. Human rights - Underdeveloped areas.
4. Economic assistance - Underdeveloped areas.
I. Series.

"Congress shall make no law . . .
abridging the freedom of speech,
or of the press."

First Amendment to the US Constitution

The basic foundation of our democracy is the first amendment
guarantee of freedom of expression. The *Opposing Viewpoints Series*
is dedicated to the concept of this basic freedom and the idea that
it is more important to practice it than to enshrine it.

Contents

Chapter 5: How Can Third World Debt Be Reduced?

Why Consider Opposing Viewpoints?

"It is better to debate a question without settling it than to settle a question without debating it."

Joseph Joubert (1754-1824)

The Importance of Examining Opposing Viewpoints

The purpose of the Opposing Viewpoints books, and this book in particular, is to present balanced, and often difficult to find, opposing points of view on complex and sensitive issues.

Probably the best way to become informed is to analyze the positions of those who are regarded as experts and well studied on issues. It is important to consider every variety of opinion in an attempt to determine the truth. Opinions from the mainstream of society should be examined. But also important are opinions that are considered radical, reactionary, or minority as well as those stigmatized by some other uncomplimentary label. An important lesson of history is the eventual acceptance of many unpopular and even despised opinions. The ideas of Socrates, Jesus, and Galileo are good examples of this.

Readers will approach this book with their own opinions on the issues debated within it. However, to have a good grasp of one's own viewpoint, it is necessary to understand the arguments of those with whom one disagrees. It can be said that those who do not completely understand their adversary's point of view do not fully understand their own.

A persuasive case for considering opposing viewpoints has been presented by John Stuart Mill in his work *On Liberty*. When examining controversial issues it may be helpful to reflect on this suggestion:

> The only way in which a human being can make some approach to knowing the whole of a subject, is by hearing what can be said about it by persons of every variety of opinion, and studying all modes in which it can be looked at by every character of mind. No wise man ever acquired his wisdom in any mode but this.

Analyzing Sources of Information

The Opposing Viewpoints books include diverse materials taken from magazines, journals, books, and newspapers, as well as statements and position papers from a wide range of individuals, organizations and governments. This broad spectrum of sources helps to develop patterns of thinking which are open to the consideration of a variety of opinions.

Pitfalls To Avoid

A pitfall to avoid in considering opposing points of view is that of regarding one's own opinion as being common sense and the most rational stance and the point of view of others as being only opinion and naturally wrong. It may be that another's opinion is correct and one's own is in error.

Another pitfall to avoid is that of closing one's mind to the opinions of those with whom one disagrees. The best way to approach a dialogue is to make one's primary purpose that of understanding the mind and arguments of the other person and not that of enlightening him or her with one's own solutions. More can be learned by listening than speaking.

It is my hope that after reading this book the reader will have a deeper understanding of the issues debated and will appreciate the complexity of even seemingly simple issues on which good and honest people disagree. This awareness is particularly important in a democratic society such as ours where people enter into public debate to determine the common good. Those with whom one disagrees should not necessarily be regarded as enemies, but perhaps simply as people who suggest different paths to a common goal.

Developing Basic Reading and Thinking Skills

In this book carefully edited opposing viewpoints are purposely placed back to back to create a running debate; each viewpoint is preceded by a short quotation that best expresses the author's main argument. This format instantly plunges the reader into the midst of a controversial issue and greatly aids that reader in mastering the basic skill of recognizing an author's point of view.

A number of basic skills for critical thinking are practiced in the activities that appear throughout the books in the series. Some of the skills are:

Evaluating Sources of Information   The ability to choose from among alternative sources the most reliable and accurate source in relation to a given subject.

Separating Fact from Opinion   The ability to make the basic distinction between factual statements (those that can be demonstrated or verified empirically) and statements of opinion (those that are beliefs or attitudes that cannot be proved).

Identifying Stereotypes The ability to identify oversimplified, exaggerated descriptions (favorable or unfavorable) about people and insulting statements about racial, religious or national groups, based upon misinformation or lack of information.

Recognizing Ethnocentrism   The ability to recognize attitudes or opinions that express the view that one's own race, culture, or group is inherently superior, or those attitudes that judge another culture or group in terms of one's own.

It is important to consider opposing viewpoints and equally important to be able to critically analyze those viewpoints. The activities in this book are designed to help the reader master these thinking skills. Statements are taken from the book's viewpoints and the reader is asked to analyze them. This technique aids the reader in developing skills that not only can be applied to the viewpoints in this book, but also to situations where opinionated spokespersons comment on controversial issues. Although the activities are helpful to the solitary reader, they are most useful when the reader can benefit from the interaction of group discussion.

Using this book and others in the series should help readers develop basic reading and thinking skills. These skills should improve the readers' ability to understand what they read. Readers should be better able to separate fact from opinion, substance from rhetoric and become better consumers of information in our media-centered culture.

This volume of the Opposing Viewpoints books does not advocate a particular point of view. Quite the contrary! The very nature of the book leaves it to the reader to formulate the opinions he or she finds most suitable. My purpose as publisher is to see that this is made possible by offering a wide range of viewpoints which are fairly presented.

David L. Bender
Publisher

11

Introduction

"People can't listen to suggestions by people from another world. They want to take advice from someone with their own background."

—G.K. Ikiara, quoted in *Psychology Today*, December 1986.

The 1980 movie *The Gods Must Be Crazy* humorously portrays the impact a Coke bottle, a symbol of Western technology, could have on a remote African tribe of bushpeople. The bottle falls from a passing airplane and a member of the tribe picks it up. He brings the unfamiliar object to his village, where the people are delighted by it. They discuss it and use it as a toy and cooking implement. But the bottle soon causes discord. The villagers begin fighting over it and discover it can also be used to hit each other. The bushman decides the gods must have been crazy to drop in his midst an object that could do such harm. He embarks on a journey to return it to the gods. The movie effectively dramatizes the impact a single Western object could have on the people of the Third World.

Today's Third World has been inundated with objects from the US, Western Europe, and the Soviet Union, ranging from machinery to movies. These nations have sent technology and invested capital in an effort to help poorer nations improve their economies and standards of living. But like the Coke bottle, outside help has been a double-edged sword. In many cases, it has challenged cherished cultural traditions and raised the question of whether the Third World must abandon its traditions to develop economically.

When economists began examining the problem of Third World development in the 1950s, many agreed with W.W. Rostow, an influential economic historian. Rostow developed theories of economic development which were applied to the Third World. He had studied how Western European countries, the US, and Japan had built strong economies. He argued that these countries developed new technology and production methods, even when doing so eliminated traditional, but less efficient ways of producing goods. As a result, Rostow wrote, these countries' economies boomed. Those who agreed with his theories believed Rostow had illustrated the cause of and solution to Third World poverty.

Instead of using efficient machines, people in the Third World were still using human labor. Third World countries could overcome poverty by taking advantage of Western technology and adopting more efficient, cost-effective ways of producing goods. The Third World then could sell more products, earn money, and eventually become as prosperous as Europe, the US, and Japan. Thus, the 1950s and 1960s were marked by ambitious development projects that used technology and Western aid. Experts hoped that this technology would modernize and bring prosperity to the Third World.

Trying to develop countries based on the West's experiences created a disturbing side-effect, however. The changes wrought by modernization programs disrupted the lives of many Third World people. In Iran, for example, tractors were imported in an effort to speed agricultural development. But these expensive machines were not suited to Iran's farmers, who were peasants with small plots of land, according to Iranian scholar and political activist Jalal Al-I Ahmad. Ahmad writes, "Go see what a graveyard for scrapped tractors the country's farmlands have become—where there are no repair stations to maintain them, no open horizons or open lands to use them on, and no highways to take them to town for repair." In addition, farm technology replaced laborers and caused massive unemployment. "The people of a village are out of work at least three months of the year and exposed to cold, floods, drought, and locusts," Ahmad observed. As a result, unemployed people in Iran and other countries migrated to overcrowded Third World cities, which were incapable of providing the new arrivals with jobs and shelter.

Examples like this one of useless and harmful projects convinced many experts that development efforts had to integrate Third World culture rather than ignore it. One of the originators of this approach was E.F. Schumacher, a British economist. In his 1973 book, *Small Is Beautiful: Economics as if People Mattered*, he argued that development agencies had to consider how aid and technology would affect rural villagers—the majority of the Third World poor. He maintained that current efforts to send technology created unemployment, forced people to migrate to cities, and replaced cultural traditions. Schumacher advocated instead sending technology appropriate to conditions in the Third World. Such technology would use unskilled laborers, be designed for rural areas, and build on techniques already used by the villagers. He believed that if development could be made more appropriate, it would "reach down to the heartland of world poverty, to two million villagers. . . . If the rural people of the developing countries are helped to help themselves, I have no doubt that a genuine development will ensue, without vast shanty towns and misery belts around every big city." Schumacher and others believed this new approach would truly help the Third World develop, not hinder it.

But Schumacher's theories, like Rostow's, have not eliminated Third World poverty. And as the world becomes more interconnected and modern, the Third World is rapidly losing the option of remaining aloof and culturally isolated. Unlike the fictional bushman in *The Gods Must Be Crazy*, it cannot simply throw back the Coke bottle.

Ultimately, Third World nations must choose the path they wish to follow—emulate the West, maintain their traditions, or find some middle route combining modernization and tradition. Among such a diverse group of nations, the choices they make will be diverse also. *Third World: Opposing Viewpoints* examines several issues raised by economic and cultural changes in the Third World. The questions probed are: Why Is the Third World Poor? Why Are Human Rights Threatened in the Third World? Does US Foreign Aid Benefit the Third World? What Policies Would Promote Third World Development? How Can Third World Debt Be Reduced? As the Third World receives machines, money, movies, and other items from the West, clearly the issues raised by modernization will remain pertinent and contentious.

Why Is the
Third World Poor?

Chapter Preface

The discrepancies in wealth between Western industrialized nations and less-developed countries are striking. Seventy percent of the people in the world are poor, and most of those people live in the Third World. While per capita income in the US is $13,451 per year and in France is $10,260 per year, in the African country of Burkina Faso it is only $150 per year. Life expectancy in most industrialized nations ranges from sixty-five to seventy years; in some Third World nations such as Bangladesh and Burundi, few people can expect to live to be fifty years old. And while the literacy rate in most Western nations is reported to be 97 to 99 percent, few Third World nations have reached such levels. Pakistan's literacy rate is 26 percent and Honduras's rate is 56 percent. Another frequent measure of a country's welfare is its infant mortality rate, which is measured by determining the number of stillborn babies per 1000 live babies. Sweden's infant mortality rate is 3.3, Great Britain's is 10, while Kenya's rate is 63, Peru's rate is 82, and Mali's rate is 173.

Why are so many people in the Third World still mired in poverty and disease while many people in the West enjoy prosperity? The following chapter presents several answers to this question.

*"Third World nations are impoverished...
because of the highly unnatural things
imperialism has been doing to them."*

Imperialism Causes
Third World Poverty

Michael Parenti

In the following viewpoint, Michael Parenti writes that Third
World nations are poor because Western imperialism has exploited
their resources and economies. Seeking to enrich themselves,
American and European capitalists have been extracting the Third
World's natural resources and treating its workers as slave
laborers, Parenti believes. He concludes that Western prosperity
was built on the exploitation of the Third World. A well-known
activist and author, Parenti's books include *Power and the Powerless,
Inventing Reality: The Politics of the Mass Media,* and *The Sword and
the Dollar: Imperialism, Revolution, and the Arms Race.*

As you read, consider the following questions:

1. What does the author believe motivates capitalists?
2. Why do US companies invest in the Third World,
   according to Parenti?
3. Why does Parenti argue that it is misleading to say the
   Third World is underdeveloped?

W e in the United States live in a capitalist society, and this fact has significance not only for us but for the rest of the world. So let us take a moment to dwell upon the nature of capitalism. The essence of the capitalist system is the accumulation of capital, the making of profits in order to invest and make still more profits. The first law of capitalism is: make a profit off the labor of others or go out of business. And the best way to accumulate capital is not to work hard but to get others to work hard for you. Private gain, not social need, is the central imperative of our economic system. As an erstwhile chairman of Castle and Cooke put it: "We are in the business of making a profit. We are not in business primarily to satisfy society. We're not going to satisfy society very long if we go out of business. So profits are the number-one consideration." . . .

Grow or Die

A capitalist economy is an unplanned and competitive one in which security is guaranteed to no one, not even the corporate giants. A corporation searches for security by increasing its hold over resources, developing new technologies (through the application of mental and physical labor), searching out cheaper labor markets, getting government to subsidize everything from production to exports, capturing a competitor's market, merging with other companies, devising new sales networks and techniques, and the like. The problem is that all the other big companies are doing the same thing. So not even the giant corporations can rest secure for very long.

Grow or die: that's the unwritten rule. To stand still amidst the growth of competitors is to decline, not only relatively but absolutely, causing a firm's financial structure to collapse. The dynamics of a market economy—the accumulation of profit and the need to invest surplus capital, the demand for strategic overseas materials and new markets, the fluctuations in consumer spending, the instabilities of old markets, the threat of recession and depression, the pressures of domestic and foreign competition—all these things force corporations into a restless, endless drive to expand, compelling them to gather as much strength as they can. Those ecologists who dream of a "no-growth capitalism," better to preserve the environment, do not seem to realize that the concept is an oxymoron.

I once heard a corporate executive explain why his company was expanding overseas: he noted that the regional firms in New England that years ago decided not to pursue *national* markets are now extinct. He could not even recall their names. The same fate awaits those companies that today do not go *international*, he concluded. Whether it really is all that drastic, the point remains that the history of capitalism is a history of expansion from local to regional to national to international arenas. About 140 years ago, Marx and Engels noted the phenomenon, describing a bourgeoisie that "chases . . . over the whole surface of the globe. It must nestle everywhere, settle everywhere, establish connections everywhere." Given its expansionist nature, capitalism can never stay home.

Investing in the Third World

The attractions of Third World investments are evident: a relative lack of competition, a vast cheap labor pool, the absence or near absence of environmental and safety regulations and corporate taxes, and the opportunity to market products at monopoly prices. As the practical limitations of investments are reached in one country and the margin of profit narrows, outlets are sought in other less advantaged and more vulnerable lands. As Harry Magdoff states:

> What matters to the business community, and to the business system as a whole, is that the option of foreign investment (and foreign trade) should remain available. For this to be meaningful, the business system requires, as a minimum, that the political and economic principles of capitalism should prevail and that the door be fully open for foreign capital at all times. Even more, it seeks a privileged open door for the capital of the home country in preference to capital from competing industrial nations.

The quality of products and services, the safety of commodities, the protection of the natural environment, the conditions supportive of community life and human development, the opportunity to do gratifying and socially useful work, the care of the vulnerable and handicapped, in sum, a whole range of values that might be basic to human happiness, are considered in the capitalist mode of production, if at all, only to the extent they advance or retard pecuniary gain. . . .

Apologists of Imperialism

Life is continually confirming that however much the apologists of imperialism try to present the American monopolies as the apostles of progress, the peoples are realising ever more clearly where the danger for their independent development comes from. Foreign monopolies, above all American ones, are ready to sacrifice entire nations if this will bring them additional profits.

V.D. Shchetinin, *US Monopolies and Developing Countries*, 1986.

For some 500 years the nations of Western Europe, and later North America, plundered the wealth of Asia, Africa, and Latin America. *This forceful expropriation of one country's land, labor, markets, and resources by another is what is here meant by im-*

perialism. Imperialism is of course older than capitalism. Neither Alexander the Great, nor the emperors of Rome, nor the Spanish conquistadores were capitalists. They did not systematically accumulate capital through the rationalized exploitation of free labor and the expansion of private markets. But these earlier plunderers all had one thing in common with capitalists: the desire to expropriate the wealth of other peoples' land and labor. They were all imperialists. Capitalist imperialism differs from these earlier forms in the systematic ways it invests in other countries and shapes the productive forces, penetrates the markets, and transforms the economies and cultures of the colonized nations, integrating their financial structures and trade into an international system for the extraction of wealth.

When the merchant capitalists replaced the mercantilist monarchs, the process of expropriation accelerated and expanded. Along with gold and silver, they took flax, hemp, indigo, silk, diamonds, timber, molasses, sugar, rum, rubber, tobacco, calico, cocoa, coffee, cotton, copper, coal, tin, iron, and later on, oil, zinc, columbite, manganese, mercury, platinum, cobalt, bauxite, aluminum, and uranium. And of course there was that most dreadful of all expropriations—of human beings themselves—slaves. Millions of people were abducted from Africa, while millions more perished in the hellish passage to the New World.

Rich Nations, Poor People

The stupendous fortunes that were—and still are being—extracted by the European and North American investors should remind us that there are very few really poor nations in what today is commonly called the Third World. Brazil is rich; Indonesia is rich; and so are the Philippines, Chile, Bolivia, Zaire, Mexico, India, and Malaysia. Only the people are poor. Of course in some areas, as in parts of Africa south of the Sahara, the land has been so ruthlessly plundered that it too is now impoverished, making life all the more desperate for its inhabitants.

In a word, the Third World is not "underdeveloped" but overexploited. The gap between rich and poor nations is not due to the "neglect" of the latter by the former as has been often claimed. For forty years or more we have heard how the nations of the North must help close the poverty gap between themselves and the nations of the South, devoting some portion of their technology and capital to the task. Yet the gap between rich and poor only widens because investments in the Third World are not designed to develop the capital resources of the poor nations but to enrich the Western investors.

From 1970 to 1980, the flow of investment capital from the United States to the Third World amounted to about $8 billion. But the return flow from the Third World to the United States in the form of dividends, interest, branch profits, management fees, and royalties was $63.7 billion. Together, all the multinational corporations and banks in the world take as much as $200 billion every year from the Third World nations. Nor should this come as a surprise since, as we already noted, the first rule of capitalism is that sooner or later more must be taken out than put into any business venture. Why else would companies and banks invest, except to make more than they started with?

The Costs of Colonialism

Third World nations would have been only too grateful if they could have escaped the attentions of the Western self-enriching nations that exploited them throughout their history. Consider India: As late as 1815, India exported 1.3 million British pounds of textile goods to Britain and imported only 26,000 British pounds from that country. But Britain placed prohibitive tariffs on Indian imports, and used its armies and gunboats in India to prevent that country from taking retaliatory protective measures. By 1830 the trade balance was reversed. As British textile goods flooded India, Indian industrial centers like Dacca fell into decay, and Indian weavers, spinners, and metal workers were driven out of business.

Intrinsically Unjust

Capitalism used painful methods, including slavery and piracy and the sacking of America, to produce the wealth that enabled it to initiate its adventures. After 400 years of development of capitalism, its growth rate is something that the socialist countries cannot hope to match. Socialist countries look for justice. Socialism began with many errors but not as many as did capitalism. . . .

Inefficiency is something we can fix. Injustice is more difficult to change. Capitalism is intrinsically unjust.

Patricio Halco, *The New York Times*, January 24, 1989.

But "you cannot continue to inundate a country with your manufactures, unless you enable it to give you some produce in return," observed Marx. Only then will it have some funds to purchase the finished goods dumped on its markets. Thus, to complete the imperialistic relationship, Britain promoted the large-scale production of agricultural raw materials in India, especially cotton plantations. Hence, writes Ernest Mandel, "a people who formerly had exported cotton goods to all parts of the world now exported only raw cotton to be worked up in Britain and sent back to India as textile goods!" Yet India's earnings from this arrangement proved insufficient and by 1853 India had accumulated a national debt of 53 million British pounds. This was financed from the labor of the common people and had an additionally regressive effect upon the economy. From 1850 to 1900, India's per capita income dropped by almost two-thirds. India was forced deeper into poverty and denied the opportunity of its own development so that it might serve as a provider for British capitalism. . . .

Neither Primitive Nor Underdeveloped

Africa has been one of the lands most often misrepresented as "primitive" and "underdeveloped" by imperialism's image makers. The truth is, as early as the 1400s, Nigeria, Mali, and the Guinea coast were making some of the world's finest fabrics and leathers. Katanga, Zambia, and Sierra Leone produced copper and iron, while Benin had a brass and bronze industry. As early as the thirteenth century, finely illuminated books and manuscripts were part of the Amharic culture of Ethiopia, and impressive stone palaces stood in Zimbabwe. Yet Africa under colonial rule soon was exporting raw materials and importing manufactured goods from Europe, like other colonized places.

The advantages Europeans possessed in seafaring and warfare proved decisive. "West Africans had developed metal casting to a fine artistic perfection in many parts of Nigeria, but when it came to the meeting with Europe, beautiful bronzes were far less relevant than the crudest cannon." Arms superiority also allowed the Europeans to impose a slave trade that decimated certain parts of Africa, set African leaders against each other in the procurement of slaves, and further retarded that continent's economic development.

Attempts by African leaders at development, including the area of arms technology, were suppressed by the British, French, and other colonizers. From the seventeenth to the twentieth centuries, Europe imposed imperialist trade relationships, forcing Africa to sell its raw materials and buy manufactured goods on increasingly disadvantageous terms. As Walter Rodney points out: "There was no objective economic law which determined that primary produce should be worth so little. Indeed, the [Western capitalist] countries sold certain raw materials like timber and wheat at much higher prices than a colony could command. The explanation is that the unequal exchange was forced upon Africa by the political and military supremacy of the colonizers."

The investors exploit not only the Third World's land and natural resources but also its labor. United Brand, Standard Fruit, Del Monte, and Cargill no doubt are in El Salvador for the sugar, bananas, and other such agribusiness export products. But they, along with Alcoa, USX, Westinghouse, Phelps-Dodge, American Standard, Pillsbury, Proctor & Gamble, Chase Manhattan Bank, Bank of America, First National Bank, Standard Oil of New Jersey,

Gary Huck. Reprinted with permission.

Texaco, and at least twenty other major companies, are in that tiny country also for the cheap labor. They reap enormous profits by paying Salvadoran workers subsistence wages to produce everything from aluminum products and baking powder to computers and steel pipes—almost all for export markets.

If Third World nations are impoverished, then, it is not because of their climate or culture or national temperament or some other "natural condition" but because of the highly unnatural things imperialism has been doing to them. It is not because they have lacked natural wealth and industries but, quite the contrary, because the plenitude of their resources proved so inviting to the foreign pillagers, and the strength of their industries so troublesomely competitive to foreign industrialists. . . .

Observing the Lever House on New York's fashionable Park Avenue, W. Alpheus Hunton mused: "You look at this tall, striking glass and steel structure and you wonder how many hours of underpaid Black labor and how many thousands of tons of underpriced palm oil and peanuts and cocoa it cost to build it." Hunton's comment graphically makes the point: Third World poverty and multinational industrial wealth are directly linked to each other. The large companies invest not to uplift impoverished countries but to enrich themselves, taking far more out than they ever put in.

Overexploited and Maldeveloped

Publications on both the Right and the Left, along with the United Nations itself, describe the Third World as composed of "developing" countries. This terminology creates the misleading impression that these countries are escaping from Western economic exploitation and emerging from their impoverishment. In fact, most of them are becoming *more* impoverished. Third World nations are neither "underdeveloped" nor "developing"; they are overexploited and maldeveloped.

24

"The Third World's poorest countries are not those that have had longer and closer exchanges with the West, but, significantly, those whose exchanges had been weaker and shorter."

Imperialism Does Not Cause Third World Poverty

Carlos Rangel

Carlos Rangel is a Venezuelan journalist. In the following viewpoint, excerpted from his book *Third World Ideology and Western Reality*, Rangel argues that blaming imperialism for Third World poverty is wrong. According to Rangel, those countries that had the most contact with European and American imperialists are now the most prosperous. Europe's spectacular prosperity, a result of capitalism, has long provided a model for impoverished nations to follow, he concludes.

As you read, consider the following questions:

1. Why are Third World nations in debt, in Rangel's opinion?
2. What point does Rangel make by discussing Napoleon Bonaparte's invasion of Egypt?
3. How has contact with the West helped the Third World, according to the author?

The charges against capitalism and its influence upon the Third World are, in synthesis, that poor countries today are worse off than ever before, or even that they were once in a state of near perfect social harmony and economic equilibrium, having lost this bliss entirely because of the complementarity that the imperialist countries have forced on them. In other words, the developed world is rich because the underdeveloped world is poor, and vice versa. We would witness a general situation in which the progress of some countries compared to other countries, but also the backwardness of the latter in opposition to the former, would be essentially explained by the reciprocal effect of the economic, cultural, and political exchanges between the advanced on the one hand and the backward on the other. Thus the links between all regions of the globe, established for the first time by capitalism, are held by the Third World ideology to have been exclusively advantageous for the capitalist centers, and exclusively detrimental to the peripheries; if those links had never been established, England perhaps would be as backward as India, or India as advanced as England, or both would have a comparable degree of prosperity, inferior to present day England, but superior to present day India.

To achieve the process by which they become and remain rich at the expense of others, the imperial countries would have deliberately degraded Third World countries and falsely persuaded them of their intrinsic inferiority. Through this clever Western trick, the consequences of imperialist exploitation, evident in the inequality of nations, could be attributed to that supposed inferiority and not to the true cause which is imperial exploitation, first through colonialism and more recently through neocolonialism and dependency.

False Allegations

All these allegations, fundamental to the Third World ideology, are false in general and false in each aspect. The Third World's poorest countries are not those that have had longer and closer exchanges with the West, but, significantly, those whose exchanges had been weaker and shorter—Ethiopia, for instance. Until 1935, when it was invaded by fascist Italy, Ethiopia had never suffered Western contacts other than the passing through of some European eccentrics searching for the sources of the Nile. There was, it is true, a British expedition (1867-68) to rescue some of those explorers held prisoner by Emperor Theodore, a military display which, its mission accomplished, turned its heels and went home. And there was a first Italian attempt at invasion (in 1896) so ragged that it was easily rejected by the Ethiopians.

The appalling poverty and backwardness of Ethiopia continue unabated or worse. These conditions—although it is no longer fashionable to recall them, since that country has now fallen into the Soviet orbit—therefore owe nothing to Western influence. In sharp contrast is Nigeria, where, prior to 1890, there was no cultivation of cocoa, peanuts or cotton. Due to the British development and commercialization of their cultivation, however, Nigeria today exports an enormous proportion of the world supply of these products. Another example, among many, is what occurred in Malaya (today part of Malaysia), which, at the end of the nineteenth century, remained a wretchedly sparsely populated territory, where practically the only economic activity was fishing by primitive methods. By the time it achieved independence in 1963 (in federation with Singapore, Sarawak, and Borneo), Malaya had become a prosperous and populous nation due to the British colonial administrations' introduction of the cultivation of rubber.

Little Evidence

There is little evidence to sustain the claim that Western imperialist powers sought and were able to impede, dismantle, or hamper the growth of native industries, making it impossible for local, self-supporting industrialization to get underway. . . .

Western capitalist competition, for instance, has often been charged with having forcibly terminated the Turkish, Middle Eastern, and Indian crafted textiles. Overlooked is the fact that Western cotton factories clothed the average Indian peasant far better than had the high-cost native handicraftsmen.

Lewis Feuer, *Imperialism and the Anti-Imperialist Mind*, 1986.

The Third World ideology reflects in terms of current world politics a very old fallacy present in all of the reincarnations of the socialist animus: the conviction that enrichment by fair means and personal or national virtues is just not possible, so that the wealth of an individual or community cannot be in any way the just result of their special and honest efforts and ingenuity, but must have been confiscated from others, who consequently must suffer a degree of impoverishment equivalent to the prosperity of their exploiters. With reference to this fallacy, the tyrants of several of the new African states unleashed a vast repression of ethnic minorities, mainly Indians, who had achieved—thanks to their diligence and capacity as tradesmen and artisans—relative prosperity compared to that of the Black populations. The ruin and expulsion of these minorities, carried out for example by Idi Amin Dada in Uganda under the allegation that they had prospered by exploiting and robbing the Black population, caused suffering and impoverishment not only among these "colored Jews," but also among the native Ugandans. In fact, Uganda remains even today an example of wretched poverty and mass suffering, clearly caused not by the colonial relationship but by its termination. . . .

Foreign Debt

Another war horse of the Third World ideology is the foreign debt of Asia, Africa and Latin America, regarded somehow as perversely inflicted on those countries by the United States, Great Britain, France, Germany, Switzerland, etc., when obviously the origin of that debt was the transference of real resources from lending to borrowing countries, under conditions frequently more advantageous both in installments and interest rates than those prevailing in the international financial markets. The thesis is just short of ridiculous that private Western and Japanese banks (but also the World Bank and the International Monetary Fund) meant to harm the Third World with their loans. But it is less surprising that that argument be put forward and be taken seriously if we realized that for radical Third World ideologists, even outright grants by the West to the Third World are harmful, since they maintain dependency and postpone the magical day of the final and irreversible split with imperialism.

Viewing the foreign debt of the Third World objectively, it is evident that the incapacity of certain countries to productively use the immense real resources that have been transferred to them from the advanced capitalist countries since 1945, is another symptom among many that reveals the typical ineptitude and large scale corruption of the majority of the Third World governments. The bankers' inexcusable sin was to lend such astronomical sums to such unworthy borrowers. Just as in the previously mentioned fallacy according to which there can be no just enrichment, and neither individual nor collective prosperity would be feasible except by despoiling others, there also exists with equal tenacity the natural resentment of debtors against lenders. Typically, a fool who has mortgaged his house to invest in an unprofitable business to gamble, without thinking of the due date of the loan, will say upon losing his house that the bank robbed him. In the case of nation-states, the private banks or the international credit agencies do not have the possibility of "foreclosing the mortgages," and paradoxically have to worry a great deal more than the debtor governments over conditions of virtual bankruptcy caused by the same perversity as that of the fool who mortgaged his house. . . .

Recognizing Inequalities

It has been only very recently that the idea arose that the inequalities in wealth and poverty between nations are an intolerable scandal. All factors that gave rise to this new attitude are of Western origin: the contact between cultures by geographic exploration; the conquest and colonization by Europeans of non-Western territories; the advance in communications that has

28

forged the world (not excluding the Socialist countries) into a single community, where everyone has information about how others live; the demonstration by capitalist social and economic development, more pronounced in some areas of the world community, that poverty, disease, ignorance and extreme social inequalities are not the ineluctable destiny of humanity; and the social tension generated by modernization.

The Problems of the Real World

To explain the disasters, repression, corruption, nepotism, and stagnation that ravage the Southern hemisphere, the key concept of *neocolonialism* is invoked. . . . Is poverty spreading like wildfire? This, of course, is because of the shameful pillage committed by multinational corporations. French colonialists, American imperialists, English overlords, and Dutch, German, and Swiss businessmen are invoked to explain illiteracy, epidemics, wars, falling standards of living, and the despotism of peoples' new leaders. . . . Instead of taking reality into account, instead of looking for causal relationships, far-off causations that pardon the states in the tropics are preferred. Thus, neocolonialism is the universal sin that becomes a way of permanently dismissing the problems of the real world.

Pascal Bruckner, *The Tears of the White Man*, 1986.

A certain degree of Third World misery has been caused by the West in this way, without a doubt. Not material poverty, which was much greater before, but rather the painful consciousness of a vast and widening gap between rich and poor, a condition for which the Third World ideology and its fallacies offer compensation. The essential impact of the West on the other countries of the world has been the revelation to those countries of their backwardness. The inevitable result has been painful: a sense of inferiority, of failure, of functioning and living below the suddenly revealed extraordinary potentials of human society, according to the demonstration made by capitalist civilization.

Napoleon Bonaparte and the Mamalukes

Today we have lost sight of the totally unpredictable and sensational character of that revelation. In this sense the meeting between the Mamalukes and Bonaparte is exemplary. The French had invaded Egypt before, in the twelfth and thirteenth centuries, when the West was actually in a condition of general inferiority to aspects of Moslem civilization, including the art of war. The medieval French knight was a less expert version of the Mamaluke, therefore suffering a severe defeat in battle and having to abandon the ambition to conquer Egypt. During the course of five-and-a-half centuries the Mamalukes remained just as they had always been, and naturally supposed that the French had changed as little. When they learned that Napoleon had had the temerity to land in Alexandria, they made ready to rout him as they had done with Saint Louis in 1250.

But while Egypt had remained virtually static or had degenerated since 1250, the development of capitalist civilization had taken place in Europe. The result, militarily, was the Battle of the Pyramids. On one side, it was the last cavalry charge of the Middle Ages; on the other side, the rational and methodical use of modern artillery. It was not a battle—it was a massacre.

Both situations, the backwardness of Egypt and the progress of France, had run their course separately. If someone had told the defeated Mamalukes that their military inferiority opposite Napoleon had been caused by Western imperialism, they wouldn't have known what he was talking about.

The Late Competitors

Napoleon's expedition to Egypt has a laboratory-like purity showing with perfect clarity the truth in the controversy about the impact of the West on the Third World. Egypt is today far from being a successful and balanced society; nevertheless, one has to be totally ignorant or completely in bad faith to argue that its situation in 1798 was preferable to what developed thereafter, starting precisely from the French expedition. The result of this was to shake Egypt from its stagnation, but moreover, as is well known, to make it revalue itself. Egypt's extraordinary specificity was a closed book until the explorations and systematic studies were brilliantly made by the scientists and artists whom Bonaparte took along with him. And this is typical of the way capitalist civilization, the only one in history that to a considerable degree has overcome ethnocentrism, has everywhere called to the attention of the non-Western countries their own cultures and identities. Alexander von Humboldt's travels in the New World and Charles Darwin's in the *Beagle* are as inseparable from the imperialist expansion of the West as the deciphering of the hieroglyphics by Jean Champollion.

France and later England essentially revealed to Egypt alternative possibilities that the Egyptians themselves could not help judging preferable to the tyranny, poverty, ignorance and ill health that characterized Egyptian life before the European intrusion; and, Egypt was forced in part by weapons but above all by the irresistible power of that revelation, to join the world capitalist market, for which Egypt was (and remains) poorly gifted. . . .

Those who have entered the path to modernization late have at their disposal for free, or at a very low cost, the example and methods fashioned by the pioneers; the theory and practice of democracy; models and techniques of public and private administration that took centuries to initiate and perfect in the West; the accumulated and freely available scientific and technological knowledge; the evidence of copiable successes and of avoidable errors in the adaptation of capitalism (or of socialism) for their own use; and above all, the very idea of the possibility of development instead of stagnation and of a reasonable welfare for the majority instead of extreme poverty, the first unsuspected and the second presumed to be unreachable before the demonstration of its feasibility by industrial, democratic, capitalistic society. . . .

Self-Defeating Mythology

There are those who will say that what the industrialized countries have done that the low-income countries have not is to exploit the low-income countries; that development is a zero-sum game; that the rich countries are rich because the poor countries are poor. This is doctrine for Marxist-Leninists, and it has wide currency throughout the Third World. To be sure, colonial powers often did derive great economic advantage from their colonies, and U.S. companies have made a lot of money in Latin America and elsewhere in the Third World, particularly during the first half of this century. But the almost exclusive focus on "imperialism" and "dependency" to explain underdevelopment has encouraged the evolution of a paralyzing and self-defeating mythology.

Lawrence E. Harrison, *Underdevelopment Is a State of Mind*, 1985.

Even the poorest and most backward of the late competitors find themselves much better off today than before the unsettling of their stagnation by the impact of capitalism; better off in measurable indexes of economic growth, public health, education, consumption; and better off in something not measurable but essential: their spiritual tone, the condition of being awake, alert and demanding. There is a vast difference for the better between present-day Arabs and those described by Joseph Renan a hundred years ago, sleeping like lizards among the ruins of Petra and Palmyra, making him exclaim: "Damned are people without wants!"

There was a time, less disoriented than ours, when this seemed what in truth it is—totally obvious. Then the greatest hope of non-Western countries was clearly perceived as residing in the impact of the West on peoples that were either primitive, or successors of great civilizations in decline and which, even at their height had been despotic, slave-based societies, indifferent to suffering and inequality and incapable of suspecting what immense productive forces could be released by the ingenuity of free men pursuing their private interest within a free society.

31

"Rapid population growth quickly absorbs any
gains made in economic development."

Overpopulation Causes Third World Poverty

Anne H. Ehrlich

Author Anne H. Ehrlich is a senior' research associate in the
biological sciences department at Stanford University in Stanford,
California. From 1976 to 1985, she served on the executive committee of the board of directors of Friends of the Earth, an en-
vironmentalist organization. In the following viewpoint, Ehrlich
contends that rising birthrates thwart poor countries' economic
progress and put pressure on their food supplies and environment.
The world's ecosystem can support only a limited number of
people, Ehrlich concludes, thus reducing population growth is a
necessary step toward reducing poverty.

As you read, consider the following questions:

1. Why does the author believe world population will
   continue to grow?
2. What factors contribute to the success of family planning
   programs, according to Ehrlich?
3. Why does Ehrlich contend that the amount of land that
   could be converted to cropland is limited?

Anne H. Ehrlich, "Development and Agriculture" in *The Cassandra Conference*, edited by
Paul R. Ehrlich and John P. Holdren. College Station, TX: Texas A & M University Press,
1988. Reprinted by permission.

At the heart of the development problem is the population dilemma. Rapid population growth quickly absorbs any gains made in economic development. Resources must be poured into an economy just to maintain the same level of essential services for a rapidly expanding population—to provide more food; more medical and sanitation services; more schools, houses, roads, and hospitals; more fuel; more supplies of every kind for more and more people. Whatever is left over can be used to improve conditions for the people.

But in Africa, where populations have been growing by 2.5 to 4 percent a year, for the past decade and a half little or nothing has been left over. In many countries, the standard of living has slid inexorably downward. Just one component of living standards, food supplies per person, declined by 10 percent in sub-Saharan Africa between 1972 and 1982; since then they have plummeted by another 10 percent or more. The shortfall has had to be made up—to the extent that it has been made up—by importing food, which those faltering economies can ill afford, or by food donated by the rich countries.

The Underexploited Lands Myth

Some African leaders still cling to the illusion that their nations can support many times the populations they now have. Resource experts have assured them that their currently "underexploited lands" can be turned to agricultural production with an abundance rivaling Iowa's, although anything of the sort has yet to be demonstrated even with well-supported local pilot projects. African leaders remained complacent about their nations' unprecedented rates of population growth. Most countries have established family-planning programs, but many of those offer birth-control services only for health and welfare reasons and are poorly supported at best by their governments. Often the family-planning services are available only in major cities and thus are inaccessible to more than two-thirds of the people.

Sub-Saharan Africa's rapid population growth and deepening poverty are only two of the starkest examples of what could become a global phenomenon. Demographers project continued growth of the world population for a century or more because of the momentum built into age compositions, especially in developing nations. The world population is now increasing by an average of about 1.7 percent a year and is projected to expand from about 5 billion today to over 10 billion before growth can be ended by humane means—that is, through limitation of births.

In Africa, with rates of natural increase averaging nearly 3 percent a year and fertility rates in some countries still rising, the outlook is for a tripling or even quadrupling of most populations before growth could be ended through birth control (assuming no rise in death rates). Rates of population growth are nearly as high in the developing nations of Latin America and Asia (averaging 2.4 and 2.1 percent, respectively, excluding China), and their gross national products (GNPs) and food production are not expanding much faster. Significant declines in birthrates have occurred in some countries, but depressingly little change has been seen in most of them.

Family-planning programs can facilitate the reduction of birthrates, but other aspects of development seem to be crucial to their success. The availability of contraceptive services does not ensure their use; people first must want smaller families. The elements of development that experience has shown to foster such desires include improvements in health, nutrition, and sanitation, which lead to lower infant mortalities and longer life expectancies, and education, especially of women. In general, birthrates have fallen in societies that have fulfilled these conditions and have strong family-planning programs, independent of other measures of development, such as increases in per capita GNP. Where these conditions have not been met, birthrates have remained high.

Overpopulation and Poverty

Overpopulation contributes to poverty, and poverty breeds overpopulation. Reckless depletion of resource "capital" often damages the environmental machinery that provides humankind with resource "income." The planet's forests—crucial mediators of the hydrologic cycle, protectors of soil, and custodians of species diversity—are threatened simultaneously by overharvesting for fuel wood and lumber, the encroachment of agricultural lands and settlements, air pollution, and acid rain; and their diminution adds to the climate-threatening burden of atmospheric carbon dioxide already swollen by the last century's binge of combustion of fossil fuels. Human poverty and environmental impoverishment compound one another.

Paul R. Ehrlich and John P. Holdren, *The Cassandra Conference*, 1988.

The most important family-planning success story has been that of the People's Republic of China, which has reduced its rate of natural increase to about 1 percent from a high of over 3 percent in the early 1960s. Besides having an extremely strong family-planning apparatus backed by other policies to encourage small families, China has met the primary social prerequisites for success: the infant mortality rate is approaching those in developed nations, average life expectancy is over 65 years and rising, basic health care is available to the entire population, and children of both sexes are almost universally educated.

But China is an exceptional case in other respects as well.

Beyond recognizing that rapid population growth was hindering progress in development, China's leaders took a cold, hard look at their nation's natural resources and concluded that no more than 650 to 700 million people could be supported on a long-term sustainable basis at a desirable standard of living. As the population passed the 1 billion mark, the Chinese government set a goal not only of ending population growth as soon as possible but of *reducing* the population to the sustainable level. To accomplish this goal, the famous "one-child family" policy was launched. Despite some problems of public acceptance and administrative abuses that have attended the program, it seems likely that on the whole it will avert more human suffering than it causes. . . .

Hunger and Malnutrition

Chronic hunger, if not starvation, is an accompaniment of life throughout the developing world (and is not unknown in some rich countries). In most low-income and many middle-income nations, food supplies are at or below the minimum required to feed the population as measured in calories available per capita, not allowing for uneven distribution. But food is never evenly distributed. In many poor countries, distribution is highly unequal; the wealthiest classes may have access to twice as many calories per person per day as the poorest groups. Among the poor, infants and small children are most vulnerable to inadequate diets and are most likely to have them.

The United Nations Food and Agriculture Organization (FAO) has very conservatively estimated that, worldwide, perhaps a half billion people—mostly children—are seriously undernourished; in 1980 the World Bank estimated that nearly 800 million people worldwide were in "absolute poverty," defined simply as being "too poor to buy food." UNICEF [United Nations Children's Fund] maintains that 15 million children die each year of malnutrition and other poverty-related causes and that one of every four children in the developing world is suffering from "invisible malnutrition," which can appreciably handicap growth and learning. The calamity now unfolding in Africa has undoubtedly swelled the numbers of the world's malnourished, and their condition is painfully visible.

In a global context, however, the numbers of African famine victims are small—only a few million. Worldwide, the *proportion* of hungry people in the world has changed little in the last few decades, although their absolute *numbers* have steadily risen in tandem with population growth. But does this prevalence of hunger arise from real resource constraints? Or is it, as some claim, just the result of inhumane and inequitable policies? Could better distribution of resources—including food itself—solve the problem?

Despite the persistence of the poor and hungry underclass, population growth has been accommodated for many decades by steadily rising food production, and the world trade network can ship emergency food supplies to famine areas quickly and efficiently. Cornucopian optimists assume that the historic trend of rising food production will continue into the indefinite future and that adjustments in economic policies will eventually solve the problems of the destitute millions. But the evidence is mounting that, although changes in policies could do much to alleviate present problems and prevent worse to come, real constraints to raising food production and expanding the human resource base do exist and are increasingly asserting themselves.

Population Must Be Stabilized

Only by stabilizing population growth can economic conditions in the Third World improve. In Kenya the average family has eight children, in Bangladesh it has six. The developing world increases by 1 million people *every five days*. (The developed world adds only 8 million every *year*.) The economies of these developing countries cannot possibly expand at a rapid enough rate to absorb their phenomenal population growth. Thus sheer numbers are outstripping the Third World's capability to produce food and create jobs.

Peter H. Kostmayer, *Los Angeles Times*, April 5, 1985.

Since World War II, global population growth has been outpaced by increases in world food production, usually measured by the harvests of cereal grains—wheat, rice, and "coarse grains" (a category including maize, sorghum, millet, and rye). Cereals form the main feeding base of humanity and comprise about two-thirds of the world's food harvest by weight.

Nearly one-third of the global grain harvest, however, is fed to livestock rather than to people. Because energy is lost in each upward step of any biological food chain, several times more grain is needed to deliver an equal number of calories in meat or dairy products than that obtained when the grain is directly consumed by human beings. In industrialized nations, two-thirds or more of the grain supply is used as feed, while in developing nations the grain fed to livestock is usually a very small fraction of that consumed.

The generally continuous upward trend of global grain production in past decades has concealed a number of significant shifts in the world food situation. One of the most important changes has been a slackening in the rate of increase in food production since the 1950s. The 1970s and early 1980s brought not only drops in some years of production *per capita* but even absolute declines of 2 percent or more in some years, which had not previously been experienced. Meanwhile, the population inexorably climbed by nearly 2 percent every year. . . .

Land

As populations continue to increase, so does the number of people that must be supported by the food produced from each hectare of arable land. New land is being added to the global cropland base, but at a far slower rate—roughly 0.2 percent a year—than that of population growth. Since the mid-1950s, the average number of people per hectare of arable land worldwide has risen by about 30 percent. Meanwhile, the rate of expansion of cropland has steadily diminished for several decades as fewer and fewer suitable areas remained available for conversion. Another reason for the slowing of cropland expansion is that development costs have risen because the remaining new land is less accessible and is generally inferior in quality to that already under cultivation.

Today, about 11 percent of Earth's ice-free land surface is under crops, about 24 percent is pasture, and over 30 percent is forest or woodland. All of the cropland and pasture and much of the forest—nearly two-thirds of the planet's land surface—are now exploited in one degree or another by human beings. . . .

Land put into crops must, of course, be removed from some other category—usually pasture or forest. Additions to cropland (about a 5 percent net increase between 1966 and 1980) have been achieved by claiming land from pasture and forest; most of that taken from pasture was compensated by converting forest to pasture. Meanwhile, sizable amounts of land, often of high quality, have been taken out of agricultural production for various kinds of development, such as urban expansion, highways, airports, energy development, and reservoirs. Large tracts of land also have been lost to agriculture as a result of deterioration.

While a quantity of land at least equal to the present cropland base is considered *potentially* arable, in practical terms little new land is likely to be cultivated in the foreseeable future. Most responsible estimates of the probable net increase in the world cropland base in the last two decades of the twentieth century are 5 percent or less.

In recent decades, as the rate of cropland expansion has fallen, a rising proportion of the gains in food production has come from increasing yields on already cultivated land.

The human population is projected to expand by over 1.5 billion—more than one-third—between 1980 and 2000. Because of the difficulties and costs of opening new land and the inferior quality of what remains, the overwhelming bulk of increases in food production needed to feed those additional people must be gained by further increasing yields on the existing cropland base.

Yet, while opportunities to open new land are becoming fewer, the quality of much of the land already under cultivation has been declining as well. . . .

The Costs of Population Growth

Kenya is one of 42 African countries where population can be expected to double in 35 years or less. Looked at one way, these figures are welcome evidence of success in cutting down infant mortality and increasing life expectancy. But they mean problems for other areas of development. African leaders know better than to equate sheer numbers with national strength. The problem, as they point out, from Senegal to Swaziland, is that they must find the means of coping with all these new faces at the national table and find them quickly before social, political, and economic systems collapse under the strain. . . .

Development is not an overnight thing. It takes time to put in place all the many elements which go to make up the mix. And with the best will in the world, Africa does not have the time. Rapid population growth overwhelms development efforts, however carefully planned.

Nafis Sadik, *Africa Report*, July/August 1988.

It should be obvious that maintaining the present inadequate living standards for a human population twice its present size, even for a few decades, without degrading the productive capabilities of Earth and reducing its carrying capacity for human life, would be a monumental, perhaps impossible, task. Yet, though demographic momentum commits the human population to substantial further growth, a doubling in size is not inevitable.

Two Choices

Two models on a smaller scale are available to civilization. Governments could continue to consider population growth of no importance until the environment became so degraded that a natural fluctuation in climatic patterns was enough to plunge vulnerable nations into massive famine—as is happening in over 20 countries in Africa today. Or the world's nations could separately and in concert assess the world's resource base and carrying capacity in relation to available and foreseeable technologies and devise population policies that fit their findings— as China has done for itself. Despite the undeniable political and social difficulties of taking this path, it would seem much easier— and much safer—to halt world population growth as quickly as is humanely possible and begin a slow decline to a permanently sustainable level.

"Overpopulation . . . is a false concept."

Overpopulation Does Not Cause Third World Poverty

Curtis Skinner

In the following viewpoint, Curtis Skinner argues that factors other than overpopulation keep the Third World poor. The Third World is underdeveloped because of unfair political and economic systems, he writes. For example, in many countries a few wealthy people own most of the productive land. To feed themselves, the poor have to clear marginal lands and forests which causes ecological damage. Skinner contends that it is wrong in this instance to blame the ecological damage on overpopulation: the real problem is a system that denies land to the people. Skinner is a writer who specializes in Latin American affairs.

As you read, consider the following questions:

1. Why does Skinner believe that the number of people the environment can support is flexible?
2. What policies does the author recommend to improve world agriculture?
3. Why does Skinner argue that it is harmful to believe the Third World is poor because it is overpopulated?

Recurrent famine in sub-Saharan Africa and the rapid ecological deterioration of the Third World environment have given new currency to the old theory of overpopulation—the Malthusian notion of human populations outgrowing their resource base. Indeed, the demographic trend looks alarming: The number of people on the planet is expected to grow by more than half to 8 billion during the next four decades, with over 80 percent of this increase occurring in the Third World. Population-linked problems of desertification and deforestation have already reached endemic proportions in much of the region and in some cases threaten to permanently deplete topsoil and groundwater resources.

The desertification of productive land by overfarming and overgrazing stock animals is most evident in the Andes and sub-Saharan Africa, but is believed to affect more than half of the world's arid and semiarid lands to some extent. Deforestation attributed to firewood gathering and clearing farming land affects virtually every Third World country, particularly India, Brazil, and most of sub-Saharan Africa.

Environmentalists' Warnings

Environmentalists warn that if current clearing rates continue, half of the world's tropical rainforests will have disappeared by the end of the century, a catastrophe that will cause the extinction of thousands of plant and animal species, impairing biological diversity and sacrificing untold potential medical, agricultural, and other benefits for humankind. By releasing carbon into the atmosphere, moreover, deforestation contributes to the "greenhouse effect" that is gradually warming the earth and will exert a huge economic and environmental cost by raising sea levels and disrupting climatic patterns. The devastating famines that have blighted Ethiopia and other African nations through most of the 1980s have dramatized this resource depletion and environmental degradation in the Third World.

But are these problems due to some absolute increase in human numbers beyond what the planet can bear or to the failure of existing socioeconomic systems to create environmentally benign sources of livelihood for growing populations? Few contentious social questions have produced such odd alliances of opinion. Liberal one-worlders join rightist xenophobes in arguing for the first position, while Marxists and Reaganite apostles of unfettered capitalism deny any population problem and press the second view. As dogma, neither of these positions is correct; both population growth and socioeconomic structures are interactively shaping the Third World environmental catastrophe. The principal obstacle to pursuing an effective solution, however, is the widely-held fallacy of overpopulation.

The argument that the sheer growth in human numbers is destroying the planet is rooted in the biological concept of the "carrying capacity" of local environments. The term was originally used to refer to the population density of a given species that a natural habitat like a fishery or grassland could sustain without exhausting itself. Contemporary neo-Malthusians like biologists Garrett Hardin and Paul and Anne Ehrlich believe that many Third World societies have violated their environmental carrying capacity, defined on a larger scale as the natural systems of an entire country. They acknowledge that human beings, unlike other animals, are capable of significantly modifying the way in which they interact with their environment by introducing new technologies and forms of social organization, but they argue that the carrying capacity concept is still relevant for looking at a given society at a given point in history.

The difficulty with the carrying capacity argument is that despite the attempts to make it relevant to dynamic social processes it remains an inherently static concept, best suited to looking at traditional, rural societies with a clearly defined impact on the resource base. Even here, changing socioeconomic conditions invariably complicate the picture.

Why the Poor Have Children

Some people in the wealthy countries think that people are poor and hungry because of many children. But reality for poor Third World people is often the reverse: people have many children *because* they are poor and hungry.

Oxfam America, *Facts for Action: Hunger and Population*, no. 7.

Land tenureship patterns and available technologies, along with pricing and marketing policies, exert a determining influence over the size of population that a given agricultural region can adequately support. In Brazil, for instance, vast tracts of fertile land held by large landowners in northeastern Pernambuco state lie completely idle, while peasants eke out a miserable living farming plots too minuscule to adequately feed themselves and their families. As the population grows, soil nutrients are exhausted and topsoil erodes from overfarming ever-smaller parcels, prompting increasing numbers of these peasants to migrate to Amazonia to carve new lands from the tropical forest under a government colonization program. The thin tropical soils there are soon exhausted, and the settlers are obliged to move on to a new patch, destroying an ever-larger swath of irreplaceable forest.

Does this escalating pattern of erosion and deforestation mean that the rural population in Pernambuco has outgrown its

41

environmental carrying capacity? No, there is more than enough farming land in the region to meet the needs of its peasant population. What is lacking is an agrarian reform program to give it to them. Land tenureship distortions like those in Brazil (where 2 percent of the landowners control 60 percent of the agricultural land) are the rule in most other Third World countries characterized by large "surplus" rural populations.

Technological factors and government agrarian policies also markedly affect agricultural carrying capacity. Japan produces almost three times as much grain per hectare as Bangladesh with an industrial agricultural system that uses high yield variety (HYV) seeds and large inputs of machinery, chemical fertilizers, and pesticides. But simpler technologies accessible to impoverished Third World countries can also dramatically boost productivity.

A shift from monocropping for export to traditional systems of intercropping, crop rotation, and mixing plant and animal production would increase soil fertility and support larger peasant populations without further degrading the environment. The problem of deforestation to meet rural fuelwood needs can be addressed by government incentives to plant trees. Government pricing policies that yield a fair return to food-staple producers—reversing the usual bias toward the urban consumer—can also act to substantially increase rural carrying capacity. . . .

Meeting Food and Energy Needs

What is the status of global food production and resource availability? What access does the Third World have to these resources? The basic resource needs considered here are food and energy, since their supply is most often cited as doubtful or environmentally destructive: shortages of other resources such as the common industrial metals are unlikely.

Let us look at the food situation first. The earth *presently* produces more than *twice* as much food as needed to provide all of its human inhabitants with a basic diet. If hundreds of millions of people are hungry today, it is not for lack of food, but because they are unable to pay for it. So simply maintaining production at current rates is theoretically sufficient to feed double today's population, or about 10 billion people—approximately the size of the stabilized world population that demographers project as a medium estimate for the early twenty-second century based on current fertility trends.

Of course, bare food sufficiency is not the legacy we wish to bequeath to future generations. Moreover, we must ask whether even today's level of production is sustainable over the long term. Happily, the outlook is hopeful for not only sustaining but substantially increasing world food production while protecting the environment, although the task is challenging.

THE LANDLESS

Rural households that have no or practically no land.

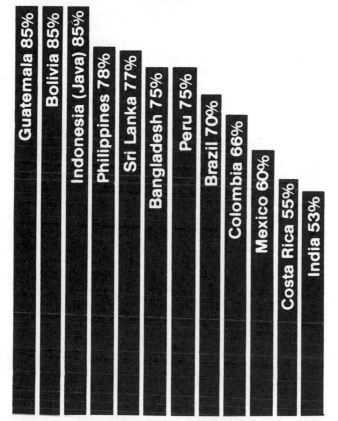

Guatemala 85%
Bolivia 85%
Indonesia (Java) 85%
Philippines 78%
Sri Lanka 77%
Bangladesh 75%
Peru 75%
Brazil 70%
Colombia 66%
Mexico 60%
Costa Rica 55%
India 53%

Reprinted with permission of New Internationalist Publications.

The key obstacles to improving agricultural yields are soil erosion—estimated at over 26 billion tons worldwide per year—and depletion of groundwater tables because of excessive irrigation and the destruction of water-retaining ground cover. A certain amount of land (Worldwatch Institute, a Washington, D.C.-based environmental think tank, estimates up to 10 percent of world cropland) should even now be taken out of production or converted to lighter uses to prevent long-term exhaustion of these resources.

Livestock herding, too, must be cut back dramatically in sub-

Saharan Africa, the Andes, and other regions to stop the over-grazing that contributes to desertification and soil and water losses. This will require a painful adjustment of traditional pastoral lifestyles, an unavoidable process that is already being forced on Sahelian tribesmen like the Tuareg and Fulani as the Sahara inexorably moves south. . . .

Other conservation measures such as increasing fallow periods and taking some land out of production altogether may prove more expensive (particularly if displaced farmers are compensated) but are certainly not beyond world society's means. The production losses that result from these conservation measures can be more than compensated for by expropriating and cultivating the vast tracts of unused agricultural land to be found in large private estates all over the Third World, particularly Latin America. Labor-intensive smallholding farming has proven to be at least as productive as capital-intensive agriculture in the Third World, and has the potential to improve its yields dramatically if environmentally benign traditional cultivation techniques are combined with appropriate inputs from modern agrarian science. . . .

The world energy picture is equally encouraging, although meeting future demand will require better conservation and a general shift from fossil fuels to environmentally benign renewable resources. As in the case of food production, this prognosis can be made on the basis of current knowledge and resources without relying on some future technological fix. Oil is running out and coal is the world's dirtiest fuel source; burning these fuels emits most of the atmospheric carbon that is heating the planet with potentially disastrous results in the greenhouse effect. . . .

Renewable Resources

According to Worldwatch Institute, 28 Third World countries now have small hydropower programs, led by China with 90,000 installed turbines. Solar and wind energy is clean, ubiquitous, and inexhaustible, and new technologies are making these sources increasingly competitive in economic terms. China and India have launched ambitious windpower programs, and the imminent development of a cheap photovoltaic cell could revolutionize energy production throughout the region.

The only real bottleneck to meeting the energy needs of the future Third World populations is the fuelwood supply. Excessive firewood harvesting has ravaged timber stands throughout the Third World, particularly in Africa and India. Worldwatch Institute estimates that more than two-thirds of Third World people rely on wood for their cooking and heating needs and that by the year 2000 more than half of these will either lack or overcut wood unless major tree-planting programs are launched. But trees are a quickly renewable resource and the problem is ultimately manageable if the political will is there to do so.

In sum, there is no absolute physical constraint to meeting the food and energy needs of a human population more than double today's size. The earth has the capacity, and mankind possesses the ingenuity and technical means to satisfy these needs without destroying the natural environment. . . .

A Plague of People?

Overpopulation as such, then, is a false concept, both in absolute and relative terms. It is rooted in the Malthusian fallacy that a surplus population means too many people and not enough resources rather than a faulty or inequitable political and economic system.

A Dangerous Myth

Of all the myths prevailing about Africa in the West, none is propagated with more vigor and regularity than the notion that over-population is a central cause of African poverty. The famine has given propagators of this myth fresh ammunition with which to press home their argument.

All myths are dangerous, especially when they become the basis of policy. But the overpopulation myth is particularly harmful because it often preempts deeper probing into the complex causes of underdevelopment.

Djibril Diallo, *The Human Life Review,* Spring 1987.

But the overpopulation theory is more than simply wrong. The idea that there are too many people in the world and that it would be good if there were fewer necessarily devalues human life. Our world appears blighted by a plague of people, tolerance ebbs, and we confront one another with the fear and hostility of survivalists. Other human beings do not belong here with us—they're "in the way." Parents feel that they must apologize for having children and hope that their offspring will somehow redeem the terrible burden they are placing on the planet. National xenophobia and anti-immigration sentiment grows.

Thus we have environmental gadfly Garrett Hardin counseling against famine relief so that starvation, "nature's last and most terrible remedy," can reduce the population to carrying capacity, and the Earth First! "direct action" environmental group hailing the AIDS epidemic as a potentially providential population-control mechanism. While the Ehrlichs and the mainstream First World environmental organizations shy away from these openly misanthropic views, their common commitment to the doctrine of overpopulation also encourages them to take a fatalistic approach to the problems of famine and disease. "Population is the only long-term solution to the human predicament," the Ehrlichs wrote in the *Amicus Journal*. "If current trends continue, no amount of redistribution can save humanity from unprecedented famines."

Pressures Exist

But to reject the dogma of overpopulation is not to deny that serious population pressures on the environment exist. The left has traditionally tended to discount any environmental limitations on human activity and believe in the power of productive technology and organization to solve all material problems. These views are now changing as it becomes evident that uncontrolled population and economic growth invariably takes a certain social and environmental toll. . . .

How, then, are we to look at the growing Third World populations? We must approach the issue not in isolation, not as a problem in and of itself, but rather as part of the socioeconomic whole. It is well-known that fertility trends are intimately linked to social and economic development as it directly affects the popular classes in society, particularly in average living standards, education, roles for women outside of the home, and mortality rates. The imperative to have many children to serve as a labor force and form of old age insurance—and to protect against the high rate of child mortality—loses much of its force when Third World peoples emerge from desperate poverty to a social and economic condition that allows them to take some control over their own destinies.

Historically, the "demographic transition" to a society with low birth and death rates has tended to follow substantial improvement in popular living standards and a broadening of social opportunities. Family planning programs put into effect without strong socioeconomic measures, on the other hand have usually failed, in the long term, to reduce population growth rates substantially. The upshot for First World environmentalists is that we can and should support voluntary family planning programs in the Third World that give people the freedom to control their reproduction, but we should harbor no illusions that these programs will lower fertility rates and must zealously fight the wide-spread notion that "overpopulation" is a leading cause of the region's environmental problems.

"There are distinct shades of Groucho Marx's: 'I have worked my way up from nothing to a state of extreme poverty' about the lot of most poor informals in Third World cities."

The Underground Economy Keeps the Third World Impoverished

Vanessa Baird

In several Third World countries, many people work unofficially—their income is not reported to the government and government regulations do not apply to them. Vanessa Baird, the author of the following viewpoint, considers the development of this underground economy unhealthy. Without the protection of labor laws and unions, informal workers can be freely exploited. Baird writes for *New Internationalist*, a monthly magazine published in Great Britain that covers issues of world poverty and Third World development.

As you read, consider the following questions:

1. Why does the author believe right-wing commentators favor the emergence of an informal sector?
2. Who benefits from an informal labor sector, according to Baird?
3. Why does the author argue that an underground economy threatens democracy?

Vanessa Baird, "The Shady World of Underground Work," *New Internationalist*, July 1987. Reprinted by permission of New International Publications.

'Can I have it in cash'? The plumber smiles broadly as he gathers up his tools and delicately tip-toes between the pools of water. 'To save me going to the bank, you understand'.

'Of course'.

Of course. A nod and a wink. Making out, off-the-books is the order of the day. It fits the mood of the times. And complicity is appealing.

Maybe a few years ago people would have disapproved. This is cheating the system after all; a system that has provided you with education, health care, roads, even the clean water which now lies in puddles on the kitchen floor. But few complain nowadays. You have to admire the ones with the guts to go it alone and make something of their lives when times are hard, even if the ways they do so are not strictly legal. The right-wing romanticism of the 'self-made man' is back in fashion.

Women and the Underground Economy

'Self-made women' you seem to hear less of. Perhaps there is a clue here. Women actually make up the bulk of underground workers in many countries. But they are largely invisible. That is until you knock on their doors. Then there is a sudden rustling of materials, a hectic ordering of children and an opening of the door only a fraction. Just enough to see a nose and one eye.

'Oh, it's only you'. She relaxes and opens the door wide. 'I always imagine it's going to be a tax-inspector'! A two-year-old is reaching excitedly out towards the hot soldering iron propped up against a saucer on the table. Meanwhile piles of brightly coloured resistors are proving irresistible to the four-year-old. There is a loud clatter as a stack of circuit boards comes tumbling down. This is piecework and it pays next to nothing. Of the 300,000 women estimated to be doing home-work in Britain today 72 per cent receive less than the legal minimum hourly wage, three quarters of those get 1 pound ($1.60) or less and some make as little as 20p (30 cents) an hour. . . .

Something is horribly twisted here. You have to ask yourself just whose interests this new 'tolerance' towards the underground economy is serving. Who stands to benefit from a growing reservoir of divided unprotected workers? And where is tax-dodging and myopic self-interest leading us? Some say straight to where most countries in the Third World stand today, with their dog-eat-dog labour relations and ever-widening divide between rich and poor.

But attitudes towards underground or informal work have been changing in developing countries too. On the face of it, this could only be a good thing. After all, just ten years ago in Lima, Peru, police were engaged in violent battles with poor hawkers trying to scrape a living on the streets. Similar things were happening in other countries.

To Third World governments, the presence of large numbers of people begging on the steps of bank buildings or roasting nuts outside five-star hotels was an insult to the progressiveness of their new skyscraper cities. And the poverty of these people was an all too visible accusing finger.

Nevertheless their energy and inventiveness were getting some development experts excited. The kettle-out-of-tin-can-makers of Accra, the barefoot engineers of Bombay, and the hawkers of everything-under-the-sun of Jakarta were showing flexibility and perhaps even salvation for the Third World poor. But at that time, the early 1970s, most governments were having none of it; migrants, hawkers and barefoot business meant mess and that was that.

Capitalism's Failure

The "informal" sector has taken on an increasingly significant role in Peru's economic and political life. The term "informal" embraces individuals engaged in a staggering array of activities, including desperately impoverished street vendors, artisans, nonunionized workers in micro-enterprises, bus owners, and petty capitalists. Such "underground" activities now occupy between 50 and 60 percent of Peru's work force and account for 38 percent of its gross domestic product. According to most analysts, the growth of the informal sector over the past 30 years reflects the failure of the "formal" economy (that is, the contractual, government-sanctioned economy) to absorb the massive internal migration of Peruvians from country to city; its existence is often held out as a glaring symbol of the failure of capitalism in Peru.

Elizabeth Farnsworth, *World Policy Journal*, Fall 1988.

Repressive measures were, of course, ineffective. The desperation that drives the rural poor to cities in the first place is not going to be quenched by water-cannon, police batons, or bulldozers crashing through shanty towns. The best the authorities could do was turn a blind eye.

But in Peru things took a turn in the early 1980s. This was largely due to a new set of studies in Lima that revealed that the informal sector accounted for 60 per cent of all economic activity and was—apart from the cocaine trade and the gold rush in the jungle—the only growth sector in a sharply declining Peruvian economy.

Politicians sat up and listened. Conservative Luis Percovich, then Interior Minister, went so far as to hail the barefoot business people as the harbingers of a 'new Peru'. Even World Bankers were saying they should be encouraged.

The Right had recognized the informal sector. But why? The studies had shown these suddenly visible 'informals' were at heart tiny capitalist individualists. Their ideology was perfectly correct. They were highly competitive, didn't belong to trade unions and lacked any notion of worker solidarity.

The benefits became clearer as companies, like the multinational Philips, fired their workers and contracted work out, often to the hundreds of small outfits that had sprung up in the surrounding Lima shanty towns of Villa El Salvador, Comas, or Independencia. This enabled companies not only to cut costs but also by-pass awkward labour-protection laws introduced during the time of the left-wing military dictatorship.

Exploitation

Informal labour relations tend to be more exploitative than those within the legitimate economy. Fly-by-night workshops only get contracts if they are prepared to do the work very cheaply. If sweatshop bosses are to be competitive they must pay their workers low wages for long hours, cut corners on health and safety and forget about such niceties as job protection. If there is a drop in demand the informal outfit has to carry the risks and absorb the shock of fluctuations in the market. The only people who really benefit from this are the larger companies that enjoy the benefits of both an informal workforce and government grants, loans and subsidies.

The same thing is happening in industrialized nations. Japan has taught much to the Western business world. It has been in the sub-contracting game for so long that about a third of Toyota or Nissan cars are to varying degrees made by other smaller firms. Italy is not far behind with companies that range from Fiat to the rapidly-growing fashion giant Benetton making use of women working in sweatshops or their own homes. California's Silicon Valley, home of computer high-tech, has more PhDs per square mile than anywhere else in the world. But it is heading for another record if the local newspapers are to be believed: that for sweat-shops employing cheap, illegal, mainly female and immigrant workers who assemble the micro-electronics parts.

In fact, sweated labour is making a comeback in the industrial-ized world. According to the *New York Times* it is very much a feature of the 1980s. The rate of recent discoveries of sweatshops in France, Britain, Italy and other countries suggests it is not just a North American phenomenon.

Unpleasant though sweatshops may be, some argue, any work is better than no work. Otherwise people would not do it. If underground outfits had to go legal many of them would go bust, their profitability often lying in their clandestine nature. So why not turn a blind eye to it in a world dogged by unemployment?

50

But you have to look at just what is being established here. Sweated labour forces down the wages of all workers, whether underground or legal. It directly threatens the poor in proper jobs and in the long term does not help the poor in underground jobs either.

Workers Who Are Not Independent

Others argue that because informals often work for themselves they are freer from exploitation than wage labour workers. This is something of a myth. Seemingly independent casual workers are often far from being so. Rubbish pickers on Mexican tips are controlled by garbage mafias. Shoeshine boys in South Korea hand over 85 per cent of their earnings to the crime syndicates that house and feed them. And even street vendors are often in the hold of middle-persons who are also their creditors.

A Funny Sort of Freedom

What had started me thinking about the underground—or the informal sector—was spending a couple of years in Latin America. You could not avoid it there. Most of the population were making a living in ways that were strictly speaking illegal. For them there were no taxes to pay, no rules to obey, but no safety nets either.

Observers said it was great: people were creating jobs for themselves in a free market. It did seem a funny sort of freedom, though, with poor people working like crazy and getting poorer, and rich people not appearing to be doing much of anything except remaining quietly rich.

Vanessa Baird, *New Internationalist*, July 1987.

For informal workers who genuinely do work for themselves the freedom of being your own boss does not often amount to much amid growing competition and soaring inflation. There are distinct shades of Groucho Marx's: 'I have worked my way up from nothing to a state of extreme poverty' about the lot of most poor informals in Third World cities. . . .

Badly battered by anti-union legislation and low morale, trade unions have responded to the new threats coming from underground with the agility of a Leviathan. The problem is that they still mainly represent those within formal work. To be fair, some, like the Transport and General Workers Union in Britain, have launched campaigns to enlist part-timers and informal workers. But it's not easy. Many informal workers are either women or black or both. These groups have no reason to feel that the white male-dominated unions have ever done much to serve their interests.

One thing is certain. Underground work is going to be with us for some time. So what can be done to protect those who are being exploited?

In the developed world we need to crack down hard on workplaces that break health and safety regulations. And there is much that local authorities can do to advise informal workers of their rights, tax and social security matters and to explain how to become legal.

Third World governments need to help the submerged economy emerge and gradually become a part of the official one. This can be done in a number of ways. Making laws is not one of them. Removing laws is. Red tape and bureaucracy are the most frequently given reasons for people working underground.

Workers Should Organize

But the most effective channel for change is underground workers themselves, organizing into groups or networks. Improbable as it may seem this has actually happened with some success. In Britain informal workers in London and the Midlands have got together to form 'Outwork' campaigns. So have Mexican immigrants in North America. In India the Self Employed Women's Association is a co-operative of informals with its own sickness benefit and welfare scheme. While in Peru informal mini-bus and taxi drivers banded together to lobby the transport ministry. The threat of a mass blockade by thousands of ramshackle vehicles proved to be an awesome bargaining weapon.

A Threat to Democracy

Finally, it is essential to recognize that, for all its apparent freedom, informality is undemocratic. It can indeed present a grave threat to democracy. Colombia is the most dramatic example of what happens to a country where informal economic activity—in this case drugs—gets control. The assassination of one justice minister who published a 'black list' of big names in the drugs business and the attempted assassination of his successor clearly illustrate the power of this underground lobby.

But there are other less openly undemocratic forces at work of which development agencies and other organizations wishing to promote the informal sector should be extremely wary. Small enterprise schemes, such as helping to set up engineering workshops in the Third World, can look very attractive on the face of it. But it is vital that supporting such ventures does not mean playing into the hands of the wrong people and so enabling exploitative interests to pluck the fruit of poor people's toil and initiative.

"In Peru, informality has turned a large number of people into entrepreneurs, into people who know how to seize opportunities. . . . This is the foundation of development."

The Underground Economy Proves the Third World Can Develop

Hernando de Soto

Hernando de Soto has been the managing director of Peru's Central Reserve Bank and a member of the United Nations Committee for Development Planning. He is also the President of the Instituto Libertad y Democracia (ILD), a think tank in Peru which did a ground-breaking study of Peru's underground economy. The following viewpoint is excerpted from de Soto's book, *The Other Path*, which was based on ILD's research. De Soto contends that Peru's underground economy arose because excessive government regulations prevented people from setting up legal businesses. This informal sector now consists of hundreds of thriving small businesspeople, de Soto argues, and it is these entrepreneurs who can help Peru's economy grow and develop.

As you read, consider the following questions:

1. What factors led to the rise of an informal sector, according to the author?
2. What does de Soto mean by the redistributive tradition?

Excerpts from THE OTHER PATH by Hernando de Soto. Copyright © 1989 by Hernando de Soto. Reprinted by permission of Harper & Row, Publishers, Inc.

Between 1940 and 1981 Peru's urban population increased almost fivefold (from 2.4 to 11.6 million), while its rural population increased barely a third (from 4.7 to 6.2 million). Thus, while 65 percent of the population lived in rural areas and 35 percent in urban areas in 1940, these percentages had been reversed by 1981. To put it more simply, in 1940, two of every three Peruvians lived in the countryside, but by 1981 two of every three lived in the city. . . .

Generally speaking, Peru's urbanization dates back to the mass migrations from the countryside to the city, which began to be recorded in the national statistics in 1940 but actually started a little earlier. This urbanization coincided with a rapid growth of the population throughout the country. Growth had hitherto been fairly slow. While not entirely accurate, the national censuses of the last two centuries reveal an average growth of 0.6 percent. In this century, on the other hand, the total population grew more than two-and-a-half times between 1940 and 1981, from 7 million to almost 18 million.

The increase was substantially greater in Lima. The population of the capital city multiplied by 7.6 times during this period. In 1940, it housed 8.6 percent of the country's population; it now contains 26 percent. The number of migrants to Lima increased 6.3 times over, from 300,000 to 1,900,000, between 1940 and 1981. . . .

A Hostile Reception

The greatest hostility the migrants encountered was from the legal system. Up to then, the system had been able to absorb or ignore the migrants because the small groups who came were hardly likely to upset the status quo. As the number of migrants grew, however, the system could no longer remain disinterested. When large groups of migrants reached the cities, they found themselves barred from legally established social and economic activities. It was tremendously difficult for them to acquire access to housing and an education and, above all, enter business or find a job. Quite simply, Peru's legal institutions had been developed over the years to meet the needs and bolster the privileges of certain dominant groups in the cities and to isolate the peasants geographically in rural areas. As long as this system worked, the implicit legal discrimination was not apparent. Once the peasants settled in the cities, however, the law began to lose social relevance.

The migrants discovered that their numbers were considerable, that the system was not prepared to accept them, that more and more barriers were being erected against them, that they had to fight to extract every right from an unwilling establishment, that they were excluded from the facilities and benefits offered by the law, and that, ultimately, the only guarantee of their freedom and prosperity lay in their own hands. In short, they discovered that they must compete not only against people but also against the system.

From Migrants to Informals

Thus it was, that in order to survive, the migrants became informals. If they were to live, trade, manufacture, transport, or even consume, the cities' new inhabitants had to do so illegally. Such illegality was not antisocial in intent, like trafficking in drugs, theft, or abduction, but was designed to achieve such essentially legal objectives as building a house, providing a service, or developing a business. As we shall see later, it is more than likely that, economically speaking, the people directly involved in these activities (as well as society in general) are better off when they violate the laws than when they respect them. We can say that informal activities burgeon when the legal system imposes rules which exceed the socially accepted legal framework—does not honor the expectations, choices, and preferences of those whom it does not admit within its framework—and when the state does not have sufficient coercive authority. . . .

The State Is the Problem

The "informal economy" is usually thought of as a problem: clandestine, unregistered, illegal companies and industries that pay no taxes, that compete unfairly with companies and industries that obey the law and pay their taxes promptly. Black-marketeers are brigands who deprive the state of funds it might use to remedy social problems and strengthen the very structure of society.

That kind of thinking is totally erroneous. In countries like Peru, the problem is not the black market but the state itself. The informal economy is the people's spontaneous and creative response to the state's incapacity to satisfy the basic needs of the impoverished masses.

Mario Vargas Llosa, in *The Other Path*, 1989.

This tells the story of the migrants who have become informals during the past forty years and attempts to show why we have come to be a country in which 48 percent of the economically active population and 61.2 percent of work hours are devoted to informal activities which contribute 38.9 percent of the gross domestic product (GDP) recorded in the national accounts. It tries to explain the reasons and the prospects for the change which is taking place in Peru by analyzing the vanguard of this change, the informals. . . .

We must now ask ourselves why bad laws predominate in Peru

and what effect this has on the country. Why does the law disrupt efficiency? Why does it limit or prevent production instead of promoting it and making it cheaper? Why does it force a large proportion of the population to work informally and impose extremely high costs and absurdly complicated requirements on the formal sector? Why does it not foster confidence in the system of social exchange? Why does it fail to encourage citizens to seize economic opportunities that would facilitate the specialization and interdependence of individuals and resources? In other words, why does our legal system make us poor?

The Redistributive Tradition

There appears to be a tradition among our country's lawmakers of using the law to redistribute wealth rather than to help create it. From this standpoint, the law is essentially a mechanism for sharing a fixed stock of wealth among the different interest groups that demand it. A state which does not realize that wealth and resources can grow and be promoted by an appropriate system of institutions, and that even the humblest members of the population can generate wealth, finds direct redistribution the only acceptable approach.

In legislating from a purely redistributive standpoint, however, our lawmakers fail to see that, in addition to its immediate distributive effect, any law will affect the functioning of the productive system as a whole. Such an approach does not consider how the law can alter the individual's economic decisions and opportunities. . . .

The redistributive tradition has created in Peru a society where almost all the country's vital forces have organized in political and economic groups, one of whose main aims is to influence government in order to obtain a redistribution which favors them or their members. This competition for privileges through the lawmaking process has resulted in a widespread politicization of our society and is directly responsible for the existence of the bad laws which give rise to the costs of formality and informality. . . .

In actual fact, the redistributive tradition is not exclusive to Peru and Latin America, it cannot be attributed solely to our cultural characteristics, nor is it historically unique. It characterizes a system of social organization in which Peru, Latin America, and possibly a large proportion of Third World countries seem to be immersed at present, as the developed countries were before them—namely, mercantilism.

The Characteristics of Mercantilism

As is well known, "mercantilism" is the name given to the economic policies pursued in Europe between the fifteenth and nineteenth centuries. According to the *UNESCO Dictionary of Social Sciences*, "mercantilism is . . . the belief that the economic welfare of the State can only be secured by government regulation of a nationalist character." According to others, who emphasize the role of the private sector in mercantilism, it is the "supply and demand for monopoly rights through the machinery of the state. . . ." The European societies of that time were politicized, bureaucratized, dominated by redistributive combines, and impoverished. The parallel between twentieth-century Peru and the European mercantilism of earlier centuries is a valid one. . . .

Bringing Prosperity to Peru

Ninety-five percent of the beat-up old cars, taxis, trucks, and buses that pass for public transport in Lima are provided by illegals, who have invested in them more than $1 billion. Fifty percent of the homes built in Lima have been built by illegals (without legal title to the land beneath them). The $8.7 billion worth of low-income housing the illegals have built is forty-seven times more than the state has provided. Without the illegals, economic life in Peru would stop dead. . . .

Peru could prosper, if it could experience at last the economic revolution of the free economy, if the law supported, rather than strangled, economic activism.

Michael Novak, *Crisis*, July/August 1987.

A revolution against mercantilism, which has been gathering momentum for decades but has only recently begun to affect it seriously, is on the move, and this revolution is informality.

Whether because of the legacy of colonialism or because of the absence of a genuine decentralizing feudal experience, the fact is that mercantilism has lasted here at least a century longer than in Europe. However, some of the phenomena we associate with its overthrow are now emerging: informal activity, frequent invasions of property, widespread lawbreaking, the first elements of a market economy, the anarchy resulting from negotiating for laws and bureaucratic favors, and many of the factors which preceded and shaped the European Industrial Revolution. There is no large-scale informal industry, but no such industry existed when the Industrial Revolution first began in the developed countries or, indeed, until the obstacles to popular participation in enterprise began to be removed and a beneficial legal system appeared which made modern production possible.

Although the basic elements of economic and social revolution already exist in Peru, the country's legal institutions are clearly still mercantilist: popular access to private enterprise is difficult or impossible for the popular classes, the legal system is excessive and obstructive, there are massive public and private bureaucracies, redistributive combines have a powerful influence on lawmaking, and the state intervenes in all areas of activity. . . .

Because they govern with mercantilist systems, the traditional left wing and right wing are both concerned more with transferring wealth than with laying the institutional bases for creating it. Having failed to create the conditions for millions of migrants to join the formal productive process, left-wingers and right-wingers alike are disconcerted by the poverty rampant in their cities and resort to the old mercantilist ploy of handing out disguised forms of charity in quantities which ultimately prove ludicrously inadequate. Today, both the left- and the right-wing view informality as the problem. Neither seems to have realized that the problem itself offers the solution—to use the energy inherent in the phenomenon to create wealth and a different order. Perhaps this is because converting a problem into a solution smacks of alchemy, or perhaps they are opposed to private initiative on a large, popular scale. Like all good mercantilists, they both feel secure only if the answers come from a higher authority within the centralized order.

The Irony of Mercantilism

A particularly good example of this tendency is the regulation on street vending, which Lima's municipal government, controlled by the Marxist left wing, enacted in 1985 through Ordinance 002. If, instead of overregulating the street vendors, the authorities had removed the obstacles to their activities and made it easier for them to form business organizations and obtain formal credit so that they could build more markets, by 1993 all of today's street vendors would be off the streets.

The irony is that, while the mayor dealt popular initiative this discriminatory blow, he openly encouraged private contractors to build markets right in the center of Lima. Thus, the policies pursued by the left wing in the municipal government were essentially mercantilist rather than socialist and did not differ significantly from what the right wing would have done in the same circumstances.

The traditional left and right wings also advocate a protective and exclusive order, and neither has proposed measures to integrate newcomers and enable them to compete. Instead of seeing how people can gain control of market forces and make them serve the country's social interests, they try to replace those forces by the system of government which preceded the Industrial Revolution in Europe.

In dealing with the problem of informality, little thought has been given to ways of reforming the legal order to adapt it to the new realities of production. No one has ever considered that most poor Peruvians are a step ahead of the revolutionaries and are already changing the country's structures, and that what the politicians should be doing is guiding the change and giving it an appropriate institutional framework so that it can be properly used and governed. . . .

The Promise of Human Capital

Competitive business people, whether formal or informal, are in fact a new breed. They have rejected the dependence proposed by the politicians. They may be neither likable nor polite—remember what many people say about minibus drivers and street vendors—but they provide a sounder basis for development than skeptical bureaucracies and traffickers in privileges. They have demonstrated their initiative by migrating, breaking with the past without any prospect of a secure future, they have learned how to identify and satisfy others' needs, and their confidence in their abilities is greater than their fear of competition. When they start something, they know there is always a risk of failure. Every day they face dilemmas: what and how are they going to produce? What are they going to make it with? At what prices will they buy and sell? Will they manage to find long-term customers? Behind every product offered or manufactured, behind all the apparent disorder or relative illegality, are their sophisticated calculations and difficult decisions.

This ability to take risks and calculate is important because it means that a broad entrepreneurial base is already being created. In Peru, informality has turned a large number of people into entrepreneurs, into people who know how to seize opportunities by managing available resources, including their own labor, relatively efficiently. This is the foundation of development, for wealth is simply the product of combining interchangeable resources and productive labor. Wealth is achieved essentially by one's own efforts. It is earned, little by little, in an active market where goods, services, and ideas are exchanged and people are constantly learning and adjusting to others' needs. Wealth comes from knowing how to use resources, not from owning them.

This new business class is a very valuable resource: it is the human capital essential for economic takeoff. It has meant survival for those who had nothing and has served as a safety valve for societal tensions. It has given mobility and productive flexibility to the wave of migrants, and is in fact doing what the state could never have done: bring large numbers of outsiders into the country's money economy. The benefits which this new business class offers Peru far outweigh the damage done it by terrorists and mercantilists. The overwhelming majority of the population has one goal in common, to overcome poverty and succeed.

Evaluating Sources of Information

A critical thinker must always question sources of information. Historians, for example, distinguish between *primary sources* (eyewitness accounts) and *secondary sources* (writings or statements based on primary or eyewitness accounts or on other secondary sources). An Indian villager's description of how Great Britain's period of rule in India affected his community is an example of a primary source. A historian writing a book on imperialism using the villager's account is an example of a secondary source.

To read and think critically, one must be able to recognize primary sources. This is not enough, however, because eyewitness accounts do not always provide accurate descriptions. The Indian villager's account of British rule may differ from the account of a British official. The historian must decide which story seems most accurate, keeping in mind the potential biases of the eyewitnesses.

Test your skill in evaluating sources of information by completing the following exercise. Imagine you are writing a paper on the causes of poverty in the Third World. You decide to include an equal number of primary and secondary sources. Listed below are a number of sources which may be useful for your research. *Place a P next to those descriptions you believe are primary sources.* Second, *rank the primary sources* assigning the number (1) to what appears to be the most accurate and fair primary source, the number (2) to the next most accurate, and so on until the ranking is finished. Next, *place an S next to those descriptions you believe are secondary sources and rank them also, using the same criteria.*

If you are doing this activity as a member of a class or group, discuss and compare your evaluation with other members of the group.

$$P = primary$$
$$S = secondary$$

_____   1. A leaflet written by an Algerian who   _____
              opposed French rule describing how
              French trading practices have affected
              local businesspeople in Algeria.

_____   2. A cover story in *Conservative Monthly*,   _____
              "Land Reform and Asian Economies:
              A Review of the Evidence."

_____   3. An interview with a Third World   _____
              woman, broadcast on national televi-
              sion news, in which she describes how
              having many children improves her
              family's economic situation.

_____   4. An editorial in the *Los Angeles Times*   _____
              discussing how environmental
              degradation has hurt Third World
              economies.

_____   5. A classroom video prepared by a uni-   _____
              versity's Center for Third World
              Studies on poverty in the Third World.

_____   6. Viewpoint 6 in this chapter.

_____   7. A book titled *Why Africa Remains Poor:*   _____
              Forty Prominent Africans Speak.

_____   8. An article in *The Journal of American*   _____
              History titled "The US and the Philip-
              pines: The Imperialist Legacy."

_____   9. A report prepared by a multinational   _____
              corporation assessing the costs and
              benefits of a new chemical processing
              plant in Colombia.

_____   10. A 1950 report by Portuguese officials   _____
              titled "How Portugal's Colonial Rule
              Improves Angola's Economy."

_____   11. A public television documentary on   _____
              the success of birth control programs
              in Asia.

Periodical Bibliography

The following articles have been selected to supplement the diverse views presented in this chapter.

Vanessa Baird "Our Earth, Our Home: Land Rights and Wrongs," *New Internationalist*, November 1987.

Noam Chomsky "Of Prussians and Traders: An Interview," *Multinational Monitor*, November 1988.

Commonweal "Reinventing the Brake: Family Planning and the Church," February 24, 1989.

Carl Haub "The World Population Crisis Was Forgotten, but Not Gone," *The Washington Post National Weekly Edition*, September 5/11, 1988.

Idriss Jazairy "Defending the Environment Means Combatting Poverty in the Rural Third World," *Los Angeles Times*, January 27, 1989.

Michael T. Kaufman "In Third World, the Legacy of Marx Takes Many Shapes," *The New York Times*, January 24, 1989.

Ernest W. Lefever "Five Myths About the Third World," *Vital Speeches of the Day*, February 15, 1988.

John P. Lewis "Government and National Economic Development," *Daedalus*, Winter 1989.

Richard U. Light "Africa and the Limits to Growth," *The Humanist*, July/August 1986.

Mario Vargas Llosa "In Defense of the Black Market," *The New York Times Magazine*, February 22, 1987.

Jeremy Main "How To Make Poor Countries Rich," *Fortune*, January 16, 1989.

Michael Novak "Why Latin America Is Poor," *Forbes*, April 17, 1989.

Amanda Root "Exporting Illusion: The New Imperialism," *New Internationalist*, January 1987.

Peter D. Whitney "Policies for Economic Development in Latin America," *Department of State Bulletin*, February 1988.

Why Are Human Rights Threatened in the Third World?

Chapter Preface

Examples of human rights abuses in the Third World are not difficult to find. Many parts of Asia, Africa, and Latin America continue to be plagued by brutal military leaders, great discrepancies between rich and poor, and massive social problems. One example occurred in Cambodia in the late 1970s, when the Khmer Rouge regime murdered over one million people, one-sixth of Cambodia's population. The reasons for the murders were horrifying: For example, it was reported that anyone with eyeglasses was considered a member of the intelligentsia who had to be purged. In Africa, the misery created by famine in Ethiopia has been exacerbated by the Ethiopian government's abuses of human rights. The government, dominated by the Amhara tribe, has used food aid as a weapon to force Tigrayans and Oromos, members of two minority tribes, to resettle in desolate, drought-stricken areas. And during the 1970s, when Argentina was ruled by a military dictatorship, hundreds of people suspected of being political dissidents were murdered or simply disappeared after being taken into police custody.

Solutions to the serious problem of human rights abuses in the Third World are far harder to find, however. The authors in the following chapter examine why so many people in the Third World suffer oppression.

"Moscow has no qualms about supporting any regime that is anti-imperialist, meaning anti-American. . . . It is indifferent to a regime's human-rights abuses."

Soviet Intervention Threatens Human Rights

Alvin Z. Rubinstein

Alvin Z. Rubinstein is a political science professor at the University of Pennsylvania in Philadelphia. In the following viewpoint, he writes that the Soviet Union has sent massive amounts of military aid to the Third World. By indiscriminately aiding any Third World leader who is anti-American, the Soviets have supplied weapons to repressive regimes, according to Rubinstein.

As you read, consider the following questions:

1. How do the US and the USSR differ in their relationships with Third World allies, according to Rubinstein?
2. What types of Third World governments does Moscow prefer to support, according to the author?
3. Why does Rubinstein write that "when Third World leaders play the power game" they lose?

Alvin Z. Rubinstein, *Moscow's Third World Strategy*, copyright © 1989 by Princeton University Press. Excerpted from pages 229-249. Reprinted with permission of Princeton University Press.

The Kremlin's courtship of the Third World began with a number of objectives: diplomatic normalization with its neighbors and the new nations of the Arab East and Southern Asia; strategic denial aimed at preventing the United States from acquiring and exploiting military-political advantages in the vast region to the south of the Soviet Union; establishment of footholds in heretofore hostile environments; expansion of trade; enhancement of the USSR's prestige; and the fostering of socialism. In casting a wide net and hoping for some kind of yield, it discovered that the biggest haul came from targeting regimes that were for various reasons at odds with regional rivals who were backed by a Western power. As these bilateral relationships took hold, Moscow accepted the reality that each party sought to use the other to defend and advance its own interests. Indeed, the asymmetry of their aims eased the cementing of ties; serious frictions were thus rare. . . .

Moscow Accepts Conflict

Moscow accepts the use of force as an integral feature of international politics and is not prone to moralize or preach to clients. It does not seriously pressure them to change even policies with which it disagrees, as when Syrian President Hafez Assad expanded into Lebanon in the mid-1970s and made efforts in the 1980s to create a PLO [Palestine Liberation Organization] alternative to Yasser Arafat's leadership. Given lavish Soviet arms transfers, this makes high-tension politics an allowable, indeed, a feasible, option for a protected client. . . .

The long-term impact of Soviet military assistance has been the militarization of politics in the Third World. There is no evidence that this was Moscow's aim in the mid-1950s when Soviet leader Nikita Khrushchev sold arms to Egypt and Afghanistan, but in a variety of unanticipated ways this development has become integral to the overall advance of Soviet foreign policy objectives. It is not limited to affecting the outcomes of particular crises or conflicts; systemically, its even greater significance lies in the corruption of democratic values, in the encouragement of coups and conflict, and in the misdirection of resources. The net effect is to lead regimes nurtured by Soviet infusions of arms to focus their attention on the institutionalization of personal power rather than on the construction of economically viable political systems.

The impact of Moscow's policy on galloping militarization is evident in the ever-increasing percentage of the gross national product devoured by defense expenditures and in the soaring imports of weapons. Given the fragility of post-colonial civilian regimes, the narrowness of the democratic base on which most of them rested, and the ease with which the military could mount coups, the proliferation of military regimes may not have been avoidable; but Moscow's arms policy made it inevitable.

First, Moscow's infusion of arms exceeded the bounds of legitimate security needs, undermining civilian rule or the paramountcy that domestic transformation had for many of the early post-independence leaders. It was Khrushchev who pioneered the policy of acceding to the requests of courted regimes regardless of the effect of the arms buildup on the government's domestic or regional policy. The open arms tap, whose responsiveness to demand corrupted Mohammed Daoud Khan, Gamal Abdel Nasser, Sukarno, Mohammed Siad Barre, and others, was to have doleful consequences for their countries. Moscow knew from the beginning that the arms they sought were intended for offensive purposes, not for defense. Its availability as an uncritical and accommodating supplier fostered a major redirection of priorities and scarce resources, away from internal development and toward high-risk foreign policies. In a number of instances it not only led to the weakening of traditional and civilian elites and authority, but also to the ascendancy of military groups for whom Soviet weapons were the bricks and mortar that buttressed their position.

Soviet-Sponsored Violence

A solid indicator of Soviet involvement in low-intensity violence is the growing Soviet support for countries which are intermediaries between the Kremlin and terrorist organizations (such as Cuba, Angola, Nicaragua, Bulgaria, Czechoslovakia, and North Korea), as well as the increase of terrorist incidents in the spheres of active Soviet penetration (including Latin America, the Middle East, and Africa). For the watchful observer of the changing pattern of international warfare, the risk assessment of violence in these areas may be very informative. "What once may have seemed the random, senseless acts of a few crazed individuals," stated John C. Whitehead, U.S. Deputy Secretary of State, "has come into clearer forms as a new pattern of low-technology and inexpensive warfare against the West and its friends."

Rett R. Ludwikowski, *Terrorism*, vol. 11, no. 3, 1988.

Second, Moscow has no qualms about supporting any regime that is anti-imperialist, meaning anti-American; if privileged access is provided, so much the better. It is indifferent to a regime's human-rights abuses or venality. The only ideological outlook that really matters is the intensity of the anti-Americanism. Moscow may well prefer to deal with military elites than with civilian leaderships who have strong commitments to internal development and the struggle against blighted socio-economic conditions that have been described [by the World Bank] as "a Malthusian nightmare." It understands that in such circumstances the West's resources have far more to offer. A Mengistu is easier to cosset than a Mugabe; an Assad and a Qaddafi easier than a Corazon Aquino or a Chadli Benjadid. For example, in Ethiopia between 1977 and 1985, the Soviets provided about $4 billion in weaponry, [according to Paul B. Henze,] "but all costs for operating this swollen military machine have had to be squeezed out of the country's own meager resources"—and this during a period of drought and famine. This cornucopia of Soviet arms, which "brought neither internal security nor external peace," has enabled Mengistu to maintain an army of approximately 300,000, a force structure more than six times the size of the one maintained by Haile Selassie. It is the antithesis of economic development. Nowhere is this more evident than in the Horn of Africa, [Henze writes]:

> The Soviets have exacerbated all the region's political problems and inhibited economic development. The whole area bristles with arms—mostly Soviet-supplied. Everyone who lives in these countries, including the rulers, enjoys less physical security than he did 25 years ago. At least half a million people in the Horn have died as a result of violence during the past two decades; at least another half million have starved. Three or four million have been uprooted and live as refugees. The Russians lack both the means and the will to remedy or reverse this situation.

In Africa, especially, Moscow's subsidies to leaders—more often than not military men playing a political role for which they are not suited—consist almost exclusively of military resources to help them retain control over a restive population. Realizing that military regimes seldom rest on a stable mass base, Moscow exploits their lack of legitimacy and consequent heightened sense of vulnerability and readiness to make concessions to the patron willing to underwrite their arrogation of power. This circumstance helps explain why the Soviet-Cuban military intervention on behalf of Ethiopia, for example, which upheld the existing territorial boundaries in the region, aroused so little criticism in Africa. The preoccupation "of most African states with domestic political stability" makes them tolerant of reliance on the USSR's weaponry and defensive shield, notwithstanding the accompanying spur to militarization, [according to Olajide Aluko].

Political Considerations

On occasion, Moscow may use arms to obtain hard currency or negotiate barter agreements for goods it needs—as in the early 1980s, when it exchanged arms for wheat with the Argentine military dictatorship; but its supply of arms to military regimes is prompted primarily by political, not commercial, considerations. Its quest in the early 1970s for naval support facilities in Somalia offers a clear instance of a courtship and readiness to persist in funneling weapons to a military dictator in order to retain the privileges it had obtained, despite evidence that the arms were being primed for aggressive purposes. Whatever the mix of considerations that affect its policy in any given situation, Moscow is not put off by the military character of any regime.

A third way in which the Soviet arms policy has militarized Third World politics is by making war a feasible option for rulers whose bent is toward regional conflict rather than regional accommodation. In his maiden speech at the U.N. General Assembly on September 24, 1985, Soviet Foreign Minister Eduard A. Shevardnadze declared, "It is not the fault of the Soviet Union that local conflicts break out and are raging in various regions of the world." Since the late 1960s, the record tells a very different story. A list of the major wars between Third World countries would show that most were made possible only because of the stockpiles and assured supplies of Soviet weapons: Egypt's war in Yemen (1962-1967), Arab-Israeli wars in 1967, 1969-1970, and

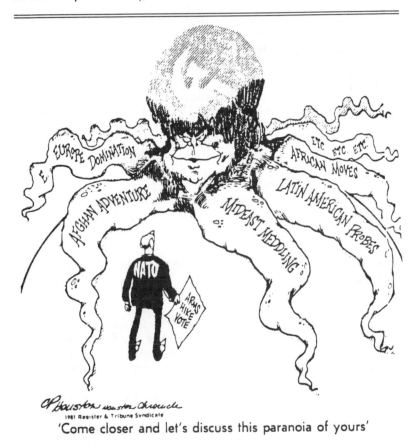

'Come closer and let's discuss this paranoia of yours'

Clyde Peterson. Reprinted with permission.

1973; Ethiopia and Somalia since 1977; Vietnam and Kampuchea since 1978; the Yemens in 1979; Iran and Iraq in 1980-1988; Libya and Chad in the 1980s. With the exception of the Indo-Pakistani war in 1965 and 1971, every major local war between Third World protagonists was started by a Soviet-armed state. . . .

Moscow did not create regional rivalries and tensions, which are the legacies of history, but it is responsible for the frequency with which they erupt into local wars. According to Dmitri Volskiy, a leading Soviet journalist, "attempts to hinder the natural, law-governed course of events in the 'Third World'" are what "creates hotbeds of tension there fraught with dangers of not only a local but also a global nature." How true. And it is the "unnatural" system-destabilizing intrusion of vast quantities of Soviet weaponry to clients whose purposes are clearly aggressive that is the single most salient catalyst of local wars in the Third World. But Soviet analysts never discuss the quantities or character of Soviet arms transfers or speculate on their consequences for domestic or regional developments in the Third World. . . .

In using arms to acquire influence and privileges, Soviet leaders try to avoid becoming involved in the local wars they make possible: their aim is "to profit from local conflicts without directly taking part in them [according to Hélène Carrère d'Encausse]." They prefer to operate behind the scenes or through surrogates, but they are deeply involved. They may not want confrontation with the United States, but they readily accept the risks entailed in priming clients bent on besting a regional adversary or undermining U.S. policy. An active participant at every critical stage of the escalation to the brink of war—and beyond—Moscow does not jeopardize its standing with major clients by curbing arms transfers. . . .

The Third World Loses

The record of the past few decades reveals that Soviet arms transfers contribute to the adoption of a high-cost military policy by assorted clients, whose one shared outlook is hostility to U.S. policy, usually as crystallized in U.S. support for their regional rivals. The process that encourages a Third World leadership to pursue a military line is insidious. Only a handful of countries have the potential to undertake large-scale military expenditures—the oil-rich Middle East countries, India, Egypt, Israel, Brazil and Argentina. In most cases, arms production and arms expenditures drain their economies of scarce resources that could otherwise be utilized for modernization. This process of militarization also tends to make countries unviable as stable political systems: it wastes resources, aggravates existing ethnic, religious, racial, and subregional cleavages, and perpetuates endemic backwardness. When Third World leaders play the power game, they are the most frequent losers, while the Soviet Union is the principal gainer.

VIEWPOINT

"The State Department offers a welcoming hand to death squad leaders from Central America, while the Justice Department prosecutes those who offer sanctuary to the victims of death squad violence."

US Intervention Threatens Human Rights

Michael Klare

In the following viewpoint, Michael Klare argues that the US intervenes in the Third World to support right-wing governments and dictators. These governments murder and torture anyone they suspect of opposing the government. US support helps these governments maintain power, Klare contends, and thwarts the efforts of Third World people who advocate change and respect for human rights. Klare directs the five-college program in peace and world security studies at Hampshire College in Amherst, Massachusetts. He is also an author and correspondent for *The Nation*.

As you read, consider the following questions:

1. How does the author define low-intensity conflict?
2. How does the strategy of low-intensity conflict affect human rights conditions in the Third World, according to Klare?
3. Why does Klare believe US support for dictators and military regimes may ultimately threaten human rights in the US?

Michael Klare, "Low-Intensity Conflict," *Christianity and Crisis*, February 1, 1988. Reprinted with permission. Copyright 1988, Christianity and Crisis, 537 West 121st Street, New York, NY 10027.

Most people have heard the term "low-intensity conflict," and have some idea of what it means. From a military perspective, LIC is warfare that falls below the threshold of full-scale military combat between modern armies (of the sort that occurred in the Korean War and at the onset of the Iran-Iraq War). Under U.S. doctrine, low-intensity conflict encompasses four particular types of operations: (1) *counterinsurgency*, combat against revolutionary guerrillas, as is now being waged in El Salvador and the Philippines; (2) *proinsurgency*, U.S. support for anticommunist insurgents, such as the contras in Nicaragua and UNITA in Angola; (3) *peacetime contingency operations*, police-type actions like the U.S. invasion of Grenada and the April 1986 bombing of Tripoli; and (4) *military "show of force,"* threatening military maneuvers of the sort the U.S. is conducting in the Persian Gulf. These are not theoretical or anticipated forms of warfare. They are military operations that the United States is conducting *now*. From an LIC point of view, *America is at war*—extensively, aggressively, and with every evidence of continuing such activity.

"Low-intensity conflict" does not necessarily imply that the level of bloodshed and savagery is low: The low-intensity conflict in Guatemala, for instance, has already claimed well over 100,000 lives. Similar numbers have perished in other LIC conflicts. What is crucial to recognize, in fact, is that low-intensity conflict is a form of warfare in which *your side* suffers very little death or destruction, while the other side suffers as much damage as possible without producing undue hardship for your own society. It is war with proxies, war with mercenaries, war with modern military systems aimed at those with the most primitive of defenses.

Avoiding the Vietnam Syndrome

In the United States today, low-intensity conflict has an even more specific meaning: Given the persistence of the Vietnam Syndrome, it means war in which U.S. involvement is kept sufficiently indistinct and inexpensive so as not to produce a hue and cry in Congress or the media. The U.S. military remembers the strident demonstrations and antimilitary attitudes of the Vietnam era, and is determined to avoid such responses for as long as it possibly can.

Low-intensity conflict, by definition, is that amount of murder, mutilation, torture, rape, and savagery that is sustainable without triggering widespread public disapproval at home. Or, to put it another way, LIC is the ultimate in "yuppie" warfare—it allows privileged Americans to go on buying condominiums, wearing chic designer clothes, eating expensive meals at posh restaurants, and generally living in style without risking their own lives, without facing conscription, without paying higher taxes, and, most important, without being overly distracted by grisly scenes on the

THE GRAND PUPPETEER

Abe Blashko/People's Daily World

television set. *That*, essentially, is the determining characteristic of low-intensity conflict in the American context today.

What, then, is low-intensity conflict aimed at? Who are its victims, and what is the nature of low-intensity combat itself?

According to U.S. military leaders, LIC is aimed at combatting terrorism, subversion, insurgency, and other forms of disruptive violence in the Third World. Such violence is generally portrayed in ideological terms, as a Soviet- or Cuban-inspired assault on the pro-Western, democratic nations of the "free world." But it is not just Marxist guerrillas whom LIC is intended to defeat, but *anyone* in the Third World who calls for a radical restructuring of the global system—whether inspired by Marx, Mao, Christ, or Mohammed.

Defense of Privilege

Perhaps the clearest and most revealing formulation of low-intensity conflict was provided by General Maxwell D. Taylor in 1974. General Taylor—a key articulator of the rationale for U.S. intervention in Vietnam—wrote at the end of the Vietnam War about U.S. military missions in the post-Vietnam era, and his words carried great weight. He said: "As the leading affluent 'have' power, we may expect to have to fight to protect our national valuables against envious 'have nots.'"

This theme, the "haves vs. the have-nots," is the underlying premise of LIC doctrine. It states, in essence, that the privileged nations of the industrialized "North" are vitally threatened by the starving, nonwhite masses of the underdeveloped "South." Accordingly, we must be prepared to combat any forces in the Third World that seek to reconstruct the world system in a way that reverses the flow of wealth from South to North.

This theme was first elaborated in a 1977 RAND Corporation study on "Military Implications of a Possible World Order Crisis in the 1980s." In this report, Guy Pauker wrote: "There is a non-negligible chance that mankind [sic] is entering a period of increased social instability and faces the possibility of a breakdown of global order as a result of a sharpening confrontation between the Third World and the industrial democracies." Because of the growing gap between rich and poor, "The North-South conflict . . . could get out of hand in ways comparable to the peasant rebellions that in past centuries engulfed large parts of Europe or Asia, spreading like uncontrolled prairie fires."

Fervent Anticommunism

In the 1980s, this sort of apocalyptic thinking became intertwined with the fervent anticommunism of President Reagan and his associates to produce the foundation for current LIC doctrine. Perhaps the strongest exponent of this thinking is Neil C. Livingstone, a Pentagon consultant and counterinsurgency expert who was a close adviser to Lt. Col. Oliver North. In a 1983 speech at the National Defense University, Livingstone observed: "Unfulfilled expectations and economic mismanagement have turned much of the developing world into a 'hothouse of conflict,' capable of spilling over and engulfing the industrial West."

The Soviet Union, in Livingstone's view, sees in this discord "a means of undermining the West," "wearing it down, nibbling away at its peripheries, denying it the strategic materials . . . critical to its commerce." Our response to this threat "cannot be half-hearted or indecisive." Given the magnitude of the threat, "the security of the United States requires a restructuring of our warmaking capabilities, placing new emphasis on the ability to fight a succession of limited wars, and to project power into the Third World."

In other words, the main thrust of American power must be turned around: Instead of facing the putative threat from the East—from the Soviet Union and the Warsaw Pact—it must be rotated 90 degrees to face the *real* peril, the threat from the South, from the envious "have-nots" who threaten to reverse the flow of global wealth.

As expressed in the crisp language of Pentagon strategists, this means (quoting from Col. James Motley in the Army's leading strategic journal): "The United States should reorient its forces and traditional policies from an almost exclusive concentration on NATO [North Atlantic Treaty Organization] to better influence politico-military outcomes in the resource-rich and strategically located Third World areas." Given the West's growing dependence on these critical areas, moreover, "The United States will require forces with greater strategic and tactical utility to counter the more likely low-intensity contingencies that will confront the United States in ever-increasing numbers for the rest of this decade and beyond."

Not only must the U.S. reorient its forces to face the growing threat from the South, LIC doctrine assumes, but it must be prepared to fight there again and again for as long as we can see into the future.

Subverting International Law

In violation of the UN Charter and in defiance of universally recognized international legal norms, the United States has been waging an undeclared war against Nicaragua, committing aggression against Grenada, conducting campaigns of intimidation against Cuba, Syria, Libya and many other countries and interfering arrogantly in El Salvador, Honduras, Guatemala and in other regions. The US administration has transformed terrorism into a tool of national policy. The President of the United States takes it for granted—and freely admits—that America has the "right" to commit crimes against independent nations and subvert governments it does not like.

Boris Dmitriev, *A Policy Keeping the World on Edge*, 1987.

What will this mean in operational terms? How does a nation go about protecting itself from a world of envious have-nots, assuming it is committed to a military solution?

Killing three-quarters of the world's population, as European settlers did in the so-called New World, doesn't seem very practical, or even profitable, since nobody would be left to buy our products; and building a Great Wall, as China did to keep the "barbarians" out, would disrupt the flow of strategic raw materials we depend on so much. So what to do? Evidently, the cheapest solution is to hire or co-opt armies of thugs and mercenaries, and use them to starve and terrorize subject populations to the point that they are too dispirited or too frightened or too weak to resist. Now, this may seem a rather extreme characterization of U.S. policy. But look at some of the so-called "success stories" of counterinsurgency—Guatemala under the generals, Nicaragua under Anastasio Somoza, Chile under August Pinochet, Iran under the Shah, the Philippines under Ferdinand Marcos, to name a few. The essence of government strategy was precisely the eradication of protest through systematic murder, torture, and the "disappearance" of disaffected social sectors (labor, the peasantry, students, the clergy, Indians, and so on). And it does not matter necessarily that the "right" people—the ones who are actually "guilty" of membership in an underground organization—are targeted. The idea is to so terrorize the population—by inculcating a constant fear of a knock on the door in the middle of the night, followed by blindfolding, torture, mutilation, and death—that it remains silent no matter what hideous crimes against humanity are being committed.

This, more than anything, is the function of the "disappearances" and the death squads and the torture in so many Third World countries. It is not some irrational product of an underdeveloped mentality, but rather a pragmatic, cheap answer to the problem of three billion envious have-nots—and it lies at the heart of the emerging LIC doctrine.

Restricting the Press

As suggested by Colonel North's mentor, Neil C. Livingstone, America failed at counterinsurgency in Vietnam because excessive television coverage inhibited use of the right tactics. However, he noted, "They have learned this lesson in Guatemala, where the Guatemalan government has restricted the press to the urban centers and prosecuted the war against the guerrillas with efficiency, brutality, and dispatch." Amnesty International reports on Guatemala, among others, demonstrate what this means: the murder, starvation, or disappearance of an estimated 100,000 peasants, Indians, labor organizers, and church activists.

To engage in low-intensity warfare, therefore, ultimately means to forge an alliance with the dictators, the death squads, and the psychopaths of the world. Such alliances, according to Livingstone, "would surely provoke an outcry from civil libertarians in the United States. . . . But the plain fact is that the United States is at war, and in wartime the only thing that counts is winning, because winning is surviving."

Similar views were expressed by another LIC expert, Professor Sam Sarkesian of Loyola University in Chicago. "The public must understand that low-intensity conflicts do not conform to democratic notions of strategy or tactics," he said in 1985. "Revolutionaries and counterrevolutionaries develop their own morality and ethics that justify any means to achieve success. Survival is the ultimate morality." . . .

It is this sort of thinking that leads me to say that low-intensity conflict represents a vital threat to America's soul.

Permanent War

LIC proponents—inside and outside the executive branch and in both parties—are quietly but consistently engaging in a permanent, offensive war. The battlefield reaches the Philippines, where U.S. dollars fund the Aquino government's war against the New People's Army. It foments civil war in Afghanistan, where Congress appropriated more aid for the rebels than the administration requested. And it finances aggression in Angola, where the U.S. collaborates with South Africa. In every case, the enemy is ostensibly communist subversion, but the targets and the victims are self-determination and the potential for a constructive, democratic U.S. foreign policy.

Marc S. Miller, *In These Times*, September 21/27, 1988.

What does it mean for a society to enjoy relative freedom and security at home, while aiding and abetting wholesale murder and mutilation abroad? Do we remain immune to the horror of it all? I think not. I do not believe that you can condone brutality somewhere else and not suffer some moral rot on your own turf. And, in fact, we have ample evidence of this fact—Congress goes on voting "humanitarian" aid for the contras (i.e., food and fuel used to sustain the killing of civilians in Nicaragua), while denying aid to the truly needy in our own country; editorial writers bemoan the incidence of censorship in Nicaragua, while failing to mention the assassination of opposition journalists in El Salvador; the State Department offers a welcoming hand to death squad leaders from Central America, while the Justice Department prosecutes those who offer sanctuary to the victims of death squad violence. When we turn away from these atrocities, when we avert our eyes from injustice, when we escape into indulgence and self-absorption, our souls descend into a slow death.

"Western-style democracy with rare exceptions
has failed to take root in the Third World and
is not likely to do so."

Cultural Tradition Prevents Third World Democracy

Ernest W. Lefever

Many Third World countries are ruled by dictatorial governments
that deny their citizens basic human rights. In the following viewpoint, Ernest W. Lefever writes that cultural attitudes among Third
World people explain this proliferation of dictators. The importance democracy places on individual rights is foreign to Third
World cultures which have been organized around a tribe, he
argues. In a tribe, individual rights are less important than the
good of the community, and power is held by a strong leader.
Lefever is an author and the president of the Ethics and Public
Policy Center, a Washington, DC organization that conducts
research and publishes material on domestic and foreign policy
issues.

As you read, consider the following questions:

1. What traditions led to the rise of democracy in the West,
   according to Lefever?
2. Why does Lefever believe the oral tradition found in many
   Third World countries limits the development of effective
   government?

Ernest W. Lefever, "Observations on the Cultural Diversity of Non-Western
Governments." This article appeared in the January 1988 issue and is reprinted with
permission of The World & I, a publication of The Washington Times Corporation.
Copyright © 1988.

Despite great differences in climate, culture, economic organization, and religious outlook, all men everywhere face the same essential political questions: How shall we be ordered? What should be the relationship between the governors and the governed, between central authority and citizen consent, between the responsibilities of the state and the rights of individuals? Differences in cultural heritage do not alter the fundamental political question, but substantially influence the response and the viability of the various kinds of government.

The modalities of government have changed over the centuries, but the essential functions of the state remain the same. Fifteen hundred years ago, St. Augustine defined the purpose of government succinctly and with a touch of humor. If it were not for the state, he said, men would devour one another as fishes. A thousand years later Martin Luther said that the function of the state was to restrain evildoers. John Calvin was in full accord with these views.

The Tasks of Government

Good and humane government has three tasks. The first is to *govern*, to maintain order and security throughout its domain. The second task of government is to govern *justly*, to uphold the rule of law. The third task of government is to govern *democratically*, to be responsive to the will of the governed. Few governments of the world perform all three tasks well. In fact, most governments barely govern, much less govern justly or democratically.

Full-fledged Western-style democracy with rare exceptions has failed to take root in the Third World and is not likely to do so in the near future because these societies have not developed the fundamental concepts, values, and traditions essential to government based on broad citizen participation. One would be hard pressed to point to a single Third World state that operates wholly along British or American lines, even though its constitution may so specify.

The Foundations of Western Democracy

The prerequisites for democracy on the Anglo-American model are exacting and rarely duplicated. Our cherished Western institutions of authority and consent are the culmination of a five-thousand-year heritage that embraces the Judeo-Christian ethic of respect for the dignity of the human person, Greek democracy and political theory, Roman law and organization, and the Magna Carta with its implicit guarantee of rights for every citizen. Our political system depends upon the operation of competing political parties secure in the concept of a "loyal opposition" and undergirded by a free press, freedom of speech, and widespread respect for the rule of law, all of which must rest on the foundation of a broad moral and political consensus.

The political culture that emerged from this rich heritage remains a vital force in the West, though even here it is challenged—from within by a failure of will and moral confusion and from without by the new barbarians who rule by coercion rather than consent, who have substituted the will of a self-anointed elite for the rule of law and who insist that the "good society" can emerge only from a violent class conflict.

It is hardly surprising, therefore, that in the Third World, where the Western political ethic is an alien concept known only by reputation, democracy is little understood and rarely practiced. Consequently, U.S. policies based on the demand for liberal and democratic governments are almost bound to fail. . . .

Majority and Unanimity

Democracy . . . depends on the will of the majority: the people are consulted, a majority emerges and it is charged to govern the country. The minority does not hesitate to criticize but it submits.

For one accustomed to the mores and practices of Black Africa, this rule is alien to the country. In the gatherings of the family, village, and tribes decisions are not made by just the majority; the rule of unanimity must be followed. They may discuss one day, two days, three days but they must arrive at a formula acceptable to all participating in the meeting. . . .

This system of "all or nothing" makes practically impossible the functioning of democracy in Black Africa because if unanimity cannot be obtained, there remains only one solution: war and dissidence.

Roland Cartigny, in *The Rise and Fall of Democracies in Third World Societies*, 1986.

Transitional Societies: Many of the countries of Asia, Africa, and Latin America are confronted by chaos and uncertainty spawned by their transition from traditional ways of thinking and doing to more "modern" ways. Traditional cultures are essentially tribal. The extended family-language group not only defines the mores, customs, and daily routines, but more important, it circumscribes the worldview of its members. This is especially pronounced in sub-Saharan Africa, where the most serious barrier to statewide cohesion and to an effective central government is the dogged persistence of tribal identity. (The word *tribe* is used generically to designate an ethnic-language-kinship group that is smaller than or not coextensive with the borders of a sovereign state.)

According to a study of Ghana in 1965 by Philip J. Foster:

Elements of traditional social structure [persist] even within the most "modern" sectors of Ghanaian society. Ethnic background, kinship affiliation, and traditional residence patterns still play a role even within the urban context and indeed may provide the basis for organizations which appear at first sight to be essentially Western.

The colonial experience in most instances has resulted in only a thin veneer of Western concepts and values, even among the so-called Westernized elite. It could hardly have been otherwise, given the brevity and superficiality of the Western contact compared with the length and depth of the tribal history and experience. The persistence of tribalism and traditional worldviews is not widely understood in the United States, where in the 1960s there were great expectations that instant decolonialization would create a score of new democracies in Africa.

Ethnic Diversity: The hard fact of ethnic diversity in most Third World countries has often been overlooked or downplayed in the West because of the lingering illusion that tribalism is politically and morally obsolete and that modern communication would succeed in replacing it with a larger national consciousness, if not with a sense of universal identity. Here, as in other areas, the idealists who believe in inevitable progress were profoundly wrong. . . .

Ethnic politics is a worldwide reality. Consider these statistics. According to one study of 132 sovereign states, only twelve (9.1 percent) were found to be composed of only one ethnic group. (Of these, only one is in Africa—Somalia.) About a third of them lacked any single dominant group. Of the 132 states, twenty-five had a dominant ethnic group comprising 90 percent or more of the population, twenty-five had a dominant group representing 75-89 percent of the population, thirty-one had a significant group comprising 50-74 percent of the population, and thirty-nine (the largest bloc) had no single group comprising half the population. . . .

Authoritarianism and Tradition

Political Orientation of Elite: The intellectual and political leaders of the Third World tend to be vaguely Marxist in ideology and authoritarian in method. The authoritarianism emerges naturally from traditional practices of social and political control where the hereditary leader or the winner of a contest does not tolerate opposition. The Leninist tactic and ideology of class struggle was imported to Asia and Africa during the latter decades of the colonial period, reflecting the most articulate social critique in Britain and France at that time. Hence, Marxist ideology with its condemnation of the West and its panoply of pejorative code words directed against the real and alleged sins of the erstwhile colonial powers has become the prevailing ideology in the Third World. . . .

It should also be noted that most black African states are ruled by one-party elites with inefficient bureaucracies characterized by widespread corruption. Corruption grows as the regime expands its power as export licenses, quotas, and market shares offer new opportunities for bribery to the well-connected. Corruption is especially rife where loyalty to the extended tribe is greater than loyalty to the impersonal and abstract state. . . .

Democracy and Individualism

Democracies . . . are based on "the rights of man"; the Declaration of Independence of 1776 in North America and those of 1789 in France are the bases of our democratic system and they engendered during the XIX century all the democracies conforming to our moral norms. That which matters is that the individual, whoever he may be, is owed respect, liberty, and security. Laws are made for him, not against him. He is the fundamental element in our entire political structure.

Now, what says one who has lived in Black Africa a while? He states that the African man does not exist as an individual; the African exists only to the extent that he belongs to his group: village, tribe, ethnic. . . . Actual life in Black Africa never really blooms unless it has a collective manifestation. In my 35 years in Africa, I have never seen a man work, hunt, play, or cry alone. No, the individual does not exist and he is being asked to be a perfect democrat by isolating himself by dropping a voting ballot in the election box. What heresy! What nonsense!

Roland Cartigny, in *The Rise and Fall of Democracies in Third World Societies,* 1986.

Most Third World states are governed by small, authoritarian elites who emphasize order over freedom in the political sphere and distribution over production in the economic sphere. To enhance their authority, Third World regimes generally co-opt the influential elites—the military, leading families, banks, businesses, intellectuals, and sometimes labor leaders. Opposition groups— press, political parties, or student organizations—may be tolerated if they are small and weak, but usually they are closely watched. When an opposition group or leader transgresses the ill-defined limits of permissible activity, swift corrective action is taken by the regime. The very concept of a "loyal opposition" is almost completely lacking among the rulers and dissenting groups. The opposition is usually seen as disloyal or subversive because it traditionally behaves that way.

Authoritarian regimes, arbitrary rule, capricious decrees, and a less-than-loyal opposition in Asia, Africa, and Latin America are all reflections of a fundamental defect as seen from the Western democratic perspective—the absence of the most precious achievement of the Western political tradition, the rule of law coextensive with the state. Tribes and other groups may have rules and customs for their own members, but this falls far short of a rule of law for all individuals, of whatever group or class, within one sovereign jurisdiction. Equal justice under law, orderly and competitive politics, wide participation in public affairs, and democracy itself are not possible without the rule of law, the codification of a moral and customary consensus developed over generations.

Oral Tradition

The concept of each individual being equal under the law is a unique achievement of the West. As Adda B. Bozeman points out:

> This has not been the case in either Africa or Asia where human groupings have been held together effectively in comprehensive orders dominated by respect for religion, etiquette, the stabilizing function of war and conflict, or perhaps the superior wisdom regularly imputed to selected men. In short, law is not recognized everywhere as a distinct idea or a paramount reference.

Professor Bozeman concludes that neither the Western concept of law nor the norms or values on which it rests "can be presumed to exist in other systems of public order." This may appear to be an exaggeration, but I believe it is dramatically the case in black Africa where oral tradition, tribal kinship loyalties, and ascribed authority to hereditary rulers or selected elders form the basis of order and justice.

The oral tradition also imposes other constraints on the quality of the political order because of its limited comprehension of time and space. Exclusive reliance on oral discourse seriously limits the future-oriented thought and planning essential to building an orderly structure of law and political authority. Oral tradition also limits the possibilities of spatial and territorial order for essentially the same reasons. When there are no written treaties or land deeds, small ethnically defined areas or even large political territories created by conquest tend to disintegrate as a result of migration or the death of the leaders. Consequently, references to precolonial African "states" and "empires" are often misleading.

This evidence suggests the validity of my central thesis—that Western-style democracy has failed to take root in the Third World and is unlikely to succeed in the near future; hence, the folly of U.S. threats to diminish or withhold support for allies for their inability to conform to our democratic model. As diplomatist George F. Kennan said: "It is difficult to see any promise in an American policy which sets out to correct and improve the political habits of large parts of the world's population," adding that authoritarian and often brutal government "has been the common tradition of most of mankind" for millennia and will remain so "for long into the future, no matter how valiantly Americans insist on tilting against the windmills.". . .

The varieties of authoritarian rule run from simple one-man dictatorships to military or civilian regimes which permit, within limits, an "independent" judiciary, a parliament, some opposition political activity, and an opposition press. Often these limits are circumscribed by emergency decrees that may be approved by a rubber-stamp legislature. Most such regimes have come to power by military coups, the majority bloodless. Others evolved incrementally by invoking one emergency power after another in the name of preserving the security of the state against subversion. Virtually all authoritarian rulers promise to return to "normal" democratic and constitutional procedures, including free elections, when the security of the country permits it.

The vast majority of the people in the Third World are disenfranchised. They live under minority ruling elites who were not elected and who cannot be voted out of office. In Asia, Africa, and Latin America a coup d'état, not an election, is the "normal" way to change governments. Bullets, whether fired or held in reserve, have been more potent than ballots. . . .

Totalitarian Regimes

In a totalitarian state, the one-party regime not only determines the political structure but also makes all significant legal, economic, social, cultural, and educational decisions. There are no oases of freedom or human choice because the elite has virtually usurped the role of the family, church, school, and the economy. The state claims the attributes of God by asserting its omniscience, and it buttresses this assertion by attempting to be omnipotent and omnipresent.

There is a profound moral difference between totalitarian North Korea and authoritarian South Korea in terms of human rights, the quality of life, and the possibilities of change toward greater political participation. The South Koreans enjoy economic and religious freedom and increasing political participation, but they do not yet enjoy the full range of rights we have in the West.

If friendly governments request our assistance or advice, we should provide help that serves our mutual interests in peace and development, but we should not force our views on our friends, much less attempt to embarrass governments that stand with us in the struggle against the totalitarians. We should extend a friendly hand to all governments that pursue a constructive and peaceful foreign policy, even if their domestic institutions and practices do not fully measure up to our standards.

"If democracy is to be a significant form of government in the developing world, it . . . must be combined with indigenous values so that it is a domestic reform, not an imported product."

Cultural Tradition Could Promote Third World Democracy

Edgar Owens

A writer and consultant, Edgar Owens served on the staff of the US Agency for International Development for twenty years. He also worked for Appropriate Technology International, a Washington, DC organization that helps Third World countries develop and adopt small-scale technologies that will increase self-sufficiency. In the following viewpoint, he argues that democracy could take root in the Third World if it were combined with cultural traditions. For example, in traditional Third World societies, power was decentralized and held by several local authorities. Owens maintains that this diffusion of power is a promising base for democracy because it gives individual people a voice in government.

As you read, consider the following questions:

1. In the author's opinion, how did the introduction of private property promote democracy in the West, but hinder democracy in the Third World?
2. How did the government agencies established by colonial administrators thwart the development of democracy?

Edgar Owens, *The Future of Freedom in the Developing World.* Elmsford, NY: Pergamon Press, 1987. Reprinted with permission.

Apologists for colonialism sometimes claim that the centuries of European world hegemony, for all its faults, at least had the merit of introducing into the developing world several of the nobler ideas of the Western tradition. On the surface, this claim may seem to have some justification. The ideas of human dignity, social justice, and political freedom that guided the reform of once feudal Western Europe eventually undermined the acceptance of colonialism, and helped bring a return to the ideas of self-determination and self-respect, which were set forth as national objectives by the newly formed—and almost everywhere democratic—governments that assumed power after independence. Further, the Western idea that poverty can be ameliorated has so captivated humankind that economic development has become an imperative of our time.

In fact, if colonial powers are judged by the extent to which they left behind partially reformed governments, then the only successful such power was Japan. Her forward wards, Taiwan and South Korea, are two of only a handful of countries in which the poor actually are involved in economic growth. Whereas Japan gave the poor of these countries limited access to production resources, public organizations and the law, the European countries and the United States did not do likewise in the countries over which they ruled.

The European colonial powers introduced three ideas that eroded the autonomy of traditional local communities in Asia and Africa, and weakened the capacity of these communities to protect themselves from exploiters—the ideas of private property, individual taxation, and monetization of taxes. That these concepts, which Westerners take for granted as almost a part of the natural order of things, could harm ordinary people, dramatizes the danger of judging other parts of the world through the blinkers of one's own culture.

Private Property

In the West, private property originated as a restraint upon the power of the king by not allowing him to take back property already given to another, most commonly a grant of land and a title. Recognition of this principle was forced upon King John by English barons at Runnymede in 1215, thus enshrining the principle of private property in the Magna Carta. As the powers of the King were gradually reduced and individual rights extended to ordinary people, private property obtained formidable protection, as in the requirements of the search warrant. So important was private property to John Locke that he originally wrote one of the most famous phrases in Western political thought as "life, liberty, and property." Thomas Jefferson changed the phrase because he and the other Founding Fathers thought the right of private property had been settled and no longer required special attention.

In Asia and Africa, land was almost everywhere controlled by local communities and allocated among individual members of the community group. These communities commonly were small villages, numbering less than a thousand people, though in some parts of Africa they were a subtribal or subclan group living in a cluster of villages similar to a township or a very small county. A family might cultivate the same plots through generations, and hold a first claim to their use, but never own them as private property. If the family disappeared from the community, the plots were reclaimed by the village and reallocated to other members. Land was neither sold nor allocated to nonmembers of the community.

The Evolution of Freedom

Westerners care about democracy not because of its forms, but because it institutionalizes what Alfred North Whitehead called "a fundamental respect for the preciousness of human life." It is this "respect," not particular forms of democracy, that is the issue of freedom in the developing world today. If today's developing countries are to become free, then freedom must evolve from within, just as it did in the developing countries in the eighteenth and nineteenth centuries—an evolution which produced the Western democracies.

Edgar Owens, *The Future of Freedom in the Developing World,* 1987.

The system kept outsiders out. Further, outsiders' contacts were with the community, rather than individuals. Taxes were levied upon the community as a whole. Once the amount was negotiated between the government agent and the community, then the governing council apportioned the taxes among individual members. The recruitment of labor (often forced) for the army or for public-works projects followed the same pattern. Since these communities were microcosms of the larger society, with a handful of privileged local elites dominating the others, the lower ranks paid more than their share of taxes and provided more than their share of labor. Nevertheless, they accepted their lot because sustaining the cohesion of the community group was their only protection against the power and greed of rulers and the attacks of roving bands of marauders, as well as their only source of support in countering the effects of natural catastrophes.

In introducing private property, individual taxation, and taxes paid in money rather than food, the colonial powers in many parts of the world required local communities, for the first time in their histories, to identify and draw fixed boundaries, and to register property descriptions and the identity of the cultivators with the local administrative office of the national government. Land taxes were then levied on the individual farmer rather than on the communal village. If individuals could not pay, the land was taken in payment and then put up for sale—often to be bought by the tax collectors. Thus, outsiders were able to force their way into the community for the first time.

Taxes

In monetizing taxes, the colonial powers forced villagers to sell a portion of their harvest, and then to grow cash crops instead of their traditional consumption crops in order to obtain hard currency to pay the taxes. In addition, villagers were forced to sell at low prices, at markets controlled by tax collectors, other officials, and those favored by the government. Thus, village farmers became victims of single-buyer markets and a sell-cheap, buy-dear price cycle that is still common in developing lands.

The new property and tax systems initiated a gradual transfer of power away from local to national governments, a change that eventually left the former almost powerless. Decisions once made by community governing bodies were transferred to administrative offices of the national government. The resolution of conflicts, once handled in customary ways of arbitration, was similarly transferred out of the local community. Thus, once highly decentralized rural societies which had exerted considerable control over local affairs, became highly centralized. By breaking down communal barriers, colonialism exposed families and individuals to the exploitation of outsiders whom they were powerless to oppose.

To give one example, the system of land tenure in British India, known as Zamindari, was established in 1793 by the same Lord Cornwallis whom George Washington defeated at Yorktown. His stated purpose was to assure adequate revenue for the East India Company, the private company that was Britain's agent in India at the time. The Zamindars were prominent individuals in local communities who agreed to deliver fixed sums to the British, in return for which they were allowed to collect as much as they could squeeze out of the people.

The Zamindars used their powers to acquire vast holdings and permitted their agents to acquire land on a smaller scale in accordance with their rank. Thus, a hierarchy of exploiters, supported by the might and majesty of the British Empire, gradually smothered local autonomy. Although Zamindari was abolished after independence, many inequities continued which are still a major obstacle to agricultural improvement in India. . . .

Near the end of colonial rule, the colonial powers began to establish those agencies of government that provide health services, education, and agriculture extension services and to build schools, hospitals, and clinics. To staff the now expanding national government, residents of the colonies were admitted to the higher ranks of the civil service for the first time. Selection was based on examinations similar to those associated with merit systems in the Western democracies. It was merit for the few, for only a handful from the higher social ranks had the education and experience to qualify. The new elite fitted easily into systems based on the assumption that villagers were incompetent and that solutions should pass downward from national agencies to the masses.

Finally, English and French became the languages of political power and government; of business and international trade; of the professions; and, to some extent, of culture. Villagers, still mostly illiterate even in their own language or dialect, were unable to communicate with their rulers. The use of foreign languages, especially as European type schools were introduced, narrowed the cultural gap between the elites of the countries and their rulers, but it widened the gap between these elites and their own people.

The Meaning of Traditionalism

The traditions of the peoples urge that the communities be strengthened through a spiritual practice which preserves their distinct nature. Traditionalism . . . is the effort to establish community identity and the internal strengthening of the community, with emphasis on the preservation of those aspects of precolonial life which make those communities distinct. It is the recognition that individuals have a responsibility to be active members and participants in the life of their community.

Traditionalism [is not] the act of seeking power for oneself: it is the effort to empower the community and, through the community, the nation. Our ancestors were not in the habit of raising up dictators as chiefs and medicine men. The Indian people of old prized individuals who were givers to their community, not takers.

John Mohawk, in *The Indigenous Voice*, 1988.

In other words, during the colonial period the access of ordinary people to the things they need to be involved in economic growth was reduced. Thanks to the private property and tax systems introduced by the colonial administrators, villagers lost land and some were converted into tenants, sharecroppers, and landless farm workers. By virtue of their lot in life, they lacked capital and also technical, managerial, and marketing skills to invest in industries. Colonial governments did not initiate special programs to help them offset these disadvantages. Ordinary people lost control over their own affairs as power was transferred from their one public organization, their local government, to national governments.

Similarly, their access to legal protection, never very great, was reduced. And so, the colonial system strengthened the power of a few to extort and exploit—except, in a limited way, in Taiwan and Korea. . . .

False Democracy

At one time or another, during the past three and a half decades, most of the noncommunist countries in the developing world have adopted a form of government described as democratic. With very few exceptions, these countries went about increasing GNP [gross national product] as if production and form of government were unrelated. They applied the tenets of the trickle down approach to economic growth, ignoring the possible use of the power of government to give the poor access to resources, public organizations, and the law. Democracy in the developing world is little more than a hollow superstructure strapped to governments that are unreformed and rife with corruption. For the great mass of the poor, still without political power, democracy is nothing more than a choice among those who are going to rule anyway. And to rule is to exploit and cheat.

Today, democracy is a tarnished ideal. Most of the self-styled democratic governments have disappeared, toppled easily, noiselessly by a mere pittance of power, commonly a small complement of soldiers. In some countries, the military seems to cling to power more or less indefinitely. In others, especially in Latin America, the pendulum appears to swing back and forth. In the 1960s, when trickle down economics masqueraded as the Alliance for Progress, democracy was ascendant. In the 1970s, the military took over. In the 1980s, elected governments rule again in a number of Latin countries, among them Argentina, Peru, Honduras, Uruguay, and Brazil. Their proclaimed respect for civil rights is welcome. However, none of these countries has created economic and social rights for the poor.

Curiously, many Westerners have accepted these false democracies as genuine. Because false democracies have failed to resolve major problems and are corrupt, some students of development say that democracy does not work in the developing world, or that a certain level of affluence must be reached before societies can become democratic, as if riches were the route to freedom. Or they claim that developing nations must pass through an authoritarian stage before they can become free. Authoritarian governments, it is argued, possess a certain combination of persuasion and coercion needed for economic growth, which cannot be matched by democracies relying on incentives and voluntary action. To assume that people without names will not respond to incentives, only to coercion, is the ultimate condescension of people of power, privilege, and plenty.

In truth, whether democracy could be an effective way of reforming government in the developing world is still an unanswered question for the simple reason that it has hardly been tried. Virtually all the governments that have been labeled democratic are false democracies. There are a handful of possible exceptions—Sri Lanka and Costa Rica, for example—but only a handful.

Extending Rights to Marginal People

To have accepted false democracies as genuine suggests that the origins of the political system of which we Westerners are justly proud have become dim in our own memory. The idea of democracy appeared in Western Europe in the seventeenth century as the modern world's first government-reform movement. It has turned out to be a truly powerful example of Alexis de Tocqueville's "idea of escape." Democracy arose at a time when poverty was assumed to be the permanent economic condition for most of the population. Nine-tenths of the population of Western Europe were illiterate subsistence farmers. Yet democracy was seen as a way of restraining the power of a privileged few to exploit, extort, and steal from them with impunity. . . .

If democracy is to be a significant form of government in the developing world, it must again become a government-reform movement, a way of giving names to the nameless, marginal people. Further, democracy must be combined with indigenous values so that it is a domestic reform, not an imported product. While it is surely true that some principles of democracy evolved in the West are universal—such as protecting the individual against the police power of the state—it is equally true that the evolution of political freedom in the developing world would lead to new forms and processes of democracy based on the values and circumstances of individual countries.

"Underlying liberation theology is a prophetic and comradely commitment to the life, cause, and struggle of . . . millions of debased and marginalized human beings."

Liberation Theology Promotes Human Rights

Leonardo Boff and Clodovis Boff

Brothers Leonardo and Clodovis Boff are two of the most well-known advocates of liberation theology. Leonardo Boff is a professor of theology in Petropolis, Brazil. Clodovis Boff teaches at the Catholic University of Sao Paulo in Brazil. Both are priests who work among Brazil's poor. The authors explain liberation theology as a response to the injustice and poverty from which Third World people suffer. The Boffs advocate a revolution of the poor to end the poverty sustained by the capitalist system.

As you read, consider the following questions:

1. What inspires liberation theology, according to the authors?
2. What do the Boffs mean by "reformism" and why do they criticize it?
3. How do the authors explain Marxism's contribution to liberation theology?

Leonardo and Clodovis Boff, *Introducing Liberation Theology.* Maryknoll, NY: Orbis Books, 1987. Reprinted with permission.

A woman of forty, but who looked as old as seventy, went up to the priest after Mass and said sorrowfully: "Father, I went to communion without going to confession first." "How come, my daughter?" asked the priest. "Father," she replied, "I arrived rather late, after you had begun the offertory. For three days I have had only water and nothing to eat; I'm dying of hunger. When I saw you handing out the hosts, those little pieces of white bread, I went to communion just out of hunger for that little bit of bread." The priest's eyes filled with tears. He recalled the words of Jesus: "My flesh [bread] is real food . . . whoever feeds on me will draw life from me" (John 6:55,57). . . .

One Saturday night I (Clodovis) went to see Manuel, a catechist of a base community. "Father," he said to me, "this community and others in the district are coming to an end. The people are dying of hunger. They are not coming: they haven't the strength to walk this far. They have to stay in their houses to save their energy."

Third World Suffering

What lies behind liberation theology? Its starting point is the perception of scandals such as those described above, which exist not only in Latin America but throughout the Third World. According to "conservative" estimates, there are in those countries held in underdevelopment:

- five-hundred million persons starving;
- one billion, six-hundred million persons whose life expectancy is less than sixty years (when a person in one of the developed countries reaches the age of forty-five, he or she is reaching middle age; in most of Africa or Latin America, a person has little hope of living to that age);
- one billion persons living in absolute poverty;
- one billion, five-hundred million persons with no access to the most basic medical care;
- five-hundred million with no work or only occasional work and a per capita income of less than $150 a year;
- eight-hundred-fourteen million who are illiterate;
- two billion with no regular, dependable water supply.

Who cannot be filled with righteous anger at such a human and social hell? Liberation theology presupposes an energetic protest at such a situation, for that situation means:

- on the social level: collective oppression, exclusion, and marginalization;
- on the individual level: injustice and denial of human rights;
- on the religious level: social sinfulness, "contrary to the plan of the Creator and to the honor that is due to him" (*Puebla and Beyond: Documentation and Commentary*, 1979).

Without a minimum of "suffering with" this suffering that affects the great majority of the human race, liberation theology can neither exist nor be understood. Underlying liberation theology is a prophetic and comradely commitment to the life, cause, and struggle of these millions of debased and marginalized human beings, a commitment to ending this historical-social iniquity. The Vatican Instruction, "Some Aspects of Liberation Theology" (August 6, 1984), put it well: "It is not possible for a single instant to forget the situations of dramatic poverty from which the challenge set to theologians springs—the challenge to work out a genuine theology of liberation."

Meeting the Poor Christ in the Poor

Every true theology springs from a spirituality—that is, from a true meeting with God in history. Liberation theology was born when faith confronted the injustice done to the poor. By "poor" we do not really mean the poor individual who knocks on the door asking for alms. We mean a collective poor, the "popular classes," which is a much wider category than the "proletariat" singled out by Karl Marx (it is a mistake to identify the poor of liberation theology with the proletariat, though many of its critics do): the poor are also the workers exploited by the capitalist system; the underemployed, those pushed aside by the production process— a reserve army always at hand to take the place of the employed; they are the laborers of the countryside, and migrant workers with only seasonal work.

God as Liberator

The historical womb from which liberation theology has emerged is the life of the poor and, in particular, of the Christian communities that have arisen within the bosom of the present-day Latin American church. This experience is the setting in which liberation theology tries to read the word of God and be alert to the challenges that faith issues to the historical process in which that people is engaged. . . . The aim is to enter more deeply into faith in a God who became one of us, and to do so on the basis of the faith-filled experience and commitment of those who acknowledge this God as their liberator.

Gustavo Gutiérrez, *A Theology of Liberation*, 1988.

All this mass of the socially and historically oppressed makes up the poor as a social phenomenon. In the light of faith, Christians see in them the challenging face of the Suffering Servant, Jesus Christ. At first there is silence, silent and sorrowful contemplation, as if in the presence of a mystery that calls for introspection and prayer. Then this presence speaks. The Crucified in these crucified persons weeps and cries out: "I was hungry . . . in prison . . . naked" (Matt. 25:31-46).

Here what is needed is not so much contemplation as effective action for liberation. The Crucified needs to be raised to life. We are on the side of the poor only when we struggle alongside them against the poverty that has been unjustly created and forced on them. Service in solidarity with the oppressed also implies an act of love for the suffering Christ, a liturgy pleasing to God. . . .

Reformism

"Reformism" seeks to improve the situation of the poor, but always within existing social relationships and the basic structuring of society, which rules out greater participation by all and diminution in the privileges enjoyed by the ruling classes. Reformism can lead to great feats of development in the poorer nations, but this development is nearly always at the expense of the oppressed poor and very rarely in their favor. For example, in 1964 the Brazilian economy ranked 46th in the world; in 1984 it ranked 8th. The last twenty years have seen undeniable technological and industrial progress, but at the same time there has been a considerable worsening of social conditions for the poor, with exploitation, destitution, and hunger on a scale previously unknown in Brazilian history. This has been the price paid by the poor for this type of elitist, exploitative, and exclusivist development in which, in the words of Pope John Paul II, the rich become ever richer at the expense of the poor who become ever poorer.

The poor can break out of their situation of oppression only by working out a strategy better able to change social conditions: the strategy of liberation. In liberation, the oppressed come together, come to understand their situation through the process of conscientization, discover the causes of their oppression, organize themselves into movements, and act in a coordinated fashion. First, they claim everything that the existing system can give: better wages, working conditions, health care, education, housing, and so forth; then they work toward the transformation of present society in the direction of a new society characterized by widespread participation, a better and more just balance among social classes and more worthy ways of life. . . .

Dreams of Freedom

Despite the massive and gospel-denying domination of the colonial centuries, dreams of freedom were never entirely extinguished. But it is only in the past few decades that a new consciousness of liberation has become widespread over the whole of Latin America. The poor, organized and conscientized, are beating at their masters' doors, demanding life, bread, liberty, and dignity. Courses of action are being taken with a view to release the liberty that is now held captive. Liberation is emerging as the strategy of the poor themselves, confident in themselves and in their instruments of struggle: free trade unions, peasant organizations, local associations, action groups and study groups, popular political parties, base Christian communities. They are being joined by groups and individuals from other social classes who have opted to change society and join the poor in their struggle to bring about change.

God's New Manifestation

The theology of the Third World has burst upon the scene with a hermeneutic challenge. Like the theology that is arising in the world of the poor, all theologies of liberation (socio-political, religious, women's, black, "theologic" and so on) mean to decipher a liberating God's new manifestation in situations of injustice and alienation. For, in the suffering of the poor, we are assisting at a new God-event. The poor are raising their consciousness and fighting for liberation. It is they, first and foremost, who "recognize" God, and who pronounce the first "word"—the first interpretation— of the God-event.

José Severino Croatto, in *Third World Liberation Theologies*, 1986.

The growth of regimes of "national security" (for which read "capital security"), of military dictatorships, with their repression of popular movements in many countries of Latin America, is a reaction against the transforming and liberating power of the organized poor. . . .

Explaining Oppression

Faced with the oppressed, the theologian's first question can only be: Why is there oppression and what are its causes?

The oppressed are to be found in many strata of society. [The 1979 Puebla document on liberation theology] lists them: young children, juveniles, indigenous peoples, campesinos, laborers, the underemployed and unemployed, the marginalized, persons living in overcrowded urban slums, the elderly. There is one overarching characteristic of the oppressed in the Third World: they are *poor* in socio-economic terms. They are the dispossessed masses on the peripheries of cities and in rural areas. . . .

If we start with the fundamental expression of oppression as socio-economic poverty, we then need to find what causes it. Here, liberation theology has found three ready-made answers, which might be called the empirical, the functional, and the dialectical explanations of poverty.

The *empirical* explanation: poverty as vice. This approach produces a short and superficial explanation. It attributes the causes of poverty to laziness, ignorance, or simply human wickedness.

96

It does not look at the collective or structural dimension of the problem: that the poor make up whole masses of a people and their numbers are growing all the time. It is the common conception of social destitution, the explanation most generally upheld in society. . . .

The *functional* explanation: poverty as backwardness. This is the liberal or bourgeois interpretation of the phenomenon of social poverty: it is attributed to economic and social backwardness. In time, thanks to the development process itself, helped in the Third World by foreign loans and technology, "progress" will arrive and hunger will disappear—so the functionalists think. . . .

The *dialectical* explanation: poverty as oppression. This sees poverty as the product of the economic organization of society itself, which *exploits* some—the workers—and *excludes* others from the production process—the underemployed, unemployed, and all those marginalized in one way or another. In his encyclical *Laborem Exercens*, Pope John Paul II defines the root of this situation as the supremacy of capital—enjoyed by the few—over labor—practiced by the many.

This explanation, also called the "historico-structural" approach, sees poverty as a *collective* and also *conflictive* phenomenon, which can be overcome only by replacing the present social system with an *alternative* system. The way out of this situation is *revolution*, understood as the transformation of the bases of the economic and social system. . . .

Relationships with Marxism

When dealing with the poor and the oppressed and seeking their liberation, how do we avoid coming into contact with Marxist groups (on the practical level) and with Marxist theory (on the academic level)? This is already hinted at in the use of such terms as "dialectical" or "historico-structural" explanation of the phenomenon of socio-economic poverty.

In liberation theology, Marxism is never treated as a subject on its own but always *from and in relation to the poor*. Placing themselves firmly on the side of the poor, liberation theologians ask Marx: "What can you tell us about the situation of poverty and ways of overcoming it?" Here Marxists are submitted to the judgment of the poor and their cause, and not the other way around.

Therefore, liberation theology uses Marxism purely as an *instrument*. It does not venerate it as it venerates the gospel. And it feels no obligation to account to social scientists for any use it may make—correct or otherwise—of Marxist terminology and ideas, though it does feel obliged to account to the poor, to their faith and hope, and to the ecclesial community, for such use. To put it in more specific terms, liberation theology freely borrows from

Marxism certain "methodological pointers" that have proved fruit-ful in understanding the world of the oppressed, such as:
- the importance of economic factors;
- attention to the class struggle;
- the mystifying power of ideologies, including religious ones. . . .

Discrimination

Liberation theology is about liberation of the oppressed—in their totality as persons, body and soul—and in their totality as a class: the poor, the subjected, the discriminated against. We cannot con-fine ourselves to the purely socio-economic aspect of oppression, the "poverty" aspect, however basic and "determinant" this may be. We have to look also to other levels of social oppression, such as:
- racist oppression: discrimination against blacks;
- ethnic oppression: discrimination against indigenous peoples or other minority groups;
- sexual oppression: discrimination against women.

Each of these various oppressions—or discriminations—and more (oppression of children, juveniles, the elderly) has its specific nature and therefore needs to be treated (in both theory and prac-tice) specifically. So we have to go beyond an exclusively "classist" concept of the oppressed, which would restrict the oppressed to the socio-economically poor. The ranks of the oppressed are filled with others besides the poor.

A Pain-Filled Cry

The theology of liberation of Jesus Christ the Liberator is the pain-filled cry of oppressed Christians. They are knocking on the door of their affluent brothers and sisters, asking for everything and yet for nothing. Indeed all they ask is to be people, to be accepted as persons. All they ask is that they be allowed to fight to regain their captive freedom.

Leonardo Boff, *Jesus Christ Liberator,* 1978.

Nevertheless, we have to observe here that the socio-economi-cally oppressed (the poor) do not simply exist *alongside* other op-pressed groups, such as blacks, indigenous peoples, women—to take the three major categories in the Third World. No, the "class-oppressed"—the socio-economically poor—are the infrastructural expression of the process of oppression. The other groups repre-sent "superstructural" expressions of oppression and because of this are deeply conditioned by the infrastructural. It is one thing to be a black taxi-driver, quite another to be a black football idol;

it is one thing to be a woman working as a domestic servant, quite another to be the first lady of the land; it is one thing to be an Amerindian thrown off your land, quite another to be an Amerindian owning your own farm.

This shows why, in a class-divided society, class struggles—which are a fact and an ethical demonstration of the presence of the injustice condemned by God and the church—are the main sort of struggle. They bring antagonistic groups, whose basic interests are irreconcilable, face to face. On the other hand, the struggles of blacks, indigenes, and women bring groups that are not naturally antagonistic into play, whose basic interests can in principle be reconciled. Although exploiting bosses and exploited workers can never finally be reconciled (so long as the former remain exploiters and the latter exploited), blacks can be reconciled with whites, indigenes with nonindigenes, and women with men. We are dealing here with nonantagonistic contradictions mixed in with the basic, antagonist class conflict in our societies. But it must also be noted that noneconomic types of oppression aggravate preexisting socio-economic oppression. The poor are additionally oppressed when, beside being poor, they are also black, indigenous, women, or old. . . .

The Dream of a Truly Free Society

Liberation theology has a spirituality at its roots and a dream of its final aim: that of a society of freed men and women. Without a dream, men and women will not mobilize themselves to transform society, nor will society seek to renew its foundations. Christians believe that such a dream belongs to the realm of reality, for they have seen it realized in anticipation by Jesus Christ, who "has broken down . . . enmity . . . , so as to create . . . a single new humanity in himself, thereby making peace" (Eph. 2:14-15). . . .

The holy city, the new Jerusalem that comes down from heaven (Rev. 21:2), can be established on earth only when men and women filled with faith and passion for the gospel, united with each other, and hungry and thirsty for justice, create the human dispositions and material conditions for it. But the earth will not then be the same earth, neither will the heavens be the same heavens; they will be a *new* heaven and a *new* earth. The old earth with its oppressions will have passed away. The new earth will be a gift of God and the fruit of human effort. What was begun in history will continue in eternity: the kingdom of the freed, living as brothers and sisters in the great house of the Father.

"*Liberation theology in Latin America is not yet practical enough.*"

Liberation Theology Does Not Promote Human Rights

Michael Novak

A prolific author, Michael Novak has been a leading critic of liberation theology. He holds the George Frederick Jewett Chair in Religion, Philosophy, and Public Policy at the American Enterprise Institute, a public policy research organization in Washington, DC. Novak was a presidential adviser to former US presidents Gerald Ford and Jimmy Carter. In the following viewpoint, he contends that liberation theology is a utopian ideology that has not specified how it would improve human rights in the Third World. Novak believes a system is already in place which vastly improves human rights and should be promoted in the Third World: the democratic capitalism found in the United States.

As you read, consider the following questions:

1. What is utopian about liberation theology, in Novak's opinion?
2. Why does the author believe that democratic capitalism has advanced human rights more than any other system in history?
3. How does Novak explain the difference between Brazil's poverty and Japan's prosperity?

"Christ led me to Marx," bluntly declares Ernesto Cardenal, the Nicaraguan priest at whom Pope John Paul II wagged an admonishing finger at the Managua airport in 1983. "I do not think the Pope understands Marxism," says the world-famous poet, and the Sandinista Minister of Culture. "For me, the four Gospels are all equally communist." Cardenal summarizes his brief against the Pope: "I'm a Marxist who believes in God, follows Christ and is a revolutionary for the sake of his kingdom."

Leonardo Boff, the Brazilian Franciscan summoned to Rome in 1984 to defend his vision of the Church today, wrote shortly afterward in the left-wing Rome newspaper *Paese Sera* that Pope John Paul II's view of Marxism is "a kind of caricature." Friar Boff says that the Vatican document, which endorses the Church's commitment to the poor while condemning Marxism, seems "to believe what is on the label of the bottle before trying the real contents." He sets aside Pope John Paul II's lifetime experience of Marxism, asserting: "Marxism is a principally European theme. In Latin America, the big enemy is not Marxism, it is capitalism." . . .

Liberation theology is a method of defining Christian faith in the political context of underdevelopment, in a side-choosing spirit committed to action. It is not distinctive for wishing to apply Christian faith to social action. It is not more concerned about "the working class" or "the poor" than Pope Leo XIII, whose 1891 encyclical underlined Catholicism's responsibility to these groups. Nor can it be universally defined as Marxist. Yet it gains its excitement from flirting with Marxist thought and speech, and from its hostility to the "North."

Third World Catholics

A majority of the world's 800 million Catholics now lives in third world nations—in Hispanic Latin America and the Philippines predominantly, but also in the burgeoning church of Africa, and in the small but vital Catholic communities of many nations of Southeast Asia. If Marxism, even of a mild sort, grows in such lands, and if it were to be blessed by Catholicism, two powerful symbolic forces would then have joined hands. In such a world, what would be the fate of civil liberties? . . .

One wishes to applaud liberation theology, in the first place, for raising the liberal question: How can human liberation be attained in practice, in the real world of flesh and blood, amid the ambiguity and contingency that constitute worldly history? Liberation theology begins by asking the right question. A next practical question then arises: Has liberation theology asked the right question *in the right way?* That is, are the teachings of liberation theology (at their present early stage of development) likely *in practice* to achieve what they hope? Liberation theology *intends* to liberate. But *does* it? What are its probable consequences?

There are two approaches to the theology of political economy, the utopian and the realistic. The utopian approach, frankly recommended by such liberation theologians as Juan Luis Segundo, S.J., argues from abstractions about a future that has never been. Permit me to take an example from Bishop Desmond Tutu of South Africa, speaking of the liberation of South Africa. Asked by a journalist whether he is a socialist, Bishop Tutu unambiguously replies "absolutely, yes." Asked then to specify the concrete socialist model he would like South Africa to follow, the bishop demurs. We have not yet seen, he says, "the kind of society" he would recommend. And he adds: "But then we are visionaries. We hope we are visionaries. And we leave it to others to try and put flesh to the things we try to dream." A better description of the utopian approach is hard to find. One encounters it frequently in socialist and Marxist writings. Grand moral principles are asserted. Bishop Tutu says: "And all I long for is a society that will be compassionate, sharing, and caring." He leaves the institutional questions—those that "put flesh to" his dreams—to others. This is one approach.

Mitchell (Australia). © 1989 Cartoonists & Writers Syndicate.

The other—the realistic approach—is quite different, not entirely different, but different in significant ways. The realistic approach, while clearly aware of its own ideals and of the open possibilities of the future, is concerned with concrete realities, proximate next steps, and comparisons based upon actual existents. Like the utopian approach, the realistic approach also has yet-unrealized ideals and, again like the utopian approach, it knows the importance of the idea of the future. But unlike the utopian approach, it takes care to use as its proximate standard of measurement the simple question: *Compared to what?* "The goal of liberation theology is a non-capitalist, socialist society," some will say; to which the realist asks: "Like what? Bulgaria? Cuba? Sweden? Identify your nearest concrete model." And if to this someone counters, "Liberation theology seeks a *new* form of society, unlike any other," the realist rejoinder is straightforward: "What concrete institutional design do you have for it? Like what? Explain to me how classic abuses will be prevented."

In suggesting that liberation theology in Latin America is not yet practical enough—does not yet offer a practical concrete model, toward whose realization institutional steps may be directed today—it is necessary for me to state the concrete ideal that informs my own thought. As a theology or philosophy of political economy, liberation theology is clearly at a pre-theoretical stage. It criticizes. It exhorts. It stimulates. But it has not yet spelled out its future *institutional* form. Until it does so, it is not yet political, but merely hortatory. Abuses of human rights are not curbed by exhortation but only by institutions functioning according to well-defined due process. Those of us who are skeptical about the claims of liberation theology must, therefore, press its thinkers to become more concrete. In doing so, we must spell out our own practical ideals of liberation. . . .

The Liberal Society

That is why I turn now to the liberation theology native to North America, "the liberal society." The first persons to be called, and to call themselves, "liberals" were so named because they sought *three* liberations. The infant United States was among the first crucibles in which their experiment was tried. They sought liberation from tyranny and torture *in the political sphere;* liberation from the tyranny of poverty *in the economic sphere;* and liberty of conscience, information and ideas *in the religious, cultural, and moral sphere.* . . .

Looking out at the world of 1800, the first liberals contemplated a world of some 800 million living souls, mostly living under tyranny, in poverty, in ignorance, in illiteracy, lacking in knowledge of basic hygiene and fundamental medicine, average age of death universally about 19. In perhaps the most developed nation, France, the average age of the oppressed sex at death was 27, the average age of death of the oppressor sex, 23. The condition of man in his natural state offered by Thomas Hobbes was taken to be reasonably descriptive of human life: "solitary, poor, nasty, brutish, and short."

As Pope John Paul II said, there are today 800 million hungry persons on this planet. That is a sad, but true, fact. The liberal task has yet to be completed. But what the Pope *didn't* say is that, 186 years after 1800, there are 4 billion people who are *not* hungry: that many more are living (because of giant strides of creativity in medicine, pharmaceuticals, immunizations, and the like), and now living to an average age worldwide of nearly 60.

Karl Marx described the bourgeois revolution as the greatest transformation ever experienced by the human race. He wrote this in 1848, when he had not seen the half of it.

Jesus and the Poor

Anybody who has tried to teach a course in the New Testament or the life of Jesus comes to an inescapable conclusion: Jesus had great empathy for the poor. To go from that, however, and to say that the inevitable economic system attached to this concern is socialism is a tremendous leap of faith, and it is not well founded theologically. The New Testament did not know socialism, and, empirically, liberation theology has to show that socialism works to make its case. I don't think that the data are there to prove that it does. And I also think that you don't have to be a Socialist to share Jesus' vision of doing something for the poor.

Rodney Grubb, in *Liberation Theology and the Liberal Society*, 1987.

So the liberal society is not solely an abstract ideal, but a real flesh-and-blood system, full of its own sins and inadequacies, a system sin-laden and yet noble, that has dramatically altered human history. In particular, I want to consider the United States as it is, as one embodiment of the liberal society. If the U.S. is not democratic, which nation is? If the U.S. is not capitalist, which nation is? If the U.S. is not pluralistic and free in conscience, what place on earth is? Yet this actual, real system we live in is based upon an idea, a conception of order, painstakingly worked out by our Founders. . . .

The US as the Second Israel

The Founders were the offspring of a biblical people. For a thousand years and more, devout readers of the Bible had reflected on its images of the person, the community, the nature and destiny of human beings, the common good, and an order worthy of what God had taught them about human dignity. They had learned of the inalienable dignity of every single person, of the need "to promote the general welfare," of the necessity for "republican virtue," and of the need to build "a new republic" worthy at last of human dignity. Thomas Jefferson, indeed, thought of the U.S. as "the second Israel." . . .

What made the *ordo* of the United States different from any in Europe or elsewhere? What was new about it? Three of its novelties were biblical in inspiration.

Sin

(1) *The Jewish-Christian notion of sin lay behind the fundamental division of systems, the division of powers in the political system, and a pervasive, systemic concern with checks and balances.* The Jewish-Christian conception of man is empirically based. It holds that every human being sometimes sins. Therefore, no person, class, or group may be entrusted with total power. . . .

The reality of human sinfulness, therefore, led to the invention of an unprecedented division of social systems, the separation of the American social system into three relatively equal, but quite different systems: political, economic, and moral-cultural. From this conception of order arises both a check upon human sinfulness, and a liberation of historical dynamism. . . .

(2) *The Jewish-Christian concept, beginning in Genesis, that humans are made in the image of God the Creator, taught the early Americans that the vocation of Christians, Jews, and humanists is not merely to be passive, resigned, and reconciled to history but, on the contrary, to change history and to be creative, to pioneer, and to persevere in being inventors of a new order.* The short answer to Adam Smith's *Inquiry into the Nature and Causes of the Wealth of Nations* is: The cause of wealth is creativity. Not natural resources. Not labor. Not planning. Rather, human wit, intelligence, inquiry, invention—in a word, the old *caput* (Latin: head), from which the name for the system, "capitalism," is appropriately derived. Until Adam Smith, wealth (identified with gold, silver, and the like) was thought to be limited. It could not be created, only taken. "If the rich get richer, the poor get poorer." This traditional conception held that wealth is a zero-sum: if some gain, others must lose. Since until that time new wealth had only rarely been created by invention and discovery, this error had a long life. It thrives in intellectual backwaters even today. The classic villain was the miser, whose hoarded coins were withheld from the common use. After Adam Smith, a new morality came into play. If wealth can be created, then, seeing the tyranny and misery inflicted by poverty, human beings must discern a new moral obligation: the moral obligation of development, the moral imperative to raise every poor person in the world out of poverty. If new wealth can be created, the miser who hoards his gold is less a villain than a fool, and thus the miser disappeared from the ranks of literary villains. And a new moral obligation to end poverty on earth arose. . . .

(3) *The distinctive Jewish-Christian idea of community—based on neither birth nor kin nor territory nor religious unity, but on free and voluntary covenant—led to the American discovery of a new principle*

of the new science of politics: the principle of voluntary association. . . .
Adam Smith called his book, not *The Wealth of Individuals,* but
The Wealth of Nations. His was the first vision of universal,
worldwide development. His is preeminently a social vision. The
vision of democratic capitalism will not be attained until a sound
material base is placed under every single person on this planet.

Religious Totalitarianism

I am worried that liberation theology is a movement whose only
function is to give religious justification for a Communist
society. . . .

What is most important is individual freedom, because religious
totalitarianism can be even more dangerous than secular authoritarianism. This is why I am afraid of this theology of liberation.

Mihajlo Mihajlov, in *Liberation Theology and the Liberal Society,* 1987.

The chief institutional invention of democratic capitalist societies is not the individual (already magnified by the aristocracy)
but the corporation and the association. These social forms provide a new way for human beings to organize themselves for
voluntary social action, including economic action, in independence from the state. . . .
The liberal society, to repeat, is based upon three liberations:
liberation of conscience, ideas, and information (the institutions
of pluralism); liberation from tyranny and from torture
(democratic institutions); and liberation from poverty (capitalist
institutions, in concert with moral-cultural and political
institutions).
Liberation theology also claims to have a "preferential option
for the poor." But, the day *after* the revolution, what sort of
economic institutions does liberation theology plan to set in place
that will actually help the poor no longer to be poor? What sort
of institutions will it set up to block tyranny and to prevent torture? What sort of institutions will it set up to guarantee liberty
of conscience, ideas, and information? If liberation theology suc-
ceeds in helping to construct such institutions as these, then it
will meet the tests of the liberal society, and achieve genuine
human liberation. Then we are all "liberation theologians." And
if not, not.

Recognizing Ethnocentrism

Ethnocentrism is the attitude or tendency of people to view their own race, religion, culture, group, or nation as superior to others, and to judge others on that basis. An American, whose custom is to eat with a fork or spoon, would be making an ethnocentric statement when saying, "The Chinese custom of eating with chopsticks is stupid."

Ethnocentrism has promoted much misunderstanding and conflict. It emphasizes cultural and religious differences and the notion that one's national institutions or group customs are superior.

Ethnocentrism limits people's ability to be objective and to learn from others. Education in the truest sense stresses the similarities of the human condition throughout the world and the basic equality and dignity of all people.

Several of the following statements are taken from the viewpoints in this book. Some have other origins. Consider each statement carefully. *Mark E for any statement you think is ethnocentric. Mark N for any statement you think is not ethnocentric. Mark U if you are undecided about any statement.*

If you are doing this activity as a member of a class or group, compare your answers with those of other class or group members. Be able to defend your answers. You may discover that others will come to different conclusions than you. Listening to the reasons others present for their answers may give you valuable insights in recognizing ethnocentric statements.

E = *ethnocentric*
N = *not ethnocentric*
U = *undecided*

1. Third World laziness and ignorance explain why Asia, Africa, and Latin America are poor.

2. The Third World tradition of group success is superior to a Western system which requires that there be winners and losers.

3. We should be friendly to all governments that pursue a constructive and peaceful foreign policy, even if human rights conditions in their countries do not measure up to our standards.

4. The poor are beating at their masters' doors, demanding life, bread, liberty, and dignity.

5. I do not believe that you can condone brutality somewhere else and not suffer some moral rot on your own turf.

6. Soviet foreign policy and arms sales lead Third World leaders to focus on increasing their own power, rather than developing good governments.

7. Already in 1776, Adam Smith had predicted that Latin America would end in poverty and tyranny because of the legacy of Spanish culture. But he believed the colonies of North America would be wealthy and free because of Judeo-Christian values.

8. From what I know about Africans, these people do not support any real progress or change. The African looks to the past.

9. The poor are additionally oppressed when besides being poor, they are also black, indigenous, women, or old.

10. Authoritarian regimes and arbitrary rule in Asia, Africa, and Latin America are reflections of a fundamental defect as seen from the Western democratic perspective.

11. Despite great differences in climate, culture, economic organization, and religious outlook, everyone faces the same essential political question: What form of government shall we have?

12. Colonialism exposed families and individuals to the exploitation of outsiders whom they were powerless to oppose.

13. Despite history's proof of the superiority of British and American governments, one would be hard pressed to find a single Third World government that operates along British or American lines.

Periodical Bibliography

The following articles have been selected to supplement the diverse views presented in this chapter.

Michael H. Armacost	"US-Soviet Relations: Coping with Conflicts in the Third World," *Department of State Bulletin*, December 1986.
Peter L. Berger	"Human Development and Economic Alternatives," *Crisis*, November 1987.
Christianity Today	"Liberation Theology's Curious Contradiction," July 10, 1987.
Charles Creekmore	"Misunderstanding Africa," *Psychology Today*, December 1986.
William W. Ellis and Margaret McMahon Ellis	"Cultures in Transition: What the West Can Learn from Developing Countries," *The Futurist*, March/April 1989.
John Kenneth Galbraith	"Economic Development: Engine of Democracy," *The New York Times*, August 25, 1987.
Ryszard Kapuscinski	"Uganda After the Terror," *The New York Times Magazine*, March 12, 1989.
Jeane Kirkpatrick	"Encouraging Democracies 'Everywhere,'" *U.S. News & World Report*, March 10, 1986.
Hans Koning	"Memories Official and Unofficial: Notes on Nationalism," *Harper's Magazine*, October 1988.
Otto Maduro, interviewed by Sharon Lavery	"Call for Liberation Comes from Christ," *Maryknoll*, April 1987.
New Internationalist	"Running for Rights," January 1988.
Michael Novak	"How About Obscene Losses?" *Forbes*, March 6, 1989.
Philip Ochieng	"The Arms Race Is a Universal Issue," *World Press Review*, January 1987.
John K. Roth	"How Latin American Liberation Theology Sees the United States and the USSR," *The World & I*, May 1988.
Russell Watson	"Dancing with Dictators," *Newsweek*, February 15, 1988.

Does US Foreign Aid Benefit the Third World?

Chapter Preface

To rebuild Europe after the devastation of World War II, US Secretary of State George C. Marshall proposed a plan to send money to Europe. Marshall feared that without US help to restore the economies of Europe, communist influence there would grow. Between 1948 and 1950, the US sent $8.7 billion to Western European nations. The result was that Europe recovered and today has some of the strongest economies in the world. The success of the Marshall Plan established a precedent and a belief; namely, that US aid could help impoverished countries while also advancing US interests and influence.

The US has applied some of the methods of the Marshall Plan to the Third World in the hope that its economies would be revitalized. Since the 1950s, US presidents have sent millions of dollars in aid to impoverished countries in Asia, Africa, and Latin America. Aid takes several forms ranging from shipments of food, to grants and loans for development projects, to military aid and weapons shipments. Yet many Third World economies are still weak, and poverty and malnutrition remain problems. Aid's defenders argue that the US has not sent enough. Others believe the US has not sent the right types of aid and has administered aid programs poorly. Still others believe that aid is doomed to fail. They contend that the Marshall Plan cannot be applied to all regions of the world with success.

The following chapter presents several views of how US foreign aid affects the Third World.

"Foreign aid promotes the humanitarian ideals and democratic values of the American people."

US Foreign Aid Helps the Third World

M. Peter McPherson

The Agency for International Development, a division of the US Department of State, is the primary distributor of US foreign aid. The author of the following viewpoint, M. Peter McPherson, was the administrator of AID from 1981 to 1987. McPherson argues that US aid has been crucial in helping many Third World countries industrialize. US aid has also saved many famine victims from starvation, McPherson contends, and has lengthened the life spans of people in the Third World.

As you read, consider the following questions:

1. Why does foreign aid promote US national interests, according to McPherson?
2. What policies does the author contend will promote economic growth in the Third World?
3. What does the author cite as accomplishments of US foreign aid programs?

M. Peter McPherson, "FY 1988 Request for Foreign Assistance Programs," *Department of State Bulletin*, June 1987.

There are important reasons why foreign aid is critical to our national interest—but these are often not well understood within our own country—especially in the face of domestic budget cuts. The health of our nation is inextricably bound up with the objectives of foreign policy, and the foreign assistance program is vital to the achievement of these objectives. U.S. national security interests in the Middle East and Central America depend upon the stability of those regions—political stability that is based on economic stability. Without effective foreign assistance from the United States, economic growth prospects are grim for many Third World countries that are increasingly important to us—economically as markets and trading partners, as well as politically. We depend on many countries that are unable to meet their security requirements and critical development needs from their own resources.

Domestic Benefits of Foreign Aid

Foreign aid has brought direct benefits to the U.S. economy with the development of new trading opportunities for American business. Indeed, without foreign assistance, our economy would suffer. Over 40% of all U.S. exports are bought by developing countries. In 1981 Korea bought more food from the United States than we had given that country in 24 years of Food for Peace shipments. High rates of economic growth by developing countries during the last several decades have benefited U.S. farmers. These countries are our fastest growing markets. Their agricultural imports from the United States increased from $1.1 billion in 1970 to a peak of $15.4 billion in 1981. In 1983 developing countries accounted for 50% of total U.S. grain and feed exports.

With our assistance, many countries—particularly in East Asia, Southeast Asia, and Latin America—previously classified as "less developed" are now "newly industrialized" and are in a position to help other countries. Finally, up to 70% of U.S. bilateral foreign assistance is spent on American commodities, equipment, and services to support overseas development programs.

Foreign aid promotes the humanitarian ideals and democratic values of the American people. In the past 25 years, American aid brought emergency relief to victims of 800 natural disasters. We can be proud of helping Africa turn the corner in fighting the effects of one of the worst droughts in history. Without our food aid, an estimated 20 million people would have died in sub-Sahara Africa. Not only has America responded to emergencies, but we have contributed to sustained development: for example, the eradication of smallpox; the reduction of child mortality by one-half; the majority of children in developing countries entering primary school; life expectancy increased by 10-20 years in the Third World; India's self-reliance in grains; and the beginnings of a "green revolution" in Africa. Democratic values have been enhanced by America's humanitarian assistance as well as through our direct support for democratic elections. Democratic processes have been gaining support throughout the Third World. In Latin America, the percentage of people living under democratically elected governments has risen from 30% in 1979 to over 90% today.

Our foreign aid is playing an important role in the war on drugs by supporting antinarcotics activities which the governments of those developing countries where narcotics are produced do not have the economic resources to launch.

Foreign Aid Achievements

I would like to cite some examples of the successful achievements of foreign aid, particularly since 1981.

Given the 100% increase in the price of oil in 1979, prolonged recession in industrial economies, historically high real interest rates, and increased trade barriers in the developed world, it is not surprising that the economies of developing countries are best characterized by decline rather than growth during the 1981-85 period. A major focus of AID [Agency for International Development] has been to assist countries that were in serious trouble to achieve economic stabilization and to make the necessary economic policy adjustments to move back on the path to growth. Countries in which significant progress has been made in adopting policy and institutional changes necessary for growth include the Dominican Republic, Costa Rica, Ecuador, Zambia, Zaire, Somalia, Niger, Bangladesh, and Israel.

Humanitarian Ideals

In the past 40 years, the United States has provided foreign countries with economic assistance totaling nearly $200 billion. This aid, which reflects American humanitarian ideals, has contributed to the development of most countries in the world.

Department of State, *Fundamentals of US Foreign Policy*, March 1988.

In the 1970s Costa Rica borrowed heavily to finance its growing public sector. In 1981 the country was forced to suspend principal and interest payments on its foreign debt. AID, in close coordination with the International Monetary Fund (IMF) and the World Bank, began extensive macroeconomic policy dialogue with the Costa Rican Government to identify necessary policy reforms. The government agreed to reduce its fiscal deficit, unify its exchange rate, and free its economy. AID supported the economy in the interim with $550 million in economic assistance from 1981 to 1985. As a result, the fiscal deficit was cut from 14.1% of GDP

[Gross Domestic Product] to 1.5% and the government is divesting many parastatals. The GDP grew by 10.6% in 1983-85; inflation dropped from 108% in 1982 to 11% in 1985, and exports of non-traditional products outside Central America rose by 31% in 1984 and 24% in 1985.

Helping the Poor

The impact of AID's effort to increase the incomes of the poor is illustrated by projects in the low-income countries of Asia and the Near East, Latin America and the Caribbean, and Africa. Honduras is an example. In the late 1970s, coffee rust disease invaded Honduras, threatening the smaller coffee producers who lacked the technical expertise and resources to combat it. AID implemented the $20 million small farmer coffee improvement project to mitigate the adverse impact of coffee rust. To date over 4,000 small farmers have received credit to plant new improved coffee varieties and to purchase inputs that combat the disease. Average yields have increased over fivefold, and net income per farm has increased by 90% as a result of the project.

In Zaire the recently completed North Shaba rural development project was instrumental in stimulating economic growth in a depressed region of the country. As a result, the marketing of foodgrains increased by 220% from 30,000 metric tons in 1977 to 96,000 metric tons in 1986. Elements of this experience are now being applied in the Central Shaba area.

In Egypt the small farmer production project provided 90,564 loans valued at $49 million to 51,000 farmers. The repayment rate is remarkable with only about 1% past due. Maize yields on the project lands doubled and are well above the all-Egypt average.

AID-supported child survival activities have already registered some striking successes around the world. Several years ago, the average immunization coverage of children in developing countries was less than 5%; today, the average in AID-assisted countries is over 30%. Other interventions are also beginning to take hold. The World Health Organization (WHO) estimates that 50% of families in developing countries (excluding China) had access to oral rehydration salts (ORS) by the end of 1985, up from only 5% in 1982. The number of ORS packets produced worldwide rose from 90 million in 1983 to 320 million in 1986. AID alone provided 100 million packets in 1986. . . .

What Remains To Be Done

We have achieved much, but we cannot be complacent for there are still problems and challenges. The good news is that our past successful investments have put us on the brink of changes from which the United States and the developing world stand to reap even greater benefits. We know that the policies of a large number of countries still inhibit the growth of economic markets and individual responsibility and decisionmaking. But through policy discussions with many countries backed up by programs, we have seen the beginning of commitment and change by many governments. The policy environments are changing to encourage free market systems and to allow the realization of individual initiatives. Fifteen African countries are privatizing government-owned enterprises, ten have devalued their currencies, and sixteen have reduced government expenditures and budget deficits. In total, two-thirds of Africa's lowest income countries are undertaking major economic restructuring. . . .

The Case for Aid

Stripped to its bare essentials, the case for development aid is that it increases growth rates in some developing countries, improves the living standards of some poor people, and offers the prospect of doing better in future on both counts.

Paul Mosley, *Foreign Aid: Its Defense and Reform*, 1987.

Twenty-five years of foreign aid have not only brought substantial accomplishments of which Americans can be proud but have given us a wealth of experience and technology upon which to base the future. To really appreciate what has happened in the last 25 years we need to be reminded of what the developed world was like then.
• One out of four children died before the age of 5.
• Only a small minority of children attended school.
• The Indian subcontinent faced massive starvation.
• Parents could not choose the size of their families.
• Life expectancy averaged about 40 years of age.
Over the past 25 years, American foreign aid has played a major role in changing these conditions.
• Child mortality has been reduced by one-half.
• Smallpox has been eliminated from the world.
• The majority of children in developing countries enter primary school.
• Safe and effective family planning methods are available.
• Life expectancy has increased 10-20 years in the Third World.
• India is self-reliant in grains.

"Four decades of experience have shown foreign aid to be largely a failure."

US Foreign Aid Harms the Third World

Doug Bandow

In the following viewpoint, Doug Bandow argues that much of the US foreign aid sent to the Third World has been wasted because it is not given to countries that support the US. Bandow believes aid should be used to advance US national interests. Bandow has been a fellow at the Cato Institute and The Heritage Foundation, two research institutions in Washington, DC. He has also edited the book, *U.S. Aid to the Developing World: A Free-Market Agenda*.

As you read, consider the following questions:

1. What does Bandow believe should be the reason for giving foreign aid?
2. Why has US development aid failed, according to the author?
3. In Bandow's opinion, what should be done to spur a reform of US aid programs?

Doug Bandow, "Rethinking US Foreign Aid," The Heritage Foundation *Backgrounder*, June 1, 1988. Reprinted with permission.

The United States gives away some $15 billion in foreign aid every year, about eight times the sum appropriated annually for its food welfare program for Women, Infants and Children (WIC) and four times that for the Strategic Defense Initiative. Much of this foreign aid goes to support avowed adversaries of the U.S. and hostile "nonaligned" nations. One estimate, for example, is that $1 billion, or 13.6 percent of 1987's bilateral assistance, went to countries that voted against the U.S. at least half the time in the United Nations, while nearly a third of the loans of the World Bank (to which the U.S. contributes about 20 percent) went to the same countries.

U.S. aid policies and aid levels rarely are determined by a dispassionate review of the national interest. Businesses and so-called private voluntary organizations lobby for more funds to serve their own ends; the Agency for International Development (AID), which has primary responsibility for U.S. foreign aid policy, rewards its managers more for spending appropriated funds quickly than for pursuing sensible development policies in poor nations; and the State Department treats increased aid spending as an opportunity to buy more access for the U.S. ambassador to the local rulers and leaders. Congress, meanwhile, treats foreign aid as a form of political symbolism, approving allocations to demonstrate concern rather than to solve problems.

Systems To Encourage Development

The U.S. foreign aid experience leads to only one conclusion: the U.S. must rethink the program completely. It should do so on the premise that the primary reason for the U.S. to transfer money to other countries is to advance U.S. interests. To be sure, emergencies and catastrophes abroad may merit a prompt American humanitarian response. In the main, however, the U.S. government's fundamental duty is to protect this nation. And protection is in part advanced by enabling poor countries to develop economically.

To best serve this U.S. objective, the foreign aid program should be cut sharply in funds and personnel. Development assistance, in particular, should be limited to countries that are moving toward democracy and have the kind of market-oriented economic system that encourages development. The White House and Congress should exercise strict oversight to assure that aid is used properly, that U.S. funds are not wasted, and that private enterprise is encouraged. . . .

Advancing National Interests

For over a quarter century, no administration has seriously questioned U.S. foreign aid or defined why U.S. national interests are advanced by giving, or lending on very generous terms, so much to foreign governments. In the early 1960s, the Agency for International Development declared that "the major objective of the U.S. foreign assistance program is to assist other countries that seek to maintain their independence and develop into self-supporting nations." Then in 1973, Congress rewrote the law to emphasize "basic human needs," turning aid that had been seen as a temporary crutch into what has become a permanent dole.

If the program were merely humanitarian, as was most U.S. assistance prior to World War II, foreign aid could be reduced to a fraction of its present levels. Disaster relief accounts for a very small portion of U.S. aid, and food assistance is used mainly to provide funds for foreign governments, not to feed hungry people. Only 10 percent to 20 percent of food aid actually goes to fight hunger.

Bankrolling Boondoggles

Foreign aid will sponsor all sorts of government boondoggles—including bailouts from debts caused by previous boondoggles.

Naturally, Third World governments prefer foreign aid, even if their economies could get more capital from private investors by relaxing the grip of politicians. Foreign aid goes into the hands of politicians, to hand out as favors—and some of it often ends up in their own pockets.

If the West truly wants to improve the standard of living of Third World peoples, it will stop bankrolling boondoggles.

Thomas Sowell, *Oasis*, October 1987.

The continued high levels of foreign aid spending suggest that policymakers believe that some broader national interest is being pursued. But the pace of development in Third World countries has proved to be unrelated to foreign aid levels. The State Department, in fact, considers aid primarily as a kind of "bribe" to curry favor with foreign governments.

This worldwide system of political payoff is evident from the flow of money with little apparent discrimination to countries that are unfriendly as well as those that are friendly, to those that are growing economically and those that stagnate, to favored trading partners and those that discriminate against U.S. exports. Example: in fiscal 1988, only $22 million of U.S. aid went to friendly Ecuador, while $35 million went to unfriendly Marxist Mozambique. The officials who manage foreign aid seem to measure success more by their ability to win approval, first from the Office of Management and Budget and then from Congress, for large appropriations, than by achieving anything positive with their spending.

Least controversial is humanitarian aid, which Ronald Reagan's

Commission on Security and Economic Assistance (the Carlucci Commission) declared in 1983 to be "deeply rooted in our national values." Since World War II, the U.S. has spent roughly $16 billion in attempting to alleviate basic human suffering, particularly that arising from natural disasters and famine that affected Third World countries.

Much of this expenditure has been made through the Food for Peace program, also known as P.L. 480. Under Title II of that program, food is given away to alleviate starvation and suffering in some 70 countries each year. But many Food for Peace crop shipments are sold under Titles I or III, either for local currency or as long-term loans to foreign governments, which then sell the food to their own people for cash. This helps the local government more than local citizens. About 32 countries currently are receiving this kind of aid. Leading recipients over the years have included Bangladesh, Guinea, India, Poland, the Sudan, and Zambia.

The U.S. has contributed $180 billion from 1946 through 1986 to other countries to promote internal development. This is more foreign aid than any other nation—or most combinations of nations—have given. These funds theoretically are intended to spur Third World development by underwriting infrastructure projects, such as farm-to-market roads, irrigation projects, commodity-storage facilities, and port facilities, promoting new technologies, and supporting basic health and welfare services. American bilateral aid, which generally flows from government to government, is administered by AID, ostensibly an independent agency, which is located, however, in State Department buildings and operated under the Department's policy guidance. The U.S. also contributes heavily to the multilateral institutions that purport to promote Third World development: the World Bank, United Nations Development Program (UNDP), Inter-American Development Bank (IDB), Asian Development Bank, and African Development Bank.

Humanitarian Aid Problems

Humanitarian aid programs are popular and have a long tradition, but U.S. humanitarian assistance, primarily food aid, has two major failings. First, it discourages self-reliance. Food for Peace crop shipments have become a permanent feature of life in many countries, sometimes handicapping the development of domestic agriculture, as in Guatemala, Haiti and elsewhere. Local farmers understandably see little point in trying to compete with free or low-cost food shipments from abroad. In 1976, for example, the U.S. shipped free corn to Guatemala after an earthquake, even though the country was still enjoying one of its best harvests ever. Prices dropped, and farmers could not earn the cash they desperately needed to rebuild their homes. Around the world,

"Food for Peace became a stumbling block to development," complains foreign development specialist Sudhir Sen.

Second, humanitarian aid sometimes helps regimes that are largely responsible for their own troubles. The Ethiopian government, for example, greatly aggravated the impact of the recent severe drought by collectivizing farmers and seizing their crops for ideological purposes. As hundreds of thousands were starving, the Marxist regime in 1984 spent as much as $150 million on a lavish celebration of its tenth anniversary in power. Peasants were later forcibly transferred from rebel-held areas to barren, government-controlled regions, a process that the French humanitarian group Doctors Without Borders estimates killed as many as 100,000 people—a death rate even higher than in the famine camps. But in spite of this the U.S. donated $276 million in food aid and $27 million for its transport to Ethiopia in 1984 and 1985 alone.

The Failure of Development Aid

Historically, development aid has been the largest component of U.S. foreign assistance. It is the sole purpose of such multilateral lending and development agencies as the World Bank and United Nations Development Program. Although some aid recipients, such as South Korea and the Republic of China on Taiwan, have succeeded economically, there is little evidence that government to government development assistance promotes economic growth abroad. Despite the post-World War II largest and most sustained transfer of wealth in history, the gap between the industrialized countries and many developing nations continues to grow. Some Third World countries, particularly in Africa, are actually slipping backwards. Perennial aid recipients such as Bangladesh, India, the Sudan, and Tanzania, have grown dependent on foreign largesse and are making little progress in lifting their people out of poverty.

A Growing Gap

We have little to show for our years of sending billions in developmental aid. Despite this massive transfer of wealth from the United States to poor nations, the gap between the industrialized countries and Third World countries is growing, not diminishing.

Phyllis Schlafly, *Manchester Union Leader*, July 6, 1988.

The reasons: foreign financial flows often subsidize the kind of domestic policies that inhibit development: large-scale, money-losing state enterprises; distorted monetary, credit, interest, and trade policies; price and supply controls; and restrictions on foreign investment. With such governmental policies, a prosperous and growing economy is impossible, whatever the level of aid. Many aid projects, moreover, have been badly designed or inadequately maintained. The wreckage left after past assistance, from deteriorating roads and storehouses to abandoned oil generators and empty hospitals, litters Africa. . . .

Why Give Any Aid?

Rarely, in fact, is the question "why give any aid?" to a particular country ever asked. Providing assistance to Third World countries has become automatic for the U.S. government. Pushing for such aid, of course, are the legions of government bureaucrats and employees of private voluntary organizations who depend on the program's continuance. These vested interests make common cause with the State Department and lobby Congress each year to keep U.S. aid levels high. Even [former] Secretary of State George Shultz pressed relentlessly for increased funds, arguing that without large amounts of aid "our ability to act as a world leader engaged abroad as a force for progress, peace and human dignity will erode."

However, U.S. aid has largely failed to fulfill its official goal of promoting a prosperous, secure international order. In fact, all too often, American funds have achieved the opposite result: retarding economic development and increasing instability in strategically important states. Foreign assistance outlays should be cut—sharply—as the essential starting point for reform. . . .

At the end of World War II, the U.S. embarked on a crusade to reshape the world economy, distributing large amounts of bilateral and multilateral funds to other countries. Four decades of experience have shown foreign aid to be largely a failure: hundreds of billions of dollars in grants and loans have done more to centralize Third World economies and strengthen anti-American governments than to promote economic growth and political freedom.

"Food aid stimulates productivity."

Food Aid Is Beneficial

Orville L. Freeman

Orville L. Freeman was US secretary of agriculture from 1961 to 1969. He has also been the governor of Minnesota and is chairman of the board of governors of the United Nations Association of the US, an organization that promotes the United Nations. In the following viewpoint, he argues that sending surplus food to the Third World is beneficial. Such a policy averts famine, feeds the hungry, and helps US farmers, Freeman maintains.

As you read, consider the following questions:

1. Why does the author believe hunger has become a serious problem?
2. How can food aid help both US and Third World agriculture, in Freeman's opinion?
3. Why does Freeman argue that US food aid is both practical and moral?

Orville L. Freeman, "Feeding the Hungry Is More Than Moral," *Los Angeles Times*, November 15, 1987. Reprinted with permission.

Hunger. Long the forgotten issue on the world agenda, it blazed briefly in public consciousness during the African famine of 1985 and abruptly faded from attention again.

But even if hunger has vanished from public debate, the gnawing problem continues—and grows. Half a billion people endure numbing malnutrition each day, often too weak to work or too debilitated even to produce the food they need to energize themselves. That number is growing, not diminishing.

The growth of chronic hunger not only presents the glaring paradox of want in the midst of plenty; in fact, the grinding poverty itself actually helps create gluts of unsold food. The ample surpluses of American agriculture, with production capacity 40% in excess of domestic needs, would find eager buyers in the fast-growing countries of the developing world if only their people could earn money with which to buy them.

Hunger as an Issue

A decade ago hunger emerged as a major issue on the global agenda. As secretary of state, Henry Kissinger went so far as to set an ambitious goal for both the United States and the world community: the elimination of world hunger by 1980. Long-range programs to accomplish both food and development strategies were established, funding was provided and considerable progress was made, even if the goal was not quite reached.

After 1980 hunger disappeared as an issue. The United States' multilateral development aid was slashed from $2.3 billion in 1980 to $949 million in 1987. Our three-year commitment to the International Fund for Agricultural Development fell from $254 million pledged for 1981-83 to $80 million pledged for 1987-89. Our Food for Peace allocation was halved in just two years, from $2 billion in 1985 to $1.1 billion in 1987. And for 1986-87, payments on our $101-million obligation to the United Nations' Food and Agriculture Organization have amounted to only $13 million.

No wonder the numbers of chronically hungry are growing once again. The United States has gone into default on a serious moral obligation, which is hardly attenuated by the episodic response to public concern about outright famine in 1985. This is the thrust of a report titled "A Time To Plant: International Cooperation to End Hunger" by the United Nations Assn. of the United States: There is an urgent need "for a renewed commitment, by our own countries and the international community, to the goal of a world where no child goes to bed hungry—to the elimination of hunger before this century's end."

This is truly a moral obligation of first priority. At the same time, it is an economic issue of inestimable importance for American agriculture. For an all-out development war to conquer world hunger is also at the core of building future markets for agricultural products.

The plain fact is that the necessary markets for American farmers are not in Japan and the countries of Western Europe. The fastest-growing markets today for U.S. food exports are the developing countries that are undergoing rapid economic growth. South Korea, once a poverty-stricken recipient of U.S. food aid, is now purchasing more than $2 billion a year in American farm products—even as its own food output grows by a healthy 3% a year. Brazil, while expanding its agricultural production by 5% a year (and becoming a stiff U.S. competitor in the soybean sector), increased the volume of its imports of U.S. farm commodities by 15% over the last decade.

Hunger and Surplus

There is, in short, a fundamental relationship between the crisis of hunger in the developing world and the crisis of surplus in U.S. agriculture. The solution to both crises lies in rapid growth of earning power in the Third World. And economic expansion in developing countries must be led by rising purchasing power in the rural sector, where the bulk of Third World people live. This underscores the importance of carefully targeted international development aid that can spark increased productivity and an economic take-off.

© Vadillo/Rothco Cartoons

It is increasingly clear that poorer nations' development policies need to be targeted to the poor in rural villages. Growth in their purchasing power both fuels local consumer industries (generating increases in urban income) and allows them to buy more varied foods. Similarly, development aid provided by wealthier countries, both directly and through multilateral institutions, should focus more on investment in productive "micro-enterprises" among the poor. Happily, initiatives in Congress to do just that have gained ground.

One of the most innovative recommendations in the U.N./U.S. Assn. report, reflecting the fundamental relationship between trade and aid, calls for re-allocating some of the budget savings from a worldwide phase-out of grower subsidies to food purchase subsidies for the poor in key developing countries. The aid, channeled back into higher food purchases, would enrich the diets of the hungry poor—and would also expand markets for our growers. Just as food stamps expanded the food purchases of America's poor by 24%, in Sri Lanka they have increased the volume of food sold to the poor by 30%.

Practical as Well as Moral

This is the epiphany that American policy makers must recognize: American interest in Third World rural development is practical as well as moral. The dollars invested in multilateral development banks are creating consumers, not competitors, and carefully targeted food aid stimulates productivity, not passivity. The possibility becomes ever more real of restoring a broad constituency against hunger amid this "action" triangle of interests: humanitarian aid, Third World development and commercial market-building.

"Tragically, Food for Peace . . . has been one of the most harmful programs of aid to Third World countries."

Food Aid Is Harmful

James Bovard

Since it was created in 1954, Food for Peace has delivered food aid from the US government to Third World countries. It has frequently been criticized, however. The author of the following viewpoint, James Bovard, believes food aid is neither humanitarian nor effective. Food aid dumps surplus US crops in Third World countries, he argues, and thus harms Third World agriculture by depressing prices and depriving farmers of a livelihood. Bovard is a Washington, DC consultant and an adjunct policy analyst for the Competitive Enterprise Institute, a Washington, DC think tank.

As you read, consider the following questions:

1. What does the author believe is the main purpose of the US Food for Peace program?
2. Why have Congressional efforts to reform Food for Peace failed, according to Bovard?
3. What does the author argue is the cause of hunger in the Third World?

James Bovard, "How American Food Aid Keeps the Third World Hungry," The Heritage Foundation *Backgrounder*, August 1, 1988. Reprinted with permission.

Americans have a proud history of being charitable, concerned about the well-being of their fellow man at home and overseas. The federal government's Food for Peace program, which provides food for less developed countries, is testimony to this. Yet ironically, and tragically, Food for Peace, formally known as P.L. [Public Law] 480, has been one of the most harmful programs of aid to Third World countries. While sometimes alleviating hunger in the short run, the program usually lowers the price at which Third World farmers can sell their crops. This depresses local food production, making it harder for poor countries to feed themselves in the long run. Food for Peace, in fact, is mainly an aid program for U.S. farmers, allowing them to dump their surplus crops in Third World countries, while the U.S. taxpayer foots the bill, and the poor in less developed countries bear the ultimate high cost. Food for Peace, despite its grand title, hinders agricultural development in such countries and makes a mockery of American humanitarian rhetoric.

Market Incentives for Farmers

As such, the Food for Peace program should be phased out. American food aid should be restricted to humanitarian relief for droughts or disasters. In place of Food for Peace, the U.S. Agency for International Development (AID) should promote policies that will give farmers in less developed countries market incentives to produce more food to feed their own people. AID should encourage and assist with technical advice the dismantling of state marketing monopolies in such countries, so that farmers will be free to sell their crops for whatever price the market will offer. . . .

American food aid to less developed countries under the P.L. 480 program, while meant to alleviate starvation, has made it more difficult for recipients to feed their peoples. Local food production has been discouraged by American food dumped in these markets. For example, in the 1950s and 1960s, massive U.S. wheat dumping in India disrupted India's agricultural market. Assistant Secretary of Agriculture George Dunlop speculated in 1984 that American food aid may have been responsible for the starvation of millions of Indians. U.S. officials have conceded that massive food aid to India, Indonesia, and Pakistan in the 1960s "restricted agricultural growth by allowing the governments to 1) postpone essential agricultural reforms, 2) fail to give agricultural investment sufficient priority, and 3) maintain a pricing system which gave farmers an inadequate incentive to increase production."

In 1976, an earthquake hit Guatemala, killing 23,000 people and leaving over a million homeless. Just prior to the disaster, the country had harvested one of the largest wheat crops on record, and food was plentiful. As earthquake relief, the U.S. rushed 27,000 metric tons of wheat to Guatemala. The U.S. "gift" knocked the bottom out of the local grain markets and depressed food prices so much that it was much harder for villages to recover. The Guatemalan government ultimately barred the import of any more basic grains.

Food for the Elites

Because most US food aid is channelled through elites, it comes as little surprise that much of it does not reach the needy. A US government study of food aid to Somalia, for example, showed that 80 per cent of the food ended up in the hands of military officers, government officials and private traders. Like other government-to-government aid, food aid is only as good as the government receiving it.

Kevin Danaher, *Race & Class*, January/March 1989.

The August 25, 1982, *Kansas City Times* reported that the Peruvian agriculture minister begged the U.S. Department of Agriculture not to send his country any more rice, fearing that it would glut the local market and drive down prices for struggling farmers. But the U.S. rice lobby turned up the heat on Washington, and the Peruvian government was told that it could either take the rice or receive no food at all.

Keeping Crops from Market

U.S. Food aid is still having devastating effects. A report by the AID Inspector General found that food aid "supported the Government of Egypt policies . . . which have a direct negative impact on domestic wheat production in Egypt." In Haiti, U.S. free food is widely sold illegally in markets next to Haitian farmers' own crops, thus driving down prices received by the Haitians. A development consultant told the House of Representatives Appropriations Subcommittee on Foreign Operations in 1979, "Farmers in Haiti are known to not even bring their crops to market the week that [P.L. 480 food] is being distributed since they are unable to get a fair price while whole bags of U.S. wheat are being sold." In May 1984, ten people were killed in Haiti when government troops fired on crowds rioting to protest corruption in the U.S. Food for Peace program.

In Jamaica, according to economist Scott D. Tollefson, Food for Peace has created a great disincentive to food production. Typical was the situation in late July 1984 when Jamaica was suffering a shortage of rice, the major staple. This led to a near political crisis. Attracted by increased prices for rice substitutes, small farmers rushed their goods to the market. Days later 4,890 metric tons of rice arrived from the U.S. under P.L. 480, the first installment of an allocated 16,000 tons costing U.S. $5 million. The U.S. rice sent the prices of substitutes tumbling, causing serious hurt to local producers.

U.S. AID helped Jamaica in 1984 design a food stamp program that was soon feeding almost half of the island's population. Carl Stone, a political scientist at the University of Jamaica observes: "The existing food stamp program is a mockery to any real commitment to local agriculture. Our poor people are being subsidized to buy imported food when our farmers can't sell their produce because of low levels of consumer buying power." . . .

Congress repeatedly has mandated that P.L. 480 should encourage private sector development in the Third World. In 1977, Congress created a Title III program to provide special bonuses to countries that changed policies to help the private sector. Yet very few countries have applied for Title III conditional aid, since they know they will get free or cheap food regardless of what policies they follow.

Congress effectively admitted the failure of Title III in 1985 by adding a new program, so-called Section 108 assistance. This is to channel P.L. 480 sales proceeds to private organizations in the Third World while encouraging expanded market opportunities for U.S. agriculture exports. Much of the Section 108 money has gone into development finance companies in poor countries which often pay large kickbacks to influential politicians. Development finance companies in general have a very poor record in the Third World and have proved a poor means for foreign donors to aid the private sector.

Misuse of Free Food

American food assistance to less developed countries often is misused by recipient governments. For example, the Congo, instead of using P.L. 480 donations to feed its people, sold free food in 1983 to buy a small arms factory from Italy. In March 1984, *The New York Times* reported that AID believed Ethiopia was selling its donated food to buy more Soviet weaponry. Mauritius insisted on receiving only the highest quality rice—and then used it in hotels to feed foreign tourists. Cape Verde begged for more emergency relief aid at the same time that it was exporting wheat donated by other countries. . . .

American food assistance programs fail to address the primary cause of the inability of Third World countries to feed themselves: government economic repression of farmers. In most less developed countries, especially in Africa, farmers must sell their crops to government marketing boards. These state monopolies usually set the price of farm products below the cost of production. In Cameroon in 1986, for example, farmers received only 29 percent of the world market price for their coffee. In Tanzania, the state marketing system is so inefficient that farmers use illegal private traders to send their crops to market. The government cracked down on this activity, leaving 300,000 tons of various crops stranded in the field. The marketing board in El Salvador, for example, pays farmers only 28 percent of the market price for their coffee. Since 1982, this monopoly, with U.S. AID indirect assistance and approval, has contributed to the 50 percent drop in Salvadoran coffee production.

A Failed Policy

Every year the United States produces far more grain than it can consume. And from the late 1960s and early 1970s the government began promoting increased agricultural production for export. The stated goals were to feed a hungry world while bringing prosperity to US farmers. Twenty years later there are now more hungry people in the world and, according to the US Department of Agriculture, 'US agriculture faces its worst economic crisis since the Great Depression'.

Kevin Danaher, *Race & Class*, January/March 1989.

Third World governments pursue such policies for the short-term political gain of securing their own power base. Food purchased from farmers for below the cost of production or world market price can be sold cheaply to urban dwellers. This keeps the potentially volatile cities, with their armies of bureaucrats, calm and loyal to the regime. In other cases, food purchased cheaply from farmers is sold at high prices on the world market with the government pocketing the profits. U.S. food policy does nothing to get at the root cause of this agricultural problem. In fact, by providing cheap food, the problem is exacerbated.

"*Development assistance should be guided by principles of entrepreneurship.*"

US Aid Should Promote the Free Market

Nicholas Eberstadt

Nicholas Eberstadt is a visiting scholar at the American Enterprise Institute, a Washington, DC think-tank. He is also a visiting fellow at the Center for Population Studies at Harvard University in Cambridge, Massachusetts. In the following viewpoint, he argues that the US has played an essential role in establishing an international economic system which operates on free-market principles. Eberstadt writes that the US should revamp its foreign aid programs to promote self-sufficiency and private enterprise in the Third World.

As you read, consider the following questions:

1. What does Eberstadt mean when he writes about the "liberal international economic order"?
2. How have the programs of the Agency for International Development thwarted US foreign policy goals, according to the author?
3. How does Eberstadt believe the US can help Third World countries make their markets healthier and more productive?

Nicholas Eberstadt, *Foreign Aid and American Purpose*. Washington, DC: American Enterprise Institute for Public Policy Research, 1988. Reprinted with permission.

With its particular political values, the United States can achieve greatest security under a world order that accepts as legitimate the free international flow of information, trade, technology, and capital; that does not question the right of people to act to improve their material well-being; and that embraces the rule of law and the propriety of enlightened governance. Conversely, the use of American power to protect a system that offers all nations and peoples opportunity—unmatched by alternative arrangements—to participate in broad-based material advance is not only a strategic goal but an objective dictated by U.S. moral and humanitarian concerns. The liberal international economic order America helped create remains the best broad hope for the world's poor and disadvantaged peoples. The United States should use its power—military, financial, moral—to protect it. . . .

Development Aid

Redirecting American development policies to the task of encouraging self-sustaining economic growth will require major changes in the operation and direction of government agencies currently charged with promoting economic advance in less-developed countries.

Within a liberal international economic order, it is not the volume of concessional foreign aid that sets the ultimate constraint on a less-developed nation's pace of economic transformation and material progress. Instead, the limit will be set, in practice, principally by the recipient government's policies, administrative competence, and willingness to take advantage of the opportunities afforded by international markets in goods, services, and finance.

Apart from their congressional budget presentations and their election-year pronouncements, current American development policy makers seem to pay strangely little attention to the policy environment in less-developed countries or to the resulting climate of economic incentives and disincentives. Judged by actions rather than words, a principal thrust of current development assistance policies would seem to be the encouragement of international transfer payments to raise living standards through social spending. The rationale for such a policy is to build "human capital." As with any other form of capital, however, the rate of return depends on the manner in which it is put to use. To a distressing extent, the social programs today justified under the rubric of human capital do not create human capital; instead, they fund unproductive public consumption in its name. Such transfers do not encourage self-sustaining growth in most recipient countries. To the contrary, they tend to distort growth processes and economic structures. Moreover, concessional budgetary transfers have often had the effect of overvaluing exchange rates and thereby reducing recipient nation's abilities to compete in, and learn from, the world economy. The consequences of such distortions on the sustainability of emergent structures and the prospects for the poor within them are predictable.

AID's Agenda

As currently directed, AID [Agency for International Development] conducts a foreign policy that often varies substantially from that of the State Department. This can be seen in AID rules that systematically circumvent the intentions of U.S. human rights legislation, "policy determinations" that undercut State Department positions toward the UN-promoted New International Economic Order or initiatives that either displace private economic activity or tie aid to the purchase of specific American products in a variant of mercantilism. This discrepancy reflects an apparent belief, often embodied in AID documents and official statements, that the international economic order that the United States officially supports cannot work for the poor—or should not be allowed to do so.

Growth-Oriented Policies

While social programs are a necessary component of assistance, U.S. foreign aid programs should focus mainly on promoting growth-oriented, free-market economic policies. Only through such policies will less developed countries become able to provide for themselves what Western aid workers now administer and thereby tackle the social problems that no amount of international welfare aid can solve.

Melanie S. Tammen, The Heritage Foundation *Executive Memorandum*, September 9, 1988.

American developmental aid should support the workings of just this liberal international economic order. Assistance should be directed toward helping governments govern more productively, rather than redressing international poverty through unsustainable transnational budget transfers. Development assistance should be guided by principles of entrepreneurship and comparative advantage: that is, of making the most productive use of scarce resources through key interventions. The experience of such nonprofit groups as the Rockefeller Foundation and the Ford Foundation in the early post-World War II period demonstrates how tremendously important such a strategic use of charitable money can be for the purposes of promoting material advance. . . .

US Funds and International Organizations

To a distressing degree, the programs funded by the United Nations and related organizations in the name of "development" are hostile to a free and open international economy. The United States should take no part in undermining the system it helped create, which has promoted prosperity in a host of once-impoverished lands. Washington should undertake a thorough review of its UN funding and stop subsidizing those programs that are found to be inconsistent with the goals of economic freedom. Washington should be neither defensive nor apologetic about disinheriting such activities; to the contrary, it should explain clearly the rationale behind each decision. . . .

As originally envisioned, the International Bank for Reconstruction and Development (IBRD), commonly known as the World Bank, was to serve as a main pillar of a free international economy. It was to promote technical assistance and to encourage the creation of a positive "investment climate" in which economic progress might be hastened. The bank was specifically expected to refrain from displacing private capital or from contributing to national policies that would restrict economic activity in borrowing countries. The bank's present activities, however, do not always seem consistent with these original purposes. The World Bank and other development banks need careful examination, evaluation, and review. Like America's own development institutions, they may usefully be reminded of the purposes for which they were established. . . .

Helping Markets Work

The "miracle of the marketplace" is a delicate and complex phenomenon and should not be taken for granted. Markets are not perfectly efficient arbiters of economic activity—if they were, there could not be such a thing as entrepreneurship. A major task confronting a less-developed country is to create the marketing infrastructure that can rapidly and cheaply convey goods and services and information and knowledge. Developing countries must also learn about and understand international markets—including financial ones—if they are to take advantage of the opportunities provided by the international system.

Making markets work, to a great extent, is simply a matter of refraining from predictably destructive interference in their operations. But societies and governments can also take positive actions to create the atmosphere and to build the links and networks upon which efficient and productive markets depend. The United States has much to offer developing countries that wish to improve the functionings of their economies. For example, U.S. business schools train students in the practical aspects of market development; these institutions could teach students and policy makers from less-developed countries as well. Making markets work also depends on the extent to which developing societies successfully build sophisticated and competent financial infrastructures. Training teams such as those developed by the Harvard Institute for International Development may be able to assist here, but in the realm of technical assistance this field remains largely *terra incognita.*

Above all, however, developing countries have much to learn about two fundamentals upon which the effective working of markets is predicated: respect for private property and rule of law. It would be reassuring to think that the United States could contribute to the instruction of low-income countries in this vital area. . . .

Promoting US Objectives

Foreign aid policies should be used to reinforce U.S. political, economic, and moral objectives throughout the world because these objectives are fundamentally sound. The converse to this argument and its implications is important as well. If America's fundamental political, economic, and moral purposes in the world are sound, then strengthening U.S. power is in itself a beneficial and effective form of foreign aid. . . .

AID Subsidizes Socialist Policies

Less than 5% of U.S. foreign assistance has gone directly to the private sector in developing countries. Instead, the U.S. government continues to subsidize statist or socialist economic policies abroad.

The main culprit in this has been the U.S. Agency for International Development. AID continues pursuing the flawed policies that for decades have substantially contributed to keeping developing nations impoverished. AID, for example, continues to distribute over 90% of its funds as "government-to-government transfers," fueling the growth of huge, bureaucratic state sectors in the Third World. It depresses domestic food prices in developing countries—and thereby farmers' incomes—with hundreds of thousands of metric tons of food aid.

Peter F. Schaefer, *The Wall Street Journal*, September 29, 1987.

No other nation has ever been in as good a position as the United States to champion the cause of the world's poor. Americans should recognize the responsibilities this implies, but they may also rejoice at the extraordinary coincidence of interests between a strong and healthy America and the prospects of advancement for the impoverished and unprotected peoples of the earth.

"How can the magic of the marketplace . . . work to end hunger if the customers are missing—that is, if people are too poor to be part of the market?"

Efforts To Promote the Free Market Are Inadequate

Frances Moore Lappé, Rachel Schurman, and Kevin Danaher

Frances Moore Lappé is a well-known specialist on Third World development. A prolific author, in 1975 she founded the Institute for Development Policy, a San Francisco organization that conducts research on Third World issues. Rachel Schurman is a former researcher at the Institute. Author Kevin Danaher is the Institute's senior analyst on Africa and US aid policies. In the following viewpoint, they argue that free-market policies cannot reduce Third World poverty. The authors contend that the first step Third World governments must take is to redistribute wealth and power so that more people can participate in the market.

As you read, consider the following questions:

1. How is current thinking about US foreign aid flawed, according to the authors?
2. Why do the authors argue that privatizing Third World economies will fail?
3. Why do Lappé, Schurman, and Danaher believe the US opposes revolutionary change in the Third World?

Despite the generosity and goodwill of most Americans, U.S. foreign aid isn't working. If its goal is to alleviate poverty abroad, we search in vain for evidence of its success. Among major recipients of U.S. aid—the Philippines, India, and Central American nations, for example—the number of people living in poverty has climbed as foreign aid has increased. Even government-sponsored studies admit that many of the best-sounding projects to help the poorest people often fail to reach them. . . .

Economic Dogma and Foreign Aid

Our government's view of the world as a battleground between "them" and "us" . . . powerfully shapes the content of the strictly economic portion of U.S. foreign aid. Washington believes that any economic system not like ours, must be like theirs. Economies are either capitalist or communist. Thus, the United States must use its foreign aid program as a lever to reform third-world economies—to make them more open to foreign investment and market-oriented like ours. The buzz-word is privatization—reducing the government's role in the economy. Increasingly, U.S. aid to third-world governments is awarded on the basis of just such "policy reforms."

In many cases, basic economic reform is needed—badly needed. But, Washington's dogmatic stance prevents it from seeing that the prerequisites for the success of its economic formula simply do not exist in many third-world countries. How can the magic of the marketplace, for example, work to end hunger if the customers are missing—that is, if people are too poor to be part of the market? How can private enterprise free people from hunger in the third world if private capital is actually fleeing Africa and Latin America in search of surer investments elsewhere? . . .

It's assumed that private investment equals growth and measurable economic return, while public investment saps an economy's vigor. Yet a 1985 World Bank report on the economic return on investments in education offers striking counterevidence. It shows that the rate of return on human investments—health, and education, for example—is higher than on capital investments. "In developing countries . . . there is a clear advantage of human versus physical capital investment," it concludes. Yet such investments in "human capital" are precisely what private wealth neglects because it can't capture the full return, which accrues not only to the individual but to society as a whole.

The goal of current policy is not merely to shift investment funds toward the private sector, however; it is to expand the private sector by trimming government's role.

Arguing that many economic activities can be performed more efficiently by private companies than by governments, AID

[Agency for International Development] urges that state corporations should be turned over to the private sector.

In many countries, increasing the efficiency of government operations is not only reasonable—it is necessary. But a key defect in AID's reasoning is that efficiency is defined strictly in financial terms. A government may save money by privatizing state corporations and laying off workers, but the savings may be lost after adding in hidden social costs. The poor and even the middle class may suffer from the cutbacks in services and employment that result because the private sector simply does not take up what government has dropped. As an AID official in the Dominican Republic admitted to us: "the private sector can't possibly create the amount of jobs needed."

Hungry People

Promoters of the 'free market' insist that its great virtue is that it responds to individual preferences. But the preference of most individuals is to eat when hungry. Yet more than half a billion people living in market economy countries lack an adequate diet.

Kevin Danaher, *Race & Class*, January/March 1989.

Honduras is just one country where AID has been pushing the government to sell state enterprises to the private sector. Guatama Fonseca, former Minister of Labor, exposes the simplemindedness of assuming that such a shift will automatically bring economic improvement.

This idea of privatization is nutty. They're touting it as if they've discovered something new. What do they think has been the predominant system here for the past century? How do they think we got in this mess to begin with?

There is nothing more inefficient and corrupt in Honduras than private enterprise. They steal millions of dollars every year from the government, from the people. Now we're supposed to sell off our public enterprises at rock-bottom prices to the thieves and mafiosos who sucked the government corporations dry to begin with.

An African might make a similar retort to U.S. advice to governments there to sell state marketing boards to private interests. These boards—government agencies with exclusive rights to market key crops—were created in many African countries in colonial times. Their purpose was to facilitate extraction of wealth from the countryside for enrichment of the colonizing country and to ensure the profits of rich farmers, especially white settlers. They are equally destructive today where wealthy farmers are a powerful political force. "Large producers are favored over small producers" by the boards, and "exports are favored over domestic production. The inefficiencies of the marketing boards and the high transport charges also fall disproportionately upon the smallholder," one study of Kenya concludes. . . .

Luring Private Investment

To spur private investment—both local and foreign—AID advises governments to lower taxes, hold down wages, and loosen restrictions on taking profits out of the country. When businessmen are asssured of a good profit, goes the theory, they will invest and thereby contribute to the development of the country.

Even if successful, attracting foreign investment is not necessarily the answer to development problems in the eyes of all third-world leaders. Selling public agencies could attract foreign investment, but some see it merely deepening a relationship of dependency. Former Honduran Labor Minister Guatama Fonseca asked us in a recent interview:

> Who has the money to buy these giant enterprises? Most Hondurans are impoverished. The only ones with enough money are the *gringos*; so privatization means selling our country, bit by bit, to foreigners. It means becoming a colony of the United States. It's worse than in the beginning of the century when we sold our land to the banana companies.

A Haitian businessman with whom we spoke echoes Fonseca's fears. "The Haitian businessmen like the sound of privatization because they think they are going to get to buy these companies cheap," he told us. "But no bank here is going to let Haitian businessmen outbid the foreigners. The U.S. private sector will swallow up the Haitian private sector because they don't need us."

The Infrastructure Is Lacking

But even if one were to accept AID's goal of increased private investment as the place to start, two problems remain.

First, how is development-stimulating investment possible without essential activities—building and maintaining roads, railways, electric grids, and water supplies, for example—which are rarely undertaken by private enterprise? Most are not profitable from the point of view of a single firm; they are only profitable from the point of view of the entire society. Such vital tasks are among the primary functions of government. But AID's current fixation on the private sector ignores this critical aspect of development necessary to get its own private investment program off the ground.

Second, how can AID's plan succeed in luring private investment if the ingredients for profit making just aren't there? Take Sub-Saharan Africa. Most Africans are too poor to constitute an attractive market, so the only kind of investors the region might attract are those interested in extraction of raw materials or production for export. Add to this the lack of infrastructure, the depletion of Africa's natural resources, and the massive foreign debt that is bankrupting many African states, and it becomes clear why capital is not just failing to come into the region, it is *deserting*. "In 1980, African countries got close to $1.5 billion, net, from private creditors; in 1985 there was a net outflow of $700 million," reports *The Economist*.

Investment in the Third World

Africa is the worst case, but it is not alone. Overall, net direct investment in third-world economies is falling. In 1983 it was $2.4 billion, forty percent below levels of just two years earlier. . . . "Every year, billions of dollars flow out of Brazil and much of Latin America . . . much of it in violation of local currency laws,"

Paul Conrad. © 1974, The Times. Reprinted by permission of Los Angeles Times Syndicate.

reports *The New York Times.* When we asked a U.S. Embassy official in Honduras where all the U.S. economic aid to that country was going, he groaned: "Most of it ends up in private bank accounts in Miami."

The lesson is clear: if a lucrative market does not exist locally, foreign firms will not be eager to invest, except to produce for export. Nor will local firms and wealthy individuals reinvest their earnings locally if more lucrative investments exist overseas. Within AID's formula, this problem has no solution. Its free enterprise dogma opposes government controls to keep profits at home. How then can governments even keep existing capital from fleeing, much less attract new capital? . . .

Lest we be misunderstood as antimarket, we want to focus for a moment on its potential role in alleviating poverty. Since any society trying to do away with the market altogether has faced monumental headaches, the goal of well-functioning markets should be a key part of ending poverty and its worst symptom, hunger. But AID's formula has it backwards. It promotes the free market and entrepreneurs. But do they need promoting? Enterprising marketers spring up wherever there are customers. In much of the third world it's the customers who are missing. They, not the market, need to be promoted!

Customers are the engine of the market. They are what is missing where poverty is widespread. As the World Bank itself acknowledges, hunger can only be alleviated "by redistributing purchasing power and resources toward those who are undernourished." But U.S. foreign assistance must remain blind to this obvious truth, for to acknowledge it calls forth a further question: how do you generate more customers?

Government's Necessary Role

Government—made accountable by active citizenry—is the only agency through which wide dispersion of control over land, credit, and other essential resources can be achieved and maintained in order to generate customers for healthy markets. And here is the hitch for the free-market ideologues. Since they proscribe a significant role for government, and deem serious redistribution a communist plot, their *own* stated goal of healthy market economies is doomed. And so are the hungry.

Ranking Concerns in Distributing Foreign Aid

This activity will allow you to rank the concerns you believe to be most important in the distribution of foreign aid. Foreign aid policy is hotly debated, in part because people and organizations disagree on what values should be used to determine when and to whom aid should be given. For instance, an organization like the Christian Children's Fund may distribute foreign aid to help the poor and to spread Christian influence in the Third World. An organization like the World Anti-Communist League, on the other hand, may distribute foreign aid to help Third World people fight communism. To further this goal, it might provide more military aid than humanitarian aid. Yet another perspective might come from a Western government, such as that of Great Britain. The British government may distribute aid partly for humanitarian reasons, but also in hopes that in return for its aid, Third World countries will adopt policies favorable to British interests and be allies of Britain. All three groups want to help the Third World, but clearly they have different concerns which will determine in what circumstances they will provide aid.

The authors in this chapter debate what type of foreign aid is beneficial. Some believe aid should be given only in times of famine and disaster, others believe aid should be given to promote self-sufficiency in the Third World. Still others argue that the US should help only those countries that are friendly and support US policies.

Part I

The class should break into groups of four to six students. Rank the foreign aid concerns listed below as though the group were staff members of the Agency for International Development. The Agency is a US governmental agency which distributes US aid to other countries. (M. Peter McPherson, the author of viewpoint 1 in this chapter, is a former administrator of AID. You may wish to review his viewpoint before completing this step.) Use 1 to designate what the group considers the most important concern, 2 for the next most important concern, and so on until all the concerns are ranked.

Foreign aid should:

_____ help the poor and suffering because there is a moral obligation to do so

_____ promote democracy and human rights

_____ compensate for the US legacy of exploitation

_____ deter communist aggression

_____ improve other countries' economies so that they can buy our products and food, thus helping our businesses and farmers

_____ help allies who will adopt policies favorable to our interests

_____ promote self-sufficiency in the Third World

Part II

Working within the same group, rank the foreign aid concerns as if the group were staff members of the private organization Church World Service. A division of the National Council of Churches, Church World Service sends food, clothing, medicines, and other supplies to famine and disaster victims. It also participates in self-help development projects in the Third World.

Part III

Step 1: After your group has come to a consensus, compare your answers with those of other groups in a class discussion.

Step 2: The entire class should discuss the following questions:

1. Was there a difference between the foreign aid concerns most important to the US government agency and the concerns most important to the private, religious organization? Why or why not?

2. How do you believe a famine victim who received food aid would respond to your ranking of concerns? How would the military leader of a Third World government who received military aid respond to your ranking?

Periodical Bibliography

The following articles have been selected to supplement the diverse views presented in this chapter.

William P. Barrett — "The Money Pit," *Forbes*, May 15, 1989.

Bill Bradley — "Fostering Worldwide Democracy," *USA Today*, September 1988.

Nicholas Eberstadt — "Restoring Purpose to Foreign Aid," *The World & I*, February 1989.

John M. Gashko — "America's Helping Hand," *The Washington Post National Weekly Edition*, September 28, 1987.

Frances Moore Lappé — "Democracy and Dogma in the Fight Against Hunger," *The Christian Century*, December 10, 1986.

Frances Moore Lappé, Kevin Danaher, and Rachel Schurman — "US Foreign Aid and the National Interest," *Zeta Magazine*, February 1988.

Robert W. Lee — "Bleeding Us Dry," *The New American*, June 19, 1989.

M. Peter McPherson — "What's Gone Right—and Wrong—with Aid," *U.S. News & World Report*, November 17, 1986.

Richard T. Montoya — "The Foreign Aid Cancer," *Vital Speeches of the Day*, August 1, 1987.

David R. Obey and Carol Lancaster — "Funding Foreign Aid," *Foreign Policy*, Summer 1988.

Jack Shepherd — "When Foreign Aid Fails," *The Atlantic Monthly*, April 1985.

Sargent Shriver — "Ideals and Imperfections," *Multinational Monitor*, September 1986.

Roy A. Stacy — "Fiscal Year 1988 Assistance Requests for Sub-Saharan Africa," *Department of State Bulletin*, May 1987.

Carol B. Thompson — "Harvests Under Fire," *Africa Report*, September/October 1988.

US Department of State — "The AID Challenge," *Department of State Bulletin*, January 1987.

What Policies Would Promote Third World Development?

Chapter Preface

Media images of the Third World paint a grim picture—millions of people live in dire poverty and unremitting misery. This poverty persists despite years of efforts to improve the economies of the Third World. Yet a few Third World nations have successful economies. Do these nations provide lessons for the rest of the Third World?

One side of the debate argues that the successes of such countries as South Korea, Taiwan, Hong Kong, and Singapore show that capitalism is the best development strategy for the Third World. These newly industrializing countries have enjoyed growth rates of 7 to 10 percent per year. Many observers attribute this success to free-market policies in these countries. Former President Richard Nixon describes the effect of economic growth on South Korea: It "has allowed a war-devastated nation with a per capita income of $50 in 1953 to develop into a potential economic giant, with a per capita income of $2,200 and a literacy rate higher than that of the United States." As these Asian countries improve the well-being of their people, Nixon believes their example will provide "incontrovertible proof" of capitalism's benefits.

But others do not consider the newly industrializing countries good models for the rest of the Third World. According to Stephen Rosskamm Shalom, a professor at William Patterson College in New Jersey, South Korea's economic growth has not helped all Koreans. In fact, it has increased the exploitation of the poor. Shalom notes that the average work week for South Koreans is 57 hours, the longest in the world.

Observers who agree with Shalom believe that rather than adopt South Korea's strategy, Third World countries should support projects similar to Bangladesh's Grameen Bank. The Bank loans money to its members—people who are poor, usually illiterate, and mostly female (80 percent). These borrowers take out small loans to buy cows, chickens, rickshaws, and other items used to make a livelihood. Many of its members have been able to establish businesses that allow them to feed themselves and their families. While Grameen supporters admit that Bangladesh on the whole is much poorer than South Korea, they maintain that its efforts to help the poorest members of society will gradually lift the country out of poverty, while the poor in South Korea will not benefit from that nation's economic growth.

The following chapter examines the economies of the Third World.

"Third World nations should be encouraged to adopt growth-oriented policies."

Capitalism Can Help the Third World Develop

Alvin Rabushka

In the following viewpoint, Alvin Rabushka describes the economic success of several Asian countries that have adopted capitalist policies. The economies of South Korea, Taiwan, Hong Kong, and Singapore have grown an average of ten percent per year, according to Rabushka, because these countries have promoted the private sector. Rabushka is an author and senior fellow at the Hoover Institution at Stanford University in California.

As you read, consider the following questions:

1. Why does the author believe many Third World countries are now adopting capitalist policies?
2. What were the effects of Sri Lanka's socialist policies, according to the author?
3. Why does Rabushka believe that the economic success of Korea, Taiwan, Singapore, and Hong Kong can be duplicated in other Third World nations?

"Great Leap Forward" by Alvin Rabushka is reprinted from the Summer 1987 issue of *Policy Review*, the quarterly publication of The Heritage Foundation, 214 Massachusetts Avenue NE, Washington, DC 20002.

Ten years ago most strategies for economic development in the Third World were state-directed and state-controlled. Development policy typically consisted of high taxation to promote national savings through government-directed capital formation; a dependence on foreign aid and massive foreign borrowing (despite official rhetoric of political and economic independence); the establishment and operation of state-owned enterprises; foreign exchange controls; limitation on overseas investment or ownership to avoid the appearance of neocolonialist influence; high tariffs, as well as quotas and other quantitative restrictions on imports; export levies; state control of businesses; the creation of agricultural marketing boards to procure domestic agricultural output on a compulsory basis at below-market prices; and, in some instances, outright central planning.

Socialism seemed especially entrenched in Africa, where only Botswana, Swaziland, and the Ivory Coast actively pursued a market-based strategy of development. Glimpses of capitalism might also be found in the Cameroon, Gabon, and Zimbabwe. But the general tendency throughout the continent was state domination of economic life.

The Heavy Hand of Intervention

The heavy hand of state economic intervention could also be found throughout the Middle East, Central and South America, and South and Southeast Asia. Only the "four Asian tigers" or "four Asian dragons"—Hong Kong, Singapore, Taiwan, and South Korea—adhered to capitalism as a strategy for development. They were growing so fast that economists were induced to define a new category of developing nation known as newly industrializing country, or NIC. But the conventional wisdom was that these were small countries with authoritarian governments and a Confucian work ethic, and that their experience would not be applicable elsewhere in the Third World.

In 1977, the foreign aid programs of the United States, the World Bank, and other donor countries and organizations reinforced the state-centered development strategies of recipient countries. Donors repeatedly stressed the objectives of redistributing income from rich to poor people and increasing spending on social programs to meet the needs of the poor. They provided grants and soft loans to inefficient, state-owned enterprises and encouraged massive commercial borrowing to finance major expansions in the scope and size of public sector activities. Partly as a result of the aid programs, many Third World countries increasingly found themselves mired in debt they could not pay, their stagnant economies overlaid by bloated public sectors that frustrated and suppressed private sector initiative.

What a difference a decade makes! Statism still dominates, but it is on the defensive, and is increasingly recognized as the cause of many Third World countries' debt crises. Today the Third World throbs with capitalism. In Buenos Aires, Calcutta, and Chiang Mai, profitable private companies running smaller buses provide better services than heavily-subsidized government-owned or regulated bus companies. In the Ivory Coast, a profitable private water company provides the most reliable urban water service in sub-Saharan Africa. Private firms do a more cost-effective job in maintaining the national road networks in Argentina and Brazil compared with government departments in previous years. In Bangladesh, the government has privatized wholesale distribution of fertilizer. Governments throughout the world are exploring ways of selling state-owned industries to private ownership, loosening trade restrictions, lowering tariff barriers, emphasizing private sector development, and reducing high marginal rates of taxation that discourage work, saving, and investment.

The Misery of Communism

In Asia we see incontrovertible proof of which social, economic, and political policies permit nations and people to live and grow and which cause them to decay and die. The world has never before had such an effective contrast in the same region between the misery produced by communism and the rich blessings of political and economic systems that permit a large measure of freedom.

Richard Nixon, *1999: Victory Without War,* 1988.

By 1987 the record of the "four Asian tigers" was unmistakable. Never before in history had four nations moved from Third World to First World status in one generation. Average annual growth rates of 9-10 percent lifted per capita income in Korea from $82 in 1962 to about $2,500 in 1987; in Taiwan, from $143 in 1960 to above $4,500 in 1987; in Hong Kong from $180 in 1949 to more than $7,000 in 1987; and in the 20 years since Singapore became an independent state in 1965, from $470 to $6,800.

Research on the magic formula of growth in the Pacific Basin is now an intellectual growth industry. Staffan Burenstam Linder, Dean of the Stockholm School of Economics and member of the board of governors of the Swedish central bank, suggests that growth among the capitalist countries of the Asian-Pacific region influenced and stimulated the Chinese reform movement and has had an electrifying effect on other countries:

There has been a demonstration effect on both economic thinking and economic policy making. . . . And there is a leverage effect: socialist setbacks have provided a painful contrast that has directed the attention of those who are disillusioned to the advantages of other systems.

The donor community has also shifted its emphasis. In 1987, the U.S. Agency for International Development (AID), the World Bank, and the International Monetary Fund all agree that as a condition of further assistance, Third World nations should be encouraged to adopt growth-oriented policies. AID, for example, set up a Bureau for Private Enterprise to encourage the growth of private sector activity in the Third World, and international donor organizations are stressing growth-oriented policy reforms as a condition of continued assistance. Four issues of the World Bank's annual *World Development Report* (1983-1986) have criticized the failed socialist policies that are so prevalent in the Third World, recommending, in their place, greater reliance on private enterprise and private investment, the elimination of state-owned enterprises and marketing boards, privatizing state-owned monopolies, swapping debt for equity, reducing subsidies to parastatals, reducing tax rates, liberalizing tariffs and other import restrictions, and so forth. The full list of recommendations constitutes a modern day *Wealth of Nations* for the Third World.

China's Transformation

The biggest transformation, of course, has been in the People's Republic of China. Since 1978, Deng Xiaoping, twice honored as *Time*'s "Man of the Year," has embarked his country on the greatest free-market experiment in the history of the world. Known as pragmatic in economic affairs, Deng and his economic colleagues are dismantling the most comprehensive system of socialist planning and practice ever attempted in the Third World in favor of an emphasis on freer markets, freer prices, private enterprise, and the replacement of the rule of man with the rule of law. . . .

China's flirtation with capitalism began with the agricultural responsibility system, under which collectively-owned fields are allocated to individual families. Households enter into 15-year contracts with the local brigade or commune. In return for the exclusive rights to farm leased plots, they agree to meet specific output quotas and payments. Households retain the rights to consume their excess production or sell it on the open market with no tax liability—a zero marginal tax rate on above-quota production. Under the new system, households, families, and individuals own the output of their work, thus injecting incentives into rural production. All restrictions have been removed on private plots, individual livestock breeding, household sideline occupations, and rural trade fairs. Farmers can own their own tractors and trucks, and enter into contractual arrangements to plow fields, transport goods, sell their services to outside parties, and set up rural processing and other sideline industries. Despite a constitutional prohibition on private ownership of land, the party tolerates transfers

151

of contracted land among peasant households as a positive concomitant of specialization and commercialization. Peasants may even hire their fellow peasants as laborers.

No Coincidence

It is no coincidence that the highly controlled centrally planned economic systems employed by underdeveloped countries perform just as miserably as they do in Eastern Europe and the Soviet Union (or worse due to the strength in many underdeveloped countries of tradition bound or non-material-based cultures, which are not conducive to economic progress). But centrally planned economies have not just failed to bring economic progress; they have led in many cases to economic decline. For instance, Cuba fell from having the fourth largest per capita GNP in Latin America to fourteenth, and the standard of living in Vietnam is now lower than it was during the height of the Vietnam War. On the other hand, it is also no coincidence that countries, and even colonies, which foster relatively free market economies, such as Hong Kong, Singapore, Taiwan, South Korea, and the Ivory Coast, are now advancing well. The governments of these areas have recognized that the secret to wealth and development is unleashing the resource of their *people*, allowing them to work and invest where *they* see personal and economic returns—not where government bureaucrats believe would be best for the "social good".

C. Brandon Crocker, *California Review*, April 1988.

From 1979 to 1985, the value of agricultural output rose at more than double the rate between 1953 and 1978. Rural per capita incomes more than doubled. Total grain harvest leapt from 300 million tons in 1978 to over 400 million tons by 1984; China became a grain exporter for the first time in its history. Large increases in grain were dwarfed by even larger annual increases in cotton, oil-bearing crops, sugar cane and beets, tea, and animal protein products. . . .

Spreading Reform

In August 1986, I had the opportunity to discuss China's current economic reforms with leading economists of the Chinese Academy of Social Sciences. They predicted that future economic reforms would unfold in labor and capital markets, which would allow these two resources to be used more efficiently. They also expressed concern that industrial reform would be far more difficult to achieve than rural reform. In particular, removing price distortions and reducing subsidies might result in inflation and unacceptable losses in too many state-owned enterprises. They were fully aware that China severely lagged the Asian tigers, and hoped they would have future opportunities to study the tigers firsthand to see what lessons could be transferred to the mainland. If the succcess of capitalism in the four Asian tigers proved irresistible to mainland China, then perhaps China's preliminary good fortune with capitalism has tempted other socialist countries to follow suit. Vietnam has begun to experiment with market reforms and reports of growing market activity are emanating from Cambodia. In the Soviet Union, Communist Party General Secretary Mikhail Gorbachev has announced a new policy of "glasnost" (openness) which has economic reform among its objectives. It is no accident that Hungary, which gives its citizens the largest measure of economic freedom among the Eastern bloc nations, has outperformed its fellow Communist nations of Poland, Rumania, Bulgaria, Czechoslovakia, and East Germany.

Sri Lanka

A major transition from socialism to capitalism has also taken place on the pearl-shaped island of Sri Lanka in the Indian Ocean, an Asian democracy without the Confucian heritage of the "four dragons." Sri Lanka's history dates back 2,500 years to its original settlement by the Sinhala people from the South Asian subcontinent. They were followed in turn by the Tamils from South India, Arab traders, Portuguese spice merchants, Dutch traders, and lastly the British. Ceylon (as the island was named under British rule) developed as a plantation economy, exporting tea, rubber, and coconuts. Its modern political evolution developed from the westernization of its indigenous elites in the early decades of the 20th century, culminating in peaceful independence in 1948.

After independence, socialism and state control steadily replaced private ownership and the market economy. The export-oriented plantation sector was heavily taxed to finance free education, free medicine, free water, sanitation, subsidized food, and cheap transport. When the plantations were finally nationalized in the mid-1970s, the public sector controlled more than 90 percent of the economy. As economic stagnation set in, further government efforts to redistribute income resulted only in a redistribution of poverty. The government of socialist-leaning Sirimavo Bandaranaike (1970-1977) ruled through a perpetual state of emergency. Her economic policies beset the economy with import controls, foreign exchange controls, price controls, and a plethora of state industrial and trading monopolies. She nationalized land, banks, and businesses. The results were food and other shortages, black markets, and widespread evasion of controls and taxes. Her strategy of import substitution fostered inefficient, overprotected industry. Low food prices and food rations for all, regardless of income, eroded producer incentives, even for those subsisting on their own land. A massive public sector smothered the remains of private sector initiative, and a great deal of the country's talent decided to migrate overseas. The country's external reserves were run down and massive budget deficits, financed by new money creation, brought a ruinous inflation. By 1975 economic life had virtually ground to a halt.

A Free-Market Course

In the 1977 elections, economic issues supplanted the traditional communal rivalry between the Sinhalese and Tamil ethnic communities. Promising a new direction in economic policy, the United National Party, under the leadership of J.R. Jayewardene, swept to a landslide victory and set out to reverse 30 years of socialist economic policies.

The new finance minister, Ronnie de Mel, charted his government's free-market course in his annual budget addresses. Over the next few years he reduced marginal tax rates, eliminated the fixed overvalued exchange rate, reduced and eliminated many state industrial and trading monopolies, curtailed consumer and producer subsidies, eased import restrictions, and established a free trade zone. In his speeches he often cited such distinguished economists as Friedrich Hayek, Milton Friedman, and Ludwig von Mises. But the most important inspiration for the government's liberal economic policies was the nearby example of Singapore.

Asian Examples

In countries such as Thailand, Singapore and South Korea, some resources were judiciously combined with sound domestic policies designed to promote broad-based growth. These policies stimulated the private sector involvement, the development and adoption of practical technologies, education and training, diversification of agriculture and industry.

Richard S. Williamson, *Human Events*, October 20, 1984.

In sharp contrast with Singapore's incredible economic growth, Sri Lanka's per capita income had stagnated for years below several hundred dollars. Sri Lanka's Jayewardene became close friends with Singapore's Lee Kuan Yew, and sent his island's public officials to Singapore for training. Virtually every official I interviewed in Sri Lanka in 1981 talked about "the Singapore model of development" as the basis of Sri Lanka's future. One treasury spokesman told me about the hostile reaction he received from the *Times of India* during a visit to India when he explained Sri Lanka's reduction in marginal tax rates. The *Times* vigorously opposed marginal tax rate cuts in India lest it turn the country away from socialism. The paper may have had reason for concern: Rajiv Gandhi sharply cut marginal tax rates after he replaced his mother as India's leader.

Although an outbreak of communal conflict between the Sinhalese and Tamil communities has marred the island's tranquility, the new free-market economic policies have worked their wonders. Between 1970 and 1976, annual economic growth averaged a meager 2.9 percent. Annual per capita income had stagnated at $190 and unemployment reached 25 percent of the labor force. Under Jayewardene's leadership, annual economic growth averaged 5.9 percent between 1977 and 1985. Per capita income almost doubled to $350 by 1985 and the unemployment rate was cut in half. . . .

Burgeoning Prosperity

Several million Americans have toured East and Southeast Asia and are aware of the burgeoning prosperity in the four Asian tigers. Those who first saw the region during the Second World War and its aftermath are especially impressed with the region's economic transformation. No one seriously questions the success of these East and Southeast Asian capitalistic economies, but skeptics question whether the wholesale adoption of the four tigers' economic policies by such giant economies as China and India, or the non-Oriental cultures of Africa and South America, will bring double-digit growth rates. I hear a variety of reasons why the experience of the four Asian tigers is not transferable to other developing nations: China is much bigger; Africa and Latin America lack the Confucian values of thrift, hard work, and a love of education; or that declining international assistance—so crucial to Taiwan and Korea during the 1950s—and rising protectionism means that export-oriented policies will not work as well in the future as they have in the past. (I find it hard to reconcile the notion that Latin Americans have a "mañana" view of human nature with the reality of millions of them entering the United States, legally or illegally, for the sole purpose of work.)

Perhaps the current generation of skeptics is correct in claiming that the four Asian tigers are unique and cannot serve as models for other developing nations. But then again, perhaps they are wrong. In 1986 I received a delegation of economic advisers to the premiers, prime ministers, and presidents of eight French-speaking, sub-Saharan African countries. They unanimously acknowledged that their countries had stagnated for two decades as a result of socialist policies and that future growth depended on the injection of market forces and foreign direct investment into their economies. They were converts to capitalism.

"Even amid desperate poverty people's lives can be sharply improved by redistributionist policies."

Capitalism Cannot Help the Third World Develop

Stephen Rosskamm Shalom

Stephen Rosskamm Shalom, a political science professor at William Paterson College in Wayne, New Jersey, is the author of *The United States and the Philippines* and co-editor of *The Philippines Reader*. In the following viewpoint, he describes the experience of Kerala, a state in India which follows the socialist policies of redistributing wealth and reducing inequality. These policies, Shalom writes, have improved Kerala and its people's standard of living.

As you read, consider the following questions:

1. Why does Shalom find it ironic that Western nations point to East Asian countries as proof that capitalism is the wave of the future?
2. What do the experiences of South Korea and Taiwan prove about development, in the author's opinion?
3. According to Shalom, how can redistribution policies improve the lives of Third World women?

Stephen Rosskamm Shalom, "Capitalism Triumphant?" *Zeta*, April 1989. Reprinted with permission.

It seems like capitalism never had it so good. Taiwan and South Korea were supposedly lifted by capitalism from the ranks of the poor to become two of the most dynamic economies in the world. Communist states are moving toward free markets or else wallowing in economic stagnation. In the Soviet Union the going joke—according to the *New York Times*—defines communism as the "longest and most painful route from capitalism to capitalism." Is socialism dead? Is capitalism the wave of the future? . . .

Ironic Proclamations

There is something rather ironic in proclamations of capitalist ideological victory coming at a time when the number of homeless on our streets has never been higher, when the U.S. economy has been bailed out once again by a massive increase in defense spending, and when Western Europe has experienced its 17th straight year of increasing unemployment. In the face of this rather abysmal showing, it has been necessary for the defenders of capitalism to try to rest their case not on the advanced capitalist nations, but on the so-called Newly Industrializing Countries— the NICs—Taiwan and South Korea. (Different writers include different countries among the NICs; many include Hong Kong and Singapore, but these are city-states, and their situations differ from those of other developing nations. But Taiwan and South Korea are on everybody's NIC roster.) Today South Korea not only produces VCRs better than the United States, but it serves as the model of capitalist development. The NICs, it is claimed, have not only achieved astonishing aggregate growth, their income distributions are among the most egalitarian in the developing world. . . .

Unique Experience

An examination of the NICs' experience makes it clear that their success will not be readily duplicated by other poor nations.

First of all, Taiwan and South Korea had rather unique colonial experiences. Typically, colonial powers groomed their colonies as sources of raw materials. Indeed, many nations actually experienced a decline in their level of industrialization while they were under colonial rule. At first Japan intended its colonies Korea and Taiwan to fulfil the same raw materials role. But this soon changed. As Alice Amsden, a leading authority on Taiwan's economy, has written: "In the 1930s, Japan reshaped its policy of transforming Taiwan into a source of food supply for the home market. The shift in policy can be understood only in the context of Japan's increasing militarism and expansionism in the Pacific. Belatedly and frantically, Japan sought to refashion Taiwan as an industrial adjunct to its own war preparations. . . . From a few industries with strong locational advantages before 1930 (e.g., sugar and cement), industry in Taiwan expanded in the 1930s to include the beginnings of chemical and metallurgical sectors, and as World War II cut off the flow of duty-free goods, some import substitution began." . . .

In Korea, the Japanese colonial authorities had issued a law designed to limit nonagricultural investment that might compete with Japanese industry. But the law was abolished in 1920. In the 1930s colonial policies shifted toward the creation of heavy industry and by 1939-1941, 29 percent of Korean output was manufactured goods (up from 7 percent in 1910-12). (A majority of the industry was in what became North Korea, but the south still had 35 percent of the heavy industry and 69 percent of the light industry and dominated in textiles, machine tools, and manufactured food.) By World War II, in the words of a specialist on the Korean economy, "manufacturing, transport, power, and the other elements of industrial infrastructure were unusually advanced for a poor country, especially one that was a colony." . . .

Land Reform

Because Japan dominated the economies of its two colonies, the confiscation of Japanese assets at the end of World War II had a significant leveling effect. Further leveling occurred as a result of land reforms—along with Japan's, the most extensive in the capitalist world. Land reform in any capitalist country runs into the entrenched power of the landlords. Unique circumstances, however, enabled both Taiwan and South Korea to carry out agrarian redistribution policies. . . .

A Bad Joke

There is no question the Third World has experienced a certain kind of 'progress' over the last three decades. Many more people now live in Third World cities—mostly in sprawling, unserviced shantytowns. There is a patina of modernization evident in capital cities from Bangkok to Bogota: high-rise buildings and fancy government offices are common. There are new airports, power dams, luxury hotels and even a few factories producing cars and electronic appliances that most Brazilians or Nigerians will never be able to afford. And of course the military is always after the latest weapons system. . . .

Inequality is built into this pattern of development and the notion that wealth will trickle down to those who need it most has become a bad joke.

Richard Swift, *New Internationalist,* May 1988.

The spread of education also had an equalizing effect in South Korea. This was not so much because of government policy (government spending on education has been quite low by international standards), but because of strong public pressures and the Korean people's willingness to finance the bulk of their educational expenses privately. By 1965, over 90 percent of primary school-age children were in school, up from two-thirds in 1953. Another factor contributing to equalization in Korea was the Korean War, which destroyed a large fraction of all physical assets.

Taiwan and South Korea thus began their periods of industrialization with considerably less inequality than most other Third World nations. . . .

Foreign Aid

Both Taiwan and South Korea, because of their particular Cold War role, were provided by the United States with extremely high levels of economic aid, among the highest in the world on a per capita basis. In the 1950s, nearly 40 percent of Taiwan's gross domestic capital formation was financed by foreign savings, almost all in the form of U.S. aid. One scholar estimated that without U.S. aid the annual growth rate of Taiwan's GNP [gross national product] would have been less than half of what it was in this period; another calculated that Taiwan would have suffered a net decline in per capita income.

In South Korea, foreign assistance—mostly U.S. aid—provided more than half the total resources available for capital accumulation in every year from 1955 to 1962; in 1960-62, foreign aid comprised 80 percent of total South Korean savings. Aid from all sources to South Korea from 1945 to 1983 exceeded $26 billion, and from the United States alone, Korea received more total aid per capita than any other country in the world except Israel and South Vietnam. . . .

Fueled by foreign assistance, Taiwan and South Korea were able to begin their process of industrialization at a very fortuitous time. The 1960s were years of worldwide economic boom and global markets were wide open. An industrialization strategy based on exports could succeed, provided there were not too many competitors pursuing the same strategy. But, as economists Robin Broad and John Cavanagh have argued in *Foreign Policy*, Fall 1988, the world of the 1970s and 1980s is a very different place. The international economic downturn has meant that export markets are no longer growing. (Not that world export markets were ever big enough for large Third World countries: as Stephen A. Marglin has noted, for India to duplicate the NIC achievement, Americans would have to change TVs as fast as they change shirts.) In any event, however, world export markets in coming years are never going to match the growth rates of the boom period of the past. . . .

It is interesting to note that those who applaud the NIC model and urge it on other countries, call only for following Taiwan and South Korea in terms of their commitment to capitalism, their ex-

IT SAYS HERE THAT THE G.N.P. HERE IN KENYA A FEW YEARS AGO...

IN PER CAPITA TERMS INDICATED $136 PER HEAD OF POPULATION...

BUT IN FACT THE WEALTHIEST 20% RECIEVED 68% OF THE TOTAL...

WHILE THE POOREST 40% OBTAINED ONLY 10% AND IT'S STILL LIKE THAT TODAY!

NOW I KNOW WHY THEY CALL IT THE GROSS NATIONAL PRODUCT...

PUNCHLINE
by ©CHRISTIAN

Christian Clark. Reprinted with permission.

port orientation, and their (alleged) openness to foreign corporations. (Some, it is true, also admire their authoritarian states.) But in fact, the NICs could be used to prove a rather different point: that a key to development is beginning with substantial equality and with thorough land reform.

Development itself, of course, is an ambiguous concept. For some it means aggregate economic growth, industrialization, and increasing per capita income. It can also be viewed, however, as the improvement in the lives of the population. These two notions are related, and in the case of Taiwan and South Korea, for example, development in both senses has occurred. But it is possible for nations with substantial GNP growth to show relatively meager improvement in the lives of their citizens, and, likewise, it is possible for nations with unimpressive aggregate growth rates to register sharp improvements in living conditions. . . .

An alternative to income-based statistics for measuring well-being is the Physical Quality of Life Index, PQLI, a composite index combining the infant mortality rate, life expectancy, and literacy. These three components are generally considered the most important indicators of physical well-being. Each of the components to some extent takes into account distributional effects, because if only the rich live long or are literate, the statistics will be low; to get a high score, a relatively large fraction of the population must be benefiting. (Per capita GNP, on the other hand, will be misleading if income is skewed.) The PQLI ranges from 0 to 100, with a score of 0 representing the worst performance of any society since 1950, and a 100 representing the best conceivable performance for any country in this century.

One study of the provision of basic human needs in Latin America found that richer countries tended to perform better than poorer ones, but not invariably so. In 1980 Cuba ranked in the middle of Latin American nations in terms of per capita income but led in PQLI. Moreover, the rate at which Cuba reduced the disparity between its 1960 PQLI and a perfect PQLI score of 100 was easily the highest in Latin America and among the highest in the world. (There are some who claim that Cuba's figures have been fudged, and the claim cannot be rejected out of hand given the lack of free information flow in Cuba; but a highly critical scholar has concluded that "current estimates of life expectancy and infant mortality are correct.")

One fascinating study of how government policies that emphasize redistribution over growth can enhance people's lives has been done by Richard W. Franke and Barbara H. Chasin in Kerala, one of India's states. . . .

India is an extremely poor country (1986 per capita GNP was $290), but Kerala is even poorer, with a per capita GNP of $182. Nevertheless, Kerala's adult literacy rate is 78 percent (compared to 43 percent for India as a whole), life expectancy is 66 years (compared to India's 57), and infant mortality is 33 deaths per 1,000 live births (compared to India's 86). The only low income countries in the world (defined by the World Bank as those with per capita income under $425 in 1986) with equally good figures for infant mortality or life expectancy are China, Sri Lanka, and Vietnam (life expectancy only), all nations with a substantial commitment to redistribution. . . .

Reform Programs

Kerala has had an extremely extensive land reform program and has enacted pensions for agricultural workers, unemployment insurance and welfare, school and nursery feeding programs, educa-

161

tional expansion, ration shops (where government subsidized food is provided), and affirmative action (for the former "untouchable" castes). The combination of these reforms has had a dramatic impact on inequality. In the village that Franke and Chasin studied, inequality declined by more than 16 percent from 1971 to 1987. In terms of quality of life, Kerala's PQLI went from 50 in 1961 to 70 in the early 1970s to 80 in the early 1980s—which put it dramatically higher than India (1981 PQLI=46), and above every other low income country except Sri Lanka. Countries with PQLIs comparable to that of Kerala typically had per capita incomes many times higher: e.g., Paraguay (per capita GNP 9 times that of Kerala) and Mexico (12 times). Moreover, Kerala's rate of improvement between the early 1960s and 1980s—given that the higher the PQLI the more difficult it is to attain each additional PQLI point—has been extremely impressive; more rapid than the rich countries, twice the average rate of middle income and poor countries, and more than three times the rate of India as a whole.

A True Measure of Development

The solution to the development puzzle cannot be measured by the usual economic indicators—Gross National Product, Balance of Payments, Balance of Trade or Foreign Exchange Reserves. While it may satisfy economists to gauge success in these terms, dry statistics don't say whether people have enough to eat or will live past the age of 50. They are a poor barometer of the pride and self-confidence so necessary for development to be effective. Development whose rewards are spread more evenly depends on the effective organization of those with a stake in more equal distribution—the poor, the landless and the marginalized.

Richard Swift, *New Internationalist*, May 1988.

Kerala's quality of life statistics are not simply higher than India's, but the benefits are distributed far more equally between urban and rural areas, between men and women, and between castes. For India, the female literacy rate is 50 percent that of males, the rural rate 50 percent that of the urban, and the rate for former "untouchables" 60 percent that of the other castes. For Kerala, on the other hand, the female rate is 88 percent that of males, the rural 90 percent that of urban, and the former "untouchables" 78 percent that of the other castes. For infant mortality rate, the rural figure for India is twice the urban figure; for Kerala it is only a third higher. For life expectancy most countries in the world have higher figures for females than males, perhaps reflecting biological differences. But for India, female life expectancy lags a year behind that of males, while for Kerala, females live four years longer than males.

Kerala is in fact the only Indian state in which there are more females than males. Traditional biases against females are strong in India and, especially where women's contribution to household income is lowest, female babies tend to receive less food and health care and stand greater risk of dying than do male babies. This phenomenon of "excess female mortality" is not just a thing of the past; the ratio of females to males has been decreasing in many Indian states since 1921. In Kerala, however, it has increased. In part this is a function of the greater female educational levels in Kerala, including the fact that women are more than half the college students. (Kerala was the first Indian state to have a woman cabinet minister.) In addition, however, Kerala has extensive social services: nursery and school feeding programs, ration shops, and readily accessible health care. Of 22 Indian states surveyed, Kerala ranked first in the percentage of its villages containing health dispensaries, health centers, hospitals, primary schools, secondary schools, higher education facilities, and ration shops. Kerala's policies have not just benefited the population in general, but especially those who are most often the victims of traditional development policies, namely women. . . .

Redistribution Helps

Kerala is a part of a larger nation and as such cannot serve as a model for most Third World countries. It does demonstrate, however, that even amid desperate poverty people's lives can be sharply improved by redistributionist policies. Export-oriented capitalist development strategies can work for some—they did for Taiwan and South Korea; but the external environment on which this strategy depends will not permit many others to follow in their path. A redistributionist approach, on the other hand, faces no such external limits, and there is no reason why everyone in the Third World could not have a better quality of life.

"Promoting smaller families throughout the Third World will benefit every segment of society."

Population Growth Defeats Development

Jodi L. Jacobson

Most of the countries with the fastest growing populations are in the Third World. The author of the following viewpoint, Jodi L. Jacobson, believes that the economic gains Third World countries make in providing food for their people are undermined by these burgeoning populations. Family planning programs, she writes, improve living standards, change attitudes about women's roles, and reduce damage to the environment. Jacobson is a senior researcher at the Worldwatch Institute, a Washington, DC organization that studies issues related to the environment.

As you read, consider the following questions:

1. How do family planning programs benefit women, according to Jacobson?
2. What policies to reduce population growth does the author suggest Third World governments adopt?
3. In the author's opinion, how would changes in women's roles help reduce population growth?

Thirty-three-year-old Socorro Cisneros de Rosales, a Central American mother of thirteen, is neither a demographer nor an economist. In describing her own plight and that of her country as "an overproduction of children and a lack of food and work," Mrs. Cisneros nevertheless speaks authoritatively on the conflict between high birthrates and declining economies that faces many in the Third World. Over the past two decades, steadily declining birthrates have contributed to significant improvements in the health and well-being of millions of people and to the growth of national economies. To date, however, only a handful of countries have reduced fertility rates sufficiently to make these gains universal or to ensure that their populations will stabilize in the foreseeable future. Countries that remain on a high fertility path will find that meeting basic subsistence needs will be increasingly difficult in the years to come.

Increasing Population

Despite lower fertility levels for the world as a whole, population increased by 86 million people in 1987, surpassing a total of 5 billion. Although birthrates continue to fall in many developing countries, the pace has slowed markedly. Declining death rates have balanced out the modest reductions in fertility of the past few years. Slower economic growth in developing countries plagued by debt, dwindling exports, and environmental degradation means that governments can no longer rely on socioeconomic gains to help reduce births. This uncertain economic outlook raises important questions. Can governments successfully encourage fertility reductions in the face of extensive poverty? What mix of policies is likely to promote smaller families, thereby reducing fertility and raising living standards?

Encouraging small families requires a two-pronged strategy of family planning and social change. Few countries have put family planning and reproductive health care at the top of their agendas. In most industrial nations, widely available contraceptive technologies enable couples to choose the number and spacing of their children. For the majority of women in many developing countries, contraceptive methods remain unavailable, inaccessible, or inappropriate. Surveys confirm that half the 463 million married women in developing countries outside of China do not want more children. Millions more would like to delay their next pregnancy. Meanwhile, the number of women who are in their childbearing years is increasing rapidly. With few exceptions, governments have not changed policies or invested in programs sufficiently to weaken the social conditions underlying high fertility rates. These conditions include, most significantly, the low status of women and the high illiteracy rates, low wages, and ill health that customarily accompany it. Until societal attitudes change, national fertility rates are unlikely to decline significantly. . . .

Reducing birthrates to speed the development process is a goal that deserves the immediate attention of the world community. Promoting smaller families throughout the Third World will benefit every segment of society. For women, bearing fewer children means better health for themselves and their offspring. For countries, reducing the average family size increases per capita investments and alleviates pressures on the natural resources underpinning national economies. For the world, slower population growth enhances the prospects for widespread security and prosperity. . . .

Each year, at least a half-million women worldwide die from pregnancy-related causes. Fully 99 percent of these deaths occur in the Third World, where complications arising from pregnancy and illegal abortions are the leading killers of women in their twenties and thirties. World Health Organization (WHO) officials caution that maternal deaths—those resulting directly or indirectly from pregnancy within forty-two days of childbirth, induced abortion, or miscarriage—may actually be twice the estimated figures. What is more, for every woman who dies, many more suffer serious, often long-term, health problems. That bearing life should bring death to so many women is a distressing irony. It is even more distressing given that family planning and preventive medicine could substantially reduce these losses. . . .

Family Planning Is Needed

Thanks to two decades of hard work and U.S. aid, almost half the women in developing countries now have access to family planning services. But about half still don't. The result is millions of unwanted pregnancies each year. Much more needs to be done.

Planned Parenthood, ad in *Ms.*, July/August 1987.

Illegal abortion is one of the major direct causes of maternal death. Rough estimates indicate that only half the estimated 54 million abortions performed annually around the world are legal. Most illegal abortions are carried out under unsanitary conditions by unskilled attendants, leaving women vulnerable to serious complications and infection. By contrast, modern abortion procedures, carried out under proper medical supervision in countries where they are legal, cause fewer maternal deaths than pregnancy or oral contraceptives do. . . .

Pregnancy itself takes a greater toll on a woman's body in regions where malnutrition and poor health are the norm. In the Third World, pregnancy is associated with a higher incidence of health-threatening infection, vitamin and mineral deficiencies, and anemia. Due to reduced immunity, common diseases such as pneumonia and influenza cause 50 to 100 percent more deaths in pregnant than in nonpregnant women. Three groups of women face the highest risk of pregnancy-related deaths: those at either end of their reproductive cycle, those who bear children in rapid succession, and those who have more than four children. Because of biological factors, women under nineteen or over thirty-five are more susceptible to complications of pregnancy. Women giving birth to children spaced less than a year apart are twice as likely to die from pregnancy-related causes than those who have children two or more years apart. In Matlab Thana, Bangladesh, health workers recorded three times as many deaths among women giving birth to their eighth child as among those giving birth to their third.

Preventing Maternal Death

At least half of all maternal deaths can be averted through a combined strategy of family planning, legal abortion, and primary health care. According to researchers Beverly Winikoff and Maureen Sullivan of the Population Council, in *Studies in Family Planning* in 1987, a fertility rate reduction of 25 to 35 percent resulting from more widely available family planning would also lower maternal mortality by one-fourth. Making abortions legal and safe could reduce the toll an additional 20 to 25 percent. Making all pregnancies safer through increased investments in prenatal health care and reducing the number of high-risk pregnancies would prevent another 20 to 25 percent of deaths. Winikoff and Sullivan point out that while, theoretically, this three-pronged strategy could reduce maternal mortality by three-fourths, a 50 percent decrease is more a realistic expectation, given prevailing social and political conditions, such as large desired family size and the opposition to legalizing abortion.

Establishing integrated family planning and health strategies will be well worth the investment. Village-based paramedics and mid-wives can teach women the benefits of birth spacing, breast-feeding, prenatal care, and contraceptive use. Small-scale maternity centers—on the order of one for every 4,000 people— could promote simple solutions to some of the most pervasive maternal health problems, by providing, for instance, iron supplements to treat anemia. Linked with regional facilities run by doctors, such clinics would constitute a pivotal link between rural populations and the often urban-based medical community. Assuming that maternal deaths run as high as 1 million per year, family planning and health care would save at least 500,000 women's lives annually and improve the health of millions more.

Ironically, new reproductive health threats may push family planning services to the top of national agendas. . . . WHO estimates that between 5 million and 10 million people around

167

the world may now be infected with the virus that can lead to AIDS, and that at least 2 million of them are in Africa. Approximately 4,000 cases have been found in Latin America and the Caribbean thus far. Current health care problems may only foreshadow far more serious public health burdens. . . .

Scientists currently believe that between 25 and 50 percent of those infected with the virus that can lead to AIDS will die in the next ten years. In developing countries, this disease will primarily afflict individuals aged twenty to forty-nine. Both pregnancy- and AIDS-related deaths thus strike at people in their prime, taking a tremendous toll on human life and productive capacity. The need for public education about reproductive health is stronger than ever. . . .

Reducing the Burden

Family planning is a highly cost-effective way of helping development in third-world countries. . . . By limiting the number of births, it reduces the burden to government of providing new schools, hospitals, and other facilities needed for raising children. Parents can better feed, clothe, and otherwise care for their fewer children.

David R. Francis, *The Christian Science Monitor*, March 23, 1989.

Without fertility declines, many governments cannot hope to make the investments necessary to improve human welfare and encourage economic development. A number of political and social obstacles remain for countries wishing to reduce fertility, improve health, and raise living standards. Attainment of these goals will depend on fundamental changes in several areas, including the way governments shape population policies, the degree to which they make contraceptive supplies and information accessible, and the steps they take to improve the status of women and increase their access to education.

Governments can use a mix of policies to hasten the transition to lower fertility. Population-related policies, such as laws governing minimum age at marriage, delivery of family planning services, and the importation or manufacture of contraceptive methods, directly affect the determinants of fertility. Official sanction of family planning efforts in the form of revised policies and legal codes is likely to increase acceptance of these services and help dispel widespread myths and misconceptions about contraception. Public policies concerning development indirectly affect fertility by influencing economic opportunities, social services, literacy, mortality, and the status of women. . . .

Countries that do not start now to reduce fertility may face stark choices later. The conflicts between individual desires and societal goals that result from excessive population growth are evident in China's one-child family program, perhaps the best known and most controversial of all fertility reduction campaigns. In 1953, the first census taken in China revealed a rapidly growing population of about 582 million. Mao Zedong, Communist party chairman at that time, did not see China's expanding millions as a problem. Fewer than thirty years later the Chinese numbered 1 billion, more than 20 percent of the world's population living on 7 percent of the world's arable land. By the late seventies, years of famine, poverty, and political upheaval had convinced the leaders in Beijing of the need for a rigorous family planning campaign.

Today's one-child family program evolved out of a series of strategies that began in the early seventies with the Wan Xi Shao (later, longer, fewer) program. This strategy encouraged delayed marriage, longer birth intervals, and smaller families. Even so, China's population continued to grow rapidly. As a result, policymakers enacted the one-child family policy in the hope of holding the population to about 1.2 billion just after the turn of the century. The policy, intended to last through the year 2000, offers a series of incentives and disincentives. Substantial pay increases, better housing, longer maternity leaves, and priority access to education are among the benefits offered to one-child families, while heavy fines and social criticism await couples who bear more than one. China's original policy, often seen as monolithic in its application, actually allows certain segments of the population to have more than one child. Urban couples are generally expected to adhere to the policy. Ethnic minorities and rural couples—80 percent of the nation's population—are allowed two or more.

Community Programs

Several other countries have turned to incentives in their attempts to influence fertility trends. Most of these programs have targeted individuals or couples, such as the programs in India and Bangladesh offering financial incentives for sterilization. Several have experienced uneven success and in some cases have incited charges of coercion. On the other hand, experimental incentive programs aimed at overall community participation and development have shown some promise. A pilot program in northeastern Thailand tested the effects of community-level incentives on contraceptive prevalence. Loan funds of $2,000 each were set up in several villages in conjunction with a family planning and health program. Initially, loans to individuals were based on character, credit-worthiness, and the project to be carried out. After the program became established, preference was given to applicants who were practicing family planning. Members of the loan fund

169

received shares and dividends on the basis of the contraceptive method used; more effective methods had higher values. As the prevalence of contraceptive use increased within a village, so did the total amount of the loan fund. . . .

'We can't seem to keep our heads above water' . . .

© Liederman/Rothco Cartoons

Women hold a paradoxical place in many societies. As mothers and wives, they often bear sole responsibility for childrearing and domestic duties. In many cultures, they are bound by custom and necessity to contribute to household income; in some, they are the only breadwinners. Despite these roles as the linchpins of society, women in some societies have few rights under the law regarding land tenure, marital relations, income, or social security.

Attitudes toward familial relationships dim the prospects of reducing fertility rates in some African societies until the status of women improves. For example, payments made by a groom's family in expectation of high fertility may increase the wealth of a bride's family. Odile Frank and Geoffrey McNicoll, in a Population Council study on population policy in Kenya, note that because men bear little financial or domestic responsibility for basic subsistence, the costs of large numbers of children are invisible to them. As a result, they write, "even an emerging land shortage is not necessarily felt by men as a reason to limit fertility." Policies aimed at capping and regulating bridewealth payments as well as those recognizing and enforcing a woman's right to lay claim to land may serve to at least partially counteract the social forces that underlie high fertility in this case. . . .

The international community, particularly the United States, has traditionally played a significant role in international family planning, giving political as well as financial support to reducing fertility and charting demographic trends. Donor countries have been spending about $500 million per year in this area. Recently, the United States—the largest contributor in terms of absolute dollars—has scaled back its commitment to international population assistance. United States funding fell 20 percent between 1985 and 1987, from $288 million to $230 million. . . .

Instead of cutting back on international family planning assistance, the United States and other industrial countries need to increase their contributions. Dr. Joseph Speidel of the Population Crisis Committee of Washington, D.C., estimates that in order to achieve population stabilization by the end of the next century, global expenditures must rise to $7 billion annually over the next decade. Industrial countries could contribute at least $2 billion of this total. . . .

Developing countries themselves need to make a greater commitment to family planning. At the moment, the Third World spends more than four times as much on weaponry and upkeep of military forces as it does on health care—$150 billion in 1986, compared with $38 billion. Increased government funding of family planning and primary health care programs is essential as part of the effort to speed fertility rate declines. Contraceptive supplies, education materials, prenatal health care, and information on family health are desperately needed in rural areas throughout the developing world. New approaches to contraceptive marketing and distribution, such as those that rely on local residents and shopkeepers to disseminate information and supplies, are now being tried in a number of countries, and they should be considered in others. . . .

Designing Effective Programs

Three decades of experience in international family planning hold important lessons for designing effective programs and for creating a social environment receptive to smaller families. Countries such as China, India, Mexico, and Thailand can serve as models for different approaches. Sub-Saharan African countries may find that regionwide cooperation on family planning, in the form of training and outreach programs through perhaps a new consortium on population growth, will strengthen the efforts of individual countries.

"In the Third World itself, population growth has often gone hand-in-hand with rapid material advance."

Population Growth Does Not Defeat Development

P.T. Bauer

P.T. Bauer is professor emeritus at the London School of Economics and a fellow at Cairns College at Cambridge University. A well-known author on the Third World, his books have included *Reality and Rhetoric: Studies in the Economics of Development* and *Equality, the Third World, and Economic Delusion.* In the following viewpoint, Bauer argues that historically, many countries became affluent as their populations increased. Thus, Bauer concludes, population growth is not harmful and Western efforts to promote family planning will not help the Third World.

As you read, consider the following questions:

1. What examples does Bauer cite to support his argument that land shortages do not hinder economic prosperity?
2. Why does Bauer believe Third World people are reluctant to use Western birth control?
3. What policies would improve Third World economies, according to the author?

P.T. Bauer, "Population Scares." Reprinted from *Commentary*, November 1987, by permission; all rights reserved.

Since the 1960's, population pressure and growth have been widely regarded as prime causes of Third World poverty and prime obstacles to economic development. For instance, Robert S. McNamara wrote in 1973: "To put it simply: the greatest single obstacle to the economic and social advancement of the majority of peoples in the underdeveloped world is rampant population growth . . . the threat of unmanageable population pressures is very much like the threat of nuclear war . . . Both threats can and will have catastrophic consequences unless they are dealt with rapidly and rationally." More recently, McNamara's successor as president of the World Bank, Barber B. Conable, has argued along similar lines, though in less colorful words, in an address to the World Resources Institute of Washington. . . .

Ideas like McNamara's, and the policies they produce, rest on the following explicit or clearly implicit assumptions: economic performance and progress depend critically on certain quantifiable resources per head, primarily land, but also capital; income per head is a sound measure of economic well-being and can serve as its proxy; population trends can be forecast reliably for decades ahead; and Third World people do not know about birth control, they procreate heedless of consequences, and the West must persuade or even force them to change their reproductive habits.

These ideas all go counter to simple evidence and to widely accepted moral principles.

Population Growth and Economic Progress

Rapid population growth has not prevented economic progress either in the West or in the contemporary Third World. The population of the Western world has more than quadrupled since the middle of the 18th century. Over the same period, real income per head is estimated to have increased fivefold at least. Much of this increase took place when population was growing as fast as in most of the contemporary Third World, or even faster.

In fact, in the Third World itself, population growth has often gone hand-in-hand with rapid material advance. In the 1890's Malaya was a sparsely-populated area of hamlets and fishing villages. By the 1930's, it had become a country with large cities and extensive plantations and mining operations. During these four decades the population rose through immigration and natural increase from about one-and-a-half million to about six million. This greatly enlarged population enjoyed much higher material standards and lived longer than the small numbers of the 1890's.

Since World War II, other Third World countries have also combined rapid population increase with rapid, even spectacular, economic growth for decades on end. These include Taiwan, Hong Kong, Kenya, the Ivory Coast, Mexico, Colombia, and Brazil. Conversely, over much of the Third World what obstructs economic advance is sparseness of population, which presents obstacles more effective than those supposedly created by population pressure. Thus, sparseness of population circumscribes the scope for enterprise by precluding the construction of transport facilities and communications and by retarding the spread of markets and of new ideas and methods.

Disputed Thesis

Promoters of government birth control have claimed a need to combat "overpopulation" with its alleged results in poverty and revolution. This thesis was disputed from the beginning by acknowledged economic development experts such as Lord Peter Bauer of the London School of Economics and Colin Clark of the Oxford University Agricultural Economic Institute.

Jacqueline R. Kasun, *Society*, July/August 1988.

In current public discourse more specific adverse effects of population growth are often also alleged: prospective shortage of food; exhaustion of minerals; and emergence of large-scale unemployment. These apprehensions are unfounded. They rest on invalid notions such as that methods of production and patterns of consumption do not respond to changes in resource availabilities; that labor and capital cannot be substituted for land in production or consumption; that there will be no technical progress; and that people procreate regardless of circumstances and do not adjust their reproductive habits to changing conditions.

Shortage of Land?

Nor is shortage of land and of investable resources a critical obstacle to economic achievement and progress. In particular, sustained prosperity (as distinct from occasional windfalls) owes little or nothing to natural resources. Examples in the past include Holland, much of it drained from the sea, and Venice, a wealthy world power built on a few mud flats. In our own time, there are West Germany, Switzerland, Japan, Singapore, Hong Kong, and Taiwan, to name only the most obvious instances of countries that have achieved prosperity without much in the way of land or natural resources.

On the other hand, amid abundant land and vast natural resources, the Indians of the Americas before Columbus remained wretchedly poor, without domestic animals and without even the wheel, when much of Europe, with far less land, was already rich. To this day many millions of extremely poor people have much cultivable land. Indeed they often live in areas where land is a free good. Shortage of land, actually or potentially cultivable, does not explain the extreme backwardness of the Indian populations of Central and South America, or of the Pygmies and Aborigines in Asia and Africa.

Furthermore, contrary to popular belief, the much-publicized famines in the Third World have nothing to do with shortage of land. Such famines do not occur in the densely-populated areas of the Far East and elsewhere, but in the sparsely-populated regions of Africa, especially Ethopia, Uganda, and the Sahel. In these areas the hazards of subsistence agriculture are exacerbated by such policies and circumstances as suppression of private trade, with consequent absence of reserve stocks and trading links; persecution, even expulsion, of productive groups, especially ethnic minorities; large-scale confiscation of property; forcible collectivization; restrictions on the inflow of capital and on the import of farming implements and of consumer goods; civil conflict and absence of public security. In some instances, maintenance of wasteful tribal systems of land tenure has also inhibited productive agriculture. . . .

Children's Contributions

In discussions concerning the need for population control, per-capita income is frequently invoked as an index of economic welfare, even of well-being as such. This practice issues in anomalies. The birth of a child immediately reduces income per head within the family, and also in the country as a whole. But do the parents feel worse off? Would they be happier if they could have no children, or if some of their children died?

The relatively large proportion of children in Third World countries is often described and decried as the burden of dependency. This terminology implies that children are merely a cost. But children give satisfaction; they are outlets for affection; and they enable people to project themselves into the future. In addition to yielding such psychic income, children often also contribute significantly to actual family income, serve as support for old age, and sometimes bring prestige and influence. In all these contexts, the benefits to the parents outweigh the costs; and the benefit from one highly successful child exceeds the cost of the others.

These considerations shed light on the difficulty Western agencies have experienced in getting people throughout the Third World to use modern birth-control devices.

For many decades now, cheap Western-style consumer goods such as hardware, cosmetics, soft drinks, watches, and cameras have been conspicuous trade goods in Southeast Asia, South Asia, the Middle East, West Africa, and Latin America. Soon after becoming available in the West, the transistor radio was ubiquitous in South Asia and the Middle East, Latin America, and in African cities. By contrast, condoms, intrauterine devices, and the pill have so far spread only slowly in much of the Third World, even when heavily subsidized. Indeed, these contraceptives are often absent where sophisticated articles of feminine hygiene are on sale. They are largely or even wholly absent in Third World areas where mortality has declined, which suggests that the reason large families are wanted there is not merely in order to replace children who die young.

It is a reasonable conclusion that the demand for cheap Western contraceptives is limited not because people in the Third World are ignorant of them but rather because they do not want to restrict their families, or prefer other, more traditional ways of doing so.

A Lack of Respect

It is very alarming to see governments in many countries launching *systematic campaigns* against birth, contrary not only to the cultural and religious identity of the countries themselves but also contrary to the nature of true development. It often happens that these campaigns are the result of pressure and financing coming from abroad, and in some cases they are made a condition for the granting of financial and economic aid and assistance. In any event, there is an *absolute lack of respect* for the freedom of choice of the parties involved, men and women often subjected to intolerable pressures, including economic ones, in order to force them to submit to this new form of oppression. It is the poorest populations which suffer such mistreatment.

Pope John Paul II, encyclical *On Social Concern*, December 30, 1987.

In short, in the Third World (as in the West) the children who are born are generally desired. To deny this amounts to saying that Third World parents procreate no matter what. This view treats people with unwarranted condescension or contempt, which in turn soon becomes a justification for coercion. . . .

From Malthus to McNamara, ambitious forecasts of long-term population trends have been an integral part of recurrent population scares. They are prominent in the current insistence on Third World population control. Yet for many reasons only the roughest forecasts of long-term population trends in the Third World are warranted.

Over the decades, major political, cultural, and economic changes will occur in much of the Third World. Both the changes and their demographic impact are unpredictable. This applies even to mortality trends, and much more so to fertility trends. People do respond in their reproductive habits to changed conditions. But they often do so in unexpected ways, which compounds the uncertainties of the changes themselves. This applies particularly in the context of such a huge and deeply diverse aggregate as the Third World.

Thus, in recent decades in some Third World countries,

economic improvement has resulted not in lower but in higher fertility. Or again, in some of these countries urban and rural fertility rates are about the same, while in others there are wide differences. The relationship of fertility to social class and occupation is also much more varied in the Third World than in the West.

Women's Attitudes

There is, however, one relationship of considerable generality which has been emphasized by John C. Caldwell. This is that systematic restriction of family size in the Third World is practiced primarily by women who have adopted Western attitudes toward childbearing and childrearing, as a result of exposure to Western education, media, and contacts. Their attitude to fertility control does not depend on income, status, or urbanization, but on modernization—that is, Westernization.

Caldwell's conclusion is more plausible and solidly-based than the widely-held view that higher incomes lead to reduced fertility. It is true that in the West, and in the Westernized parts of the Third World, higher incomes and lower fertility are often, though by no means always, associated. But it is not the case that higher incomes as such lead to smaller families. Both the higher incomes and the smaller families reflect greater ambition for material welfare for oneself and one's family. Both, in other words, reflect a change in motivation. By contrast, when parental incomes are increased as a result of subsidies or windfalls, without a change in attitudes, the parents are likely to have more children, not fewer. This last point is pertinent to the proposals of many Western observers who contradictorily urge both population control and also more aid to the poor with large families. . . .

Promoting Economic Growth

The economic achievement of the peoples of the Third World will not depend on their numbers. It will depend on personal, cultural, and political factors—that is, on their attitudes and mores.

Anyone wishing to influence those attitudes and mores in a direction favorable to economic development and general well-being can best do so by extending the range of external commercial contacts available to ordinary people in the Third World, especially contacts with the West. In the past such contacts have been powerful agents of voluntary changes in attitudes and mores, especially those bearing on economic advance. There is no reason to doubt that similar contacts can have the same effect in the future—and without the damaging and morally objectionable political and economic effects of official pressure on people in their most private and vital concerns.

"AT [Appropriate Technology] offers the promise of bringing better lives and stronger social bonds to some of the world's poor."

Appropriate Technology Can Help the Third World Develop

George Ovitt Jr.

By the late 1960s, many development experts became disillusioned about the effectiveness of exporting technology to the Third World. In several countries, Western machines were sitting idle because they were too costly to maintain and did not fit the needs of Third World people. In response to this problem, many experts began advocating appropriate technology: machines that consumed little energy, were easy to operate and repair, and used the resources of the local area. George Ovitt Jr. describes the benefits of appropriate technology in the following viewpoint. Ovitt teaches at Drexel University in Philadelphia.

As you read, consider the following questions:

1. What institutions does appropriate technology challenge, according to the author?
2. How has technology from multinational corporations failed the Third World, according to the author?
3. What does the author believe are the limitations of appropriate technology?

On a sprawling hacienda just outside the southern Nicaraguan coastal town of San Juan del Sur, a lanky North American engineer and machinist named David Parkhurst has established a workshop for repairing windmills. In the 1930s, about 5,000 U.S.-made Chicago Motor Company windmills were constructed on Nicaragua's Pacific coast to pump water for livestock. Today, more than half of these windmills are broken, victims of time and the U.S. economic boycott. For David Parkhurst, windmill repair represents an important contribution to Nicaragua's agrarian economy: access to potable water is a problem for the rural population, especially since heavy utilization of pesticides by U.S. agroexport firms prior to 1979 polluted much of the available groundwater.

A Lack of Spare Parts

The windmills are in place; the problem is fixing them without the necessary spare parts. For example, one common problem is that the windmill towers have been bent out of alignment by the cattle that are tied to their pliable bases. Repair is difficult because of an acute shortage of timber for bracing, steel for restructuring, and welding equipment (and technicians) for replacements. Particles of grit trapped in the windmills' gears wear out ball bearings that are likewise impossible to find. Thus, thousands of windmills stand idle, a potentially rich technological resource in a developing nation that is struggling for economic autonomy.

While David Parkhurst seeks innovative solutions to these technical problems, other engineers and technicians work on solutions to problems faced not only by Nicaragua but by developing nations around the world. Simple solar cookers built from cardboard and aluminum foil, as well as the wonderfully efficient Lorena stove (a simple mud cookstove designed by appropriate technology in Guatemala), fulfill a vital function in a country that was long ago deforested by multinational timber companies. Biomass collection and conversion to methane offers another potential source of cheap energy while small-scale hydroelectric generators, such as the one Ben Linder was constructing in San José de Bocay, also offer the hope of cheap energy to isolated rural communities that have never had electricity.

Appropriate technology (AT) is a form of engineering rich in political possibilities. The ideas that lie behind AT—democratic empowerment, grassroots decisionmaking, economic self-sufficiency—represent a direct challenge to manipulation by transnational corporations or repressive governments. The reliance on locally produced raw materials, on preexisting resources, on local needs and local abilities, all undercut "technology transfer" with its built-in bias toward continued dependency on spare parts, foreign expertise, and expensive energy inputs. As is the case in

Nicaragua, AT can help to consolidate a government's revolutionary goal of breaking the cycle of dependency on Western capital that enthralls most other Latin American nations. Thus, when Nicaraguan *campesinos* working on a cooperative north of Esteli abandoned their broken tractor and shifted back to using oxen to pull their plows and harrows, they were moving toward a more "primitive" technology, but one which is surprisingly efficient, durable, and, best of all, independent of any need for externally-produced fuel or spare parts.

Western Assumptions

Most Western policymakers assume that technological progress holds the key to development for the world's poor. "Development" for these experts includes the importation of capital and experts, the adoption of measures to control labor and labor unions, and lower import duties. The perpetuation of dependency inherent in technology transfer allows bankers, engineers, and businesspeople—the modern conquistadors—to ensure continued control of developing nations while at the same time presenting themselves as altruists. Their assistance is usually channeled through elite institutions in the underdeveloped countries, thereby creating a development bureaucracy that is narrowly controlled, urban-based, and dependent.

Local Knowledge

Technology often is not really "appropriate" unless it has been developed in the country where it is to be used. Where Africa is concerned, technological progress has always been directed by the nations of the North. They have preferred to ignore local knowledge and technologies in order to impose a system under which their own, modern skills are "adapted" to traditional needs.

Hélène Agbessi dos Santos, *AfricAsia*, October 1986.

This "technology from above" has little to offer the masses of men and women whose daily lives are a struggle for potable water, nourishing food, and sufficient fuel. Multinational corporations and U.S. banks fund massive irrigation projects for agro-export firms, not water systems for remote villages. The promise of AT is that it can help provide the necessities of life to those living in rural communities and on the margins of urban centers. AT has the potential to transform "development" into a process that respects local needs, resources, and culture. While AT cannot bring wealth to the world's poor, it can bring the essential structure upon which a decent life is built: food, shelter, clean water, and energy. . . .

180

The principles underlying AT are clear. The foundations of AT (or, as it is called in England, "intermediate technology") were prepared at a meeting held in Oxford, England in 1968. The idea of a humane and nonalienating community-based technology was advanced at this meeting, and then expressed in broadly accessible form in E.F. Schumacher's *Small is Beautiful: Economics as if People Mattered.* Schumacher's book provides the theoretical underpinnings for the AT movement in that it examines the attitudes and assumptions underlying growth-orientated, large-scale economics. Schumacher argues for a "Buddhist economics," an economics that places human needs and well-being above commodity production: "[The modern economist] is used to measuring the 'standard of living' by the amount of annual consumption, assuming all the time that a man [sic] who consumes more is 'better off' than a man who consumes less. A Buddhist economist would consider this approach excessively irrational: since consumption is merely a means to human well-being, the aim should be to obtain the maximum of well-being with the minimum of consumption."

Schumacher also argues for a "technology with a human face," that is, a technology that does not deprive workers of useful and creative labor. He also argues against the technology of mass production because such technology is "inherently violent, ecologically damaging, self-defeating in terms of non-renewable resources, and stultifying for the human person." Schumacher proposes intermediate technology—intermediate between "primitive" and "super technology"—in support of "production by the masses." By keeping in mind the existence of the "self-limiting principle," that is, by recognizing the need to find simple, inexpensive, and appropriate solutions to local problems, the humane engineer can offer meaningful assistance to those in greatest need. Under AT, the expert becomes a comrade, a person who lives and works with those who are sharing his or her expertise; democratic sharing of skills replaces top-down advising. Instead of being seen and treated as tenders of machines, recipients of aid, or victims of underdevelopment—all passive, helpless roles that correspond to the self-image of the Western "expert"—the people who are engaged in AT projects are active partners in development as workers, critics, or trainees. . . .

The Politics of Appropriate Technology

By itself, appropriate technology cannot solve the problems of underdevelopment, nor does it pretend to be able to do so. AT makes one little thing right, and then it moves on to the next little thing. While the purveyors of big technology—manufacturing plants that arrive complete with machinery, Western managers, pro-management unions, energy, and capital—tend to make claims

that link their form of development with democracy, free enterprise, and progress, those who push AT speak in rather quieter
tones about local self-sufficiency, community action, and the conservation of resources. This is only proper. AT does nothing to
bridge the gap between the wealthy elites and the poor masses:
it does not redistribute land, diminish racism, or dismantle the
occupying armies that many underdeveloped nations deploy
against their own populations. AT redirects some material
resources from the industrialized nations to poorer people, but
this transfer does nothing to ease the burden of debt that lays so
heavily on the backs of the world's poor. The political thrust of
AT is subtle, and many of its practitioners are more interested in
the enticements of interesting engineering than in the political implications of what they do.

The South's Role

It is quite apparent to all of us in the South that the North has no
wish to transfer technology freely. If we obtain it at all it is at very
high cost and often third-rate and not appropriate to our needs. As
a solution to this problem, the South should . . . [establish] on a
regional basis a requisite framework under which research and
development into appropriate technology may be carried out or
strengthened.

Robert G. Mugabe, speech at the South-South Conference in Harare, Zimbabwe,
November 11, 1985.

A realistic assessment of the political value of appropriate
technology must take these facts into account. Yet for those of us
who remain committed to an essential change in the world's
balance of power, AT offers the promise of bringing better lives
and stronger social bonds to some of the world's poor. Insofar as
a proper revolutionary goal is to strengthen the poor and to weaken
the rich, appropriate technology must be considered a constructive tool in the long-term struggle.

"U.S. multinationals have been the key agents for technology transfer . . . in many developing countries."

Corporate Technology Can Help the Third World Develop

Alan Woods

The Agency for International Development is the major distributor of US foreign aid programs. In 1989 AID issued a report advocating free-market policies for Third World economies. The following viewpoint is an excerpt from that report. Alan Woods, the administrator of AID, argues that corporate investment in Third World economies has been beneficial. He contends that corporations have brought technology to the Third World, encouraged and trained local people to use the technology, and created jobs.

As you read, consider the following questions:

1. Why does Woods believe that corporate investment in such raw materials industries as mining and petroleum has been beneficial?
2. Why do US companies invest in the Third World, according to Woods?
3. What policies does Woods suggest Third World countries adopt to promote foreign investment?

Alan Woods, *Development and the National Interest: US Economic Assistance into the 21st Century.* Report from the Agency for International Development, February 17, 1989.

Multinational corporations such as Ford, Citibank, IBM, AT&T, Merck Pharmaceutical, and Caltex Petroleum have made an enormous contribution to development in many LDCs [Less Developed Countries]. Altruism has played little role in the globalization of particular businesses. Expansion overseas, as at home, has been motivated by profits and, increasingly, by competitive necessity: Failure to invest abroad would mean losing domestic U.S. markets. Overseas expansion triggered by the profit motive has, however, generated many businesses which are now much more important to many developing countries than U.S. Government foreign aid flows. The following are but a few examples of private business contributions to development.

• The flow of direct foreign investment to developing countries, which excludes commercial bank credit, is now larger than bilateral U.S. economic assistance ($9.4 billion in 1987). The outstanding stock of direct foreign investment is almost $84 billion and is evenly divided between extractive sectors such as mining or oil and manufacturing and services.

• For decades, U.S. firms operating in developing countries have provided extensive training of host country nationals. Over the past 40 years just one services and construction firm has provided 15,000 person-years of management and industrial training.

• American multinationals bring 40,000 citizens from developing countries to the U.S. for training each year.

Creating Jobs

• Subsidiaries of U.S. businesses have created over two million jobs in developing countries in the last decade. In 1986, they produced $15 billion worth of manufactured exports. Viewed the other way around, about 20 percent of all manufactured goods imported from developing countries by the U.S. comes from the subsidiaries of American businesses operating abroad.

• U.S. multinationals have accounted for an increasing share of developing country manufactured exports. In 1960, about four percent were built by local subsidiaries of U.S. firms. By 1986, fully ten percent of the very much larger total industrial export volume had been produced at American-owned plants.

• U.S. multinationals have been the key agents for technology transfer in the manufacturing, communications, and transportation sectors in many developing countries. For example, the automobile business, now the largest industrial sector in Latin America, was built around U.S. technology, largely by the subsidiaries of U.S. firms. More generally, over 40 percent of the patents registered in all developing countries were owned by U.S. multinationals.

• U.S.-pioneered financial services and capital markets have been critical to the dramatic growth in developing country trade flows.

Despite growing competition in services, particularly from Japanese banks, virtually all developing country trade remains denominated in U.S. dollars. Most short-term trade finance, including that for transactions unrelated to the U.S., remains tied to U.S. capital markets and banking regulations.

U.S. commercial ties to developing countries vary considerably, country by country and region by region. In Africa, U.S. Government flows are larger than trade, credit, or direct foreign investment flows. In East Asia, trade now dwarfs U.S. Government development assistance or Ex-Im [export-import] activity, although direct foreign investment remains modest compared to Latin America.

Multinationals can prove to be a mixed blessing for LDCs if monopolistic, or protectionist policies are pursued. But their collective impact is positive and provides an economic base for grass roots development that, over the long-run, can lead to more prosperous, evolved economies in the host countries.

Extractive Industries

U.S. multinationals' investments in extractive industries such as mining or petroleum were their first major commitments to developing countries. Despite a conventional view that populations derive few benefits from their presence, the economic and social experience throughout the world suggests otherwise.

Developing the Private Sector

A multinational can not only create new industries, but can also help form a basic domestic private sector that is missing in many developing countries. The development of a local private sector which allocates resources efficiently, as opposed to state run industry rife with bureaucratic impediments, can make the difference between countries that grow over the long-term and those that stagnate.

Alan Woods, *Development and the National Interest*, February 17, 1989.

The biggest development success story in the Arab world was largely managed by an extractive company, the Arabian American Oil Company (ARAMCO). Although something of a special case because of the vast profits involved and the special U.S.-Saudi relationship, the accomplishment nevertheless remains an impressive one. Since 1938, ARAMCO has been responsible for nearly $50 billion worth of non-oil development in Saudi Arabia. ARAMCO's original development effort came to provide better living conditions for its employees. But the positive spin-off of benefits to the host population was almost as immediate. The

185

primitive environment in the Eastern Province of Saudi Arabia ensured that ARAMCO's efforts would go well beyond the precincts of the oil workers and their families. There were no paved roads, no port facilities to handle anything much bigger than a dhow, no renewable water supplies, no electricity, no medical facilities, and no one with either the capability or the means of repairing anything in any area of modern technology.

Along with the accoutrements of the oil industry, ARAMCO built up every aspect of the Eastern Province's infrastructure and tied its development there into parallel efforts both in Riyadh and in the Hejaz adjacent to the Red Sea.

Professional Management

The positive impact of U.S. business investment in developing countries has gone far beyond the immediate jobs, earnings, and products generated. U.S. management practices, particularly organizational expertise, have had a marked impact on local businesses in host countries. Introduction of American management skills has shaped the way many developing countries do business. The American practice of creating line managers responsible for discrete business areas such as marketing and finance has broken down the restrictive traditional pattern of consensual family ownership and decision making and introduced more professional, competitive business leadership. In many developing nations, the oligarchy has begun to give way to the publicly held and professionally managed enterprise.

Financial Practice

The spin-off benefits of the transfer of management and managerial skills may be even greater when local personnel who are trained for managerial, financial, and technical posts in multinational firms or banking institutions later leave and help stimulate indigenous enterprises.

Spin-offs in business practices can be as important as personnel spin-offs. In *Citibank, 1812-1970*, Harold van B. Cleveland and Thomas F. Huertas describe how this phenomenon worked to the ultimate benefit of developing economies in Latin America and Asia:

> Traditionally, the bank has confined its local business lending to self-liquidating loans to prime names. In the 1960s, the bank began making term loans and soliciting customers whose credit standing was less than prime. To do so without heavy losses, the bank introduced into its Latin American and Far Eastern operations techniques of credit analysis and account management that had worked successfully in the Specialized Industries Group in the United States. Frequently, they required the customer to adapt his own accounting and management to the requirements of modern banking, U.S. style.

Why have U.S. manufacturing firms invested in developing countries? Henry Ford II declared in the spring of 1961:

> Whether we like it or not, Africa, Asia, and Latin America are going all-out into the industrial age. . . . It does no good to tell them this is all very unsound, that they ought not to try to do so much so fast, that they should relax and buy from us a lot cheaper than they can make it. They just won't go along; they are deeply committed to fast industrialization.
>
> If we want to share in those markets, rich and vast as they will some day surely be . . . we are going to have to go in with our capital and tools and know-how and help them get the things they want.

EXPORTS TO THE THIRD WORLD

© Holland/Rothco Cartoons

Henry Ford's observation was put into practice by his company in Brazil. Government pressure and tariffs on imported automobiles led Ford to set up Brazil's first factory in the 1950s. Initially oriented towards assembling imported parts, Ford's Brazilian factories soon became sites of more and more value-added work. By the mid-1980s, Ford was producing 90 percent of the inputs needed for a working car within Brazil. Its factories were also big exporters of components used by other overseas affiliates of Ford and even by its U.S. operations.

Ford's experience in Brazil has come to serve as a model of why U.S. multinationals invest in developing countries. This "product cycle" explanation focuses on the changing but mutually beneficial relationship between the U.S. parent manufacturing enterprise and its developing country affiliates.

The process starts with a new product developed initially for the U.S. domestic market being exported. Assembly or production plants are then set up in a few of the largest developed country importers. As time goes on, there is increasing competitive pressure. More labor intensive aspects of manufacturing are then gradually relocated in low labor cost developing countries. At the same time, however, research and new product development for the world as a whole are kept in the U.S.

Ford's experience with the product life cycle evolved considerably between the 1950s and 1980s. In the 1950s, Ford designs and technologies were shipped out to Latin America to produce outdated U.S. car models. Now production in Latin America has shortened the product life cycle as new products begin to be produced while they are still sold in developed country markets. For example, the Ford Escort was introduced in the U.S. and Europe in 1980. It was being produced and sold in Brazil by 1983. The competitive international market and the maturity of developing country markets have shortened, but not eliminated, the product life cycle.

Overseas investment has permitted U.S. multinationals to maintain their share of world trade in increasingly competitive markets by producing overseas. Research and development (R&D) and new production plants have remained open to the service component of assembly operations abroad. The U.S. multinationals' product, including overseas inputs, has thus stayed competitive even when U.S. based manufacturing alone has become uneconomic. . . .

A Spur to Development

Just as the profit-driven American private sector has proven to be an unequalled engine for human progress on the national level, profit-based American activity in developing countries has been a powerful spur to development. Healthy economic policies are a prerequisite to sustained LDC progress in the whole range of social indicators. Those developing countries that have charted sound economic courses tend to be the ones with the best sustainable records in health, education, and, over the long-term, individual opportunity and choice, the heart of what development is all about.

Good results can be more valuable than good intentions. While it is understood that American investments overseas are made on the basis of sound business principles, not charity, the spin-off benefits they engender in their host countries include important developmental assets on a scale, and sometimes of a class, that government-to-government development assistance is incapable of achieving. One of the cases we have cited, the experience of ARAMCO in Saudi Arabia, is an example of an American corporation single-handedly creating a national infrastructure from scratch without an extant trained, indigenous cadre or any pre-existing economic foundation to build upon. This is something no government development program has ever achieved.

Enlist Multinationals' Help

Multinationals can contribute more to development than can many governmental entities, either within the developing or the developed world. There is a realistic kind of Damocles sword hanging over their heads, in that they either perform well—which means economically soundly—or they are out of business. Moreover, we can say that multinationals are a kind of entity that is going to be necessary for the development needed in the years to come. Instead of writing them off as monsters, we should try to enlist their support in a task that needs all the intelligence, creativity, and resources it can muster.

Theodore M. Hesburgh, in *Multinational Managers and Poverty in the Third World*, 1982.

While less dramatic, thousands of typical American investments in developing countries have generated much-needed jobs, upgraded both on-the-job skill training and higher educational opportunities, created modern health care systems that sometimes serve as a model for later host efforts, and facilitated technology transfer and the creation over time of a highly trained native cadre of managers and technicians. Few, if any, of these achievements could be equalled by government-to-government programs. The same economic policies that attract foreign investment also create a friendlier climate for domestic savings and investment, and those developing countries which pursue such policies tend to fare better than countries in comparable circumstances that do not. The U.S. Government can make a substantial, and cost-free, contribution to development simply by encouraging A.I.D. [Agency for International Development] recipients to foster an investment-friendly economic climate.

Distinguishing Between Fact and Opinion

This activity is designed to help develop the basic reading and thinking skill of distinguishing between fact and opinion. Consider the following statement: "Korea's per capita income increased from $82 in 1962 to $2,500 in 1987." This is a factual statement that could be verified by checking world almanacs for 1962 and 1987. The statement, "Korea's economic success can be attributed to generous foreign aid from the US," is an opinion, however. Few experts agree on what policies lead to a successful economy, and there is no one source which could definitively answer the question of why Korea's economy has improved.

When investigating controversial issues it is important that one be able to distinguish between statements of fact and statements of opinion. It is also important to recognize that not all statements of fact are true. They may appear to be true, but some are based on inaccurate or false information. For this activity, however, we are concerned with understanding the difference between those statements which appear to be factual and those which appear to be based primarily on opinion.

Most of the following statements are taken from the viewpoints in this chapter. Consider each statement carefully. *Mark O for any statement you believe is an opinion or interpretation of facts. Mark F for any statement you believe is a fact. Mark I for any statement you believe is impossible to judge.*

If you are doing this activity as a member of a class or group, compare your answers with those of other class or group members. Be able to defend your answers. You may discover that others come to different conclusions than you do. Listening to the reasons others present for their answers may give you valuable insights in distinguishing between fact and opinion.

> O = *opinion*
> F = *fact*
> I = *impossible to judge*

1. The literacy rate for women in India is 50 percent that of men.

2. Multinational corporations have enormously helped many less developed countries.

3. Only half of the estimated 54 million abortions performed annually around the world are legal.

4. Until the status of women improves, prospects for reducing birth rates in some African societies remain dim.

5. Today the Third World throbs with capitalism.

6. Children often contribute significantly to family income and help support the elderly.

7. US businesses have created over two million jobs in developing countries in the 1980s.

8. Under China's new agricultural system, households, families, and individuals own the output of their work.

9. Sri Lanka's socialist leader nationalized banks and businesses, thus leading to food shortages and a thriving black market.

10. Kerala's policies have benefited those who are most often the victims of traditional development policies, namely women.

11. Rapid population growth has not prevented economic progress either in the West or in the contemporary Third World.

12. By the late 1970s, many Third World countries increasingly found themselves mired in debt.

13. Heavy use of pesticides by US agricultural exporting firms polluted much of Nicaragua's groundwater.

14. Wasteful tribal systems of land ownership have hurt agricultural production.

15. In most industrial nations, widely available contraceptives allow couples to choose the number and spacing of their children.

16. In the 1950s, nearly 40 percent of Taiwan's gross domestic capital came from foreign savings.

17. A proper revolutionary goal is to strengthen the poor and weaken the rich.

18. The Ford Escort was produced and sold in Brazil in 1983.

Periodical Bibliography

The following articles have been selected to supplement the diverse views presented in this chapter.

Tom Bethell	"The Riches of the Orient," *National Review*, November 7, 1986.
Alan B. Durning	"Saving the Planet," *The Progressive*, April 1989.
David R. Gergen	"The Boiling Pot," *U.S. News & World Report*, May 15, 1989.
Kaval Gulhati	"The Role of Women in Development," *Social Education*, April/May 1989.
Yacob Haile-Mariam and Berhanu Mengistu	"Public Enterprises and the Privatisation Thesis in the Third World," *Third World Quarterly*, October 1988.
Garrett Hardin	"There Is No Global Population Problem," *The Humanist*, July/August 1989.
Michael Harrington	"Toward a New Socialism," *Dissent*, Spring 1989.
Stephen J. Kobrin	"Are Multinationals Better After the Yankees Go Home?" *The Wall Street Journal*, May 8, 1989.
Louis Kraar	"How To Sell to Cashless Buyers," *Fortune*, November 7, 1988.
William McGurn	"Preferential Option: Why Manila Is Poor and Hong Kong Is Rich," *Crisis*, June 1989.
New Internationalist	"Families to Order: Population and Human Rights," October 1987.
Randall B. Purcell	"Develop Their Agriculture To Save Ours," *The Wall Street Journal*, January 23, 1987.
L.G. Rawl	"Let's Look at the Whole Picture," *The Lamp*, Fall 1988. Available from *The Lamp*, Exxon Corporation, PO Box 101, Florham Park, NJ 07932.
Frances Stewart	"The Case for Appropriate Technology," *Issues in Science and Technology*, Summer 1987.
John Summa	"Killing Them Sweetly," *Multinational Monitor*, November 1988.

How Can Third World Debt Be Reduced?

Chapter Preface

Sub-Saharan Africa and Latin America: Total Debt and Its Percentage of the Gross National Product, 1987

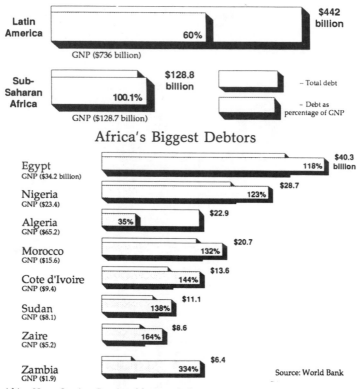

Latin America
GNP ($736 billion)
60%
$442 billion

Sub-Saharan Africa
GNP ($128.7 billion)
100.1%
$128.8 billion

– Total debt
– Debt as percentage of GNP

Africa's Biggest Debtors

Egypt
GNP ($34.2 billion)
118%
$40.3 billion

Nigeria
GNP ($23.4)
123%
$28.7

Algeria
GNP ($65.2)
35%
$22.9

Morocco
GNP ($15.6)
132%
$20.7

Cote d'Ivoire
GNP ($9.4)
144%
$13.6

Sudan
GNP ($8.1)
138%
$11.1

Zaire
GNP ($5.2)
164%
$8.6

Zambia
GNP ($1.9)
334%
$6.4

Source: World Bank

Africa News Service. Reprinted by permission.

The above graph dramatically illustrates the seriousness of Third World debt. In fact, the debts of several nations far exceed their yearly gross national products, the total amount of goods and services a nation produces. When an economically struggling nation owes this much money, paying back or refinancing the debt is clearly a monumental, perhaps impossible, task. Yet forgiving the debt may cause hardship to those who lent the money or may disrupt the international economy.

The reduction of Third World debt is a vital issue facing policymakers around the world. The authors in the following chapter present several ways to accomplish this.

"We can provide substantial benefits for debtor nations in the form of more manageable debt service obligations."

Third World Debt Should Be Refinanced

Nicholas F. Brady

Nicholas F. Brady became the secretary of the US treasury in 1988. The following viewpoint is excerpted from Brady's 1989 proposal to reduce Third World debt. He argues that an effective debt policy must promote economic growth in the Third World so that indebted countries can earn the money to repay their debts. Brady recommends a three-part strategy: Third World governments must reform their domestic policies to improve their economies, banks must agree to provide new loans to Third World nations, and international monetary organizations must help debtors acquire flexible financing.

As you read, consider the following questions:

1. What strategy was adopted in 1985 to deal with the debt problem, according to Brady?
2. What economic policies does the author suggest debtor nations adopt?
3. How can commercial banks reduce Third World debt, according to the author?

Nicholas F. Brady, a speech delivered to the Brookings Institution and the Bretton Woods Committee Conference on Third World Debt on March 10, 1989.

Since 1982 the world community has endeavored to come to terms with international debt. In 1985 we paused and took stock of our progress in addressing the problem. As a result of that review, together we brought forth a new strategy, centered on economic growth. This still makes sense. However, it is appropriate that we again take stock. Thus we have undertaken to look afresh at the international debt situation. The purpose was to discover what progress has been made: to see where we as a community of nations have succeeded and where we have not. And, where our success has not met our expectations, to understand why we have not achieved our goals. We have studied in depth, we have consulted widely—seeking and taking into account the views of debtor nations, multilateral institutions, commercial banks and legislatures. We have also consulted closely with Japan and other industrial countries in order to begin to lay the basis for a common approach to the debt problem by the creditor countries. . . .

Sound Principles

Experience demonstrates that the fundamental principles of the current strategy remain sound:

- Growth is essential to the resolution of debt problems;
- Debtor nations will not achieve sufficient levels of growth without reform;
- Debtor nations have a continuing need for external resources;
- Solutions must be undertaken on a case-by-case basis.

In recent years, we have seen positive growth occur in many debtor nations. In 1988 six major debtor nations realized more than four percent positive growth. This is primarily due to the debtors' own efforts. The political leadership of many of these nations has demonstrated their commitment to implement vital macroeconomic and structural reforms. In many countries this has been reflected in the privatization of nationalized industries. In some countries there has also been a move towards opening their shores to greater foreign trade and investment. Current account deficits have been sharply reduced, and the portion of export earnings going to pay interest on external debt has declined. These are significant achievements. All the more so, since in parallel progress, a number of debtor nations have advanced towards more democratic regimes. This has required great courage and persistence. The people of these countries have made substantial sacrifices for which they've earned our admiration. We must work together to transform these sacrifices into tangible and lasting benefits. . . .

However, despite the accomplishments, we must acknowledge

that serious problems and impediments to a successful resolution of the debt crisis remain. Clearly, in many of the major debtor nations, growth has not been sufficient. Nor has the level of economic policy reform been adequate. Capital flight has drained resources from debtor nations' economies. Meanwhile, neither investment nor domestic savings has shown much improvement. In many cases, inflation has not been brought under control. Commercial bank lending has not always been timely. The force of these circumstances has overshadowed the progress achieved. Despite progress, prosperity remains, for many, out of reach. . . .

Strengthening the Current Strategy

Any new approach must continue to emphasize the importance of stronger growth in debtor nations, as well as the need for debtor reforms and adequate financial support to achieve that growth. We will have success only if our efforts are truly cooperative. And, to succeed we must have the commitment and involvement of all parties.

Finding Additional Financial Resources

Further progress on adjustment programs will require the release of additional financial resources as well as an easing of debt service burdens in order to bring about sustained growth. It is recognized that the debt strategy needs to be strengthened especially in this area. In addition to new lending, negotiated reductions in debt and debt service burdens can provide important external financial support. Other non-debt creating methods, which we continue to strongly advocate, are direct and portfolio investment, debt/equity swaps, and, importantly, the return of flight capital.

David C. Mulford, statement before the House Subcommittee on International Development Finance, Trade, and Monetary Policy, March 16, 1989.

First and foremost, debtor nations must focus particular attention on the adoption of policies which can better encourage new investment flows, strengthen domestic savings, and promote the return of flight capital. This requires sound growth policies which foster confidence in both domestic and foreign investors. These are essential ingredients for reducing the future stock of debt and sustaining strong growth. Specific policy measures in these areas should be part of any new IMF [International Monetary Fund] and World Bank programs. It is worth noting that total capital flight for most major debtors is roughly comparable to their total debt.

Second, the creditor community—the commercial banks, international financial institutions, and creditor governments—should provide more effective and timely financial support. A number of steps are needed in this area.

Commercial banks need to work with debtor nations to provide a broader range of alternatives for financial support, including greater efforts to achieve both debt and debt service reduction and to provide new lending. The approach to this problem must be realistic. The path towards greater creditworthiness and a return to the markets for many debtor countries needs to involve debt reduction. Diversified forms of financial support need to flourish and constraints should be relaxed. To be specific, the sharing and negative pledge clauses included in existing loan agreements are a substantial barrier to debt reduction. In addition, the banking community's interests have become more diverse in recent years. This needs to be recognized by both banks and debtors to take advantage of various preferences.

A key element of this approach, therefore, would be the negotiation of a general waiver of the sharing and negative pledge clauses for each performing debtor, to permit an orderly process whereby banks which wish to do so, negotiate debt or debt service reduction transactions. Such waivers might have a three year life, to stimulate activity within a short but measurable timeframe. We expect these waivers to accelerate sharply the pace of debt reduction and pass the benefits directly to the debtor nations. We would expect debtor nations also to maintain viable debt/equity swap programs for the duration of this endeavor, and would encourage them to permit domestic nationals to engage in such transactions.

Of course, banks will remain interested in providing new money, especially if creditworthiness improves over the three year period. They should be encouraged to do so, for new financing will still be required. In this connection, consideration could be given in some cases to ways of differentiating new from old debt.

The World Bank and the IMF

The international financial institutions will need to continue to play central roles. The heart of their effort would be to promote sound policies in the debtor countries through advice and financial support. With steady performance under IMF and World Bank programs, these institutions can catalyze new financing. In addition, to support and encourage debtor and commercial bank efforts to reduce debt and debt service burdens, the IMF and World Bank could provide funding, as part of their policy-based lending programs, for debt or debt service reduction purposes. This financial support would be available to countries which elect to undertake a debt reduction program. A portion of their policy-based loans could be used to finance specific debt reduction plans. These funds could support collateralized debt for bond exchanges involving a significant discount on outstanding debt. They could also be used to replenish reserves following a cash buyback.

Moreover, both institutions could offer new, additional financial support to collateralize a portion of interest payments for debt or debt service reduction transactions. By offering direct financial support for debt and debt service operations, the IMF and the World Bank could provide new incentives, which would act simultaneously to strengthen prospects for greater creditworthiness and to restore voluntary private financing in the future. This could lead to considerable improvements in the cash flow positions of the debtor countries.

An Important Turning Point

This plan is more than Treasury Secretary Nicholas F. Brady's debut on the stage of international economics—it marks an important turning point in the long-running debt debacle. Shocked by the human, economic and—perhaps most of all—the political consequences of a capital flow from the world's poor countries to the rich, now running on the order of $35 billion per year, the powers-that-be in the international monetary system have determined the time has come to reduce the debt by up to $70 billion over the next few years.

Walter Russell Mead, *Los Angeles Times*, April 9, 1989.

While the IMF and World Bank will want to set guidelines on how their funds are used, the negotiation of transactions will remain in the market place—encouraged and supported but not managed by the international institutions. . . .

Creditor governments should continue to reschedule or restructure their own exposure and to maintain export credit cover for countries with sound reform programs. In addition, creditor countries which are in a position to provide additional financing in support of this effort may wish to consider doing so. This could contribute significantly to the overall success of this effort. We believe that creditor governments should also consider how to reduce regulatory, accounting, or tax impediments to debt reduction, where these exist.

More Timely Support

The third key element of our thinking involves more timely and flexible financial support. The current manner in which "financial gaps" are estimated and filled is cumbersome and rigid. We should seek to change this mentality and make the process work better. At the same time, we must maintain the close association between economic performance and external financial support.

While we believe the IMF should continue to estimate debtor financing needs, we question whether the international financial institutions should delay their initial disbursements until firm, detailed commitments have been provided by all other creditors to fill the financing "gap." In many instances, this has served to provide a false sense of security rather than meaningful financial support. The banks will themselves need to provide diverse, active, and timely support in order to facilitate servicing of the commercial debt remaining after debt reduction. Debtor nations should set goals for both new investment and the repatriation of flight capital, and to adopt policy measures designed to achieve those targets. Debtor nations and commercial banks should determine through negotiations the portion of financing needs to be met via concerted or voluntary lending, and the contribution to be made by voluntary debt or debt service reduction.

Finally, sound policies and open, growing markets within the industrial nations will continue to be an essential foundation for efforts to make progress on the debt problem. We cannot reasonably expect the debtor nations to increase their exports and strengthen their economies without access to industrial country markets. The Uruguay Round of trade negotiations provides an important opportunity to advance an open trading system. We must all strive to make this a success.

More Manageable Debt

Taken together, the ideas I have discussed represent a basis on which we can work to revitalize the current debt strategy. We believe that through our efforts we can provide substantial benefits for debtor nations in the form of more manageable debt service obligations, smaller and more realistic financing needs, stronger economic growth, and higher standards of living for their people.

"Paying the debt is immoral."

Third World Debt Should Be Forgiven

Carlos Rafael Rodriguez

The author of the following viewpoint, Carlos Rafael Rodriguez, is the deputy chairman of Cuba's Council of State and Council of Ministers. Rodriguez explains why the Cuban government believes all Third World debt should be forgiven. He contends that in many countries, the debts were acquired by corrupt governments that have since been overthrown. Furthermore, he maintains that the debt is so colossal that it can never be repaid without completely bankrupting the Third World.

As you read, consider the following questions:

1. Why does the author believe it is wrong for Third World governments to repay their loans?
2. How have world economic trends affected Latin America, according to Rodriguez?
3. Why does Rodriguez believe refinancing the debt is futile?

Carlos Rafael Rodriguez, "Cuba: Trying to Pay the Debt is a Political Error," *Information Bulletin*, October 1988. Reprinted by permission of *Information Bulletin*, published by Progress Books, Toronto.

Cuba has set forth its view of the external debt: it cannot be paid. So long as there is the view that the original capital has to be returned, the problem cannot be solved by any payment formula or by any combination of rescheduling or periods of grace. The idea of forgetting the capital and paying the interest is likewise a plunderous one, for it turns us into perpetual debtors.

We have also said that paying the debt is immoral. Our peoples have little to do with this indebtedness. They have found themselves in debt through a combination of deals between rulers disposed to receive and to spend, and bankers yearning to lend, at times of excessive liquidity when money accumulates at the banks unproductively.

On the other hand, we believe that any attempt to pay the debt is a political error, because this leads to an ever more violent contradiction between the governments intending to pay and their peoples, who, after all, are the ones who suffer the consequences of meeting debt obligations contracted by others.

Latin America's Debt

The case is most dramatic for Latin America because the debts accumulated under the military tyrannies alien to any popular responsibility now have to be met by popular governments, by reorganized and incipient democracies running the risk of increasing estrangement from their peoples to the extent to which they are forced to demand of them social sacrifices, to put off their aspirations for decent living standards; eventually to renounce their efforts for development to which the external debt is the major obstacle.

The data on Latin America's external debt bear out what has been said. In 1975 it stood at only $42 billion; according to the UN Economic Commission for Latin America (ECLA), it had multiplied almost 10-fold by 1987, to $409.805 billion.

The growth of the external debt has been in no way connected with an increase in investment, even if nominal investment. The external debt of some countries has grown because the decline of the dollar has increased the international cost of the debt, and also because the interest has kept going up while the prices of our export goods kept plunging.

Between 1981 and 1988 Latin America has paid out more than $200 billion through profit transfers and interest payments. While the external debt has gone up by $120 billion, the net transfers of funds have reached $159 billion.

In order to set right its balance of payments, Latin America has sharply cut back on its imports, thereby lowering the real living standards of its population. But that has been of little import, because, despite the efforts to boost exports and despite the temporary successes of some countries in this area, the value of Latin

America's exports still diminished by 11.7 per cent in 1984, by 5.9 per cent in 1985, and by 14.8 per cent in 1986.

It would appear that, from 1986 on, the situation in Latin America should have improved, because since mid-1986 the external debt has grown more slowly, while the interest rate has dropped, and the exchange rate of the U.S. dollar in which the external debt is denominated, has declined. But the results were not so appreciable. An analysis of the situation in 1987 shows that the external debt has continued to grow and has gone up from $392.9 billion to $409.8 billion. That year, interest payments came to $32.3 billion, that is, they remained virtually on the level of the earlier years, while the debt-export relation was still at 387 per cent.

That is the state of things, despite the changed situation in Venezuela and Mexico, and the diminution of the external debt of Brazil, Costa Rica, Chile, Haiti, and the Dominican Republic.

Consequently, Latin America's efforts to reduce its imports from $98.7 billion in 1981 to $59.7 billion in 1986 have scarcely yielded any tangible results. While there has been some improvement of economic growth indicators on the continent since 1984, in global terms it came to only 10 per cent of the figure in 1980—8 years ago; the gross domestic product per head went down from 945.6 pesos to 892.1 pesos, and the population in that period went up by 60 million. All of that without account of the annual growth of inflation: it has dropped from 275.3 per cent in 1985 to 187.0 per cent, but it is now three times faster than it was in 1981.

Already Paid

Countless studies reveal the Third World's foreign debt has already been paid back through interest and service charges. The tens of billions now being paid to the monopoly banks are gravy.

Marc Frank, *People's Daily World*, May 4, 1988.

Latin America now has to allocate from 30 to 35 per cent of its total exports of goods and services every year to pay the interest, while our net transfers are negative, which means that since 1982 we have been decapitalizing ourselves.

If we add to this the heavy burden falling on our economies from the drop in the prices of our basic products, which has meant a net loss of more than $72 billion, we shall need no eloquent rhetoric to describe a truly tragic picture.

What can be done when there is no change in the trends in world economic development? After all, even in the distant future there is no sign of anything that could indicate the prospect of positive change in exchange between our depressed prices and the prices of manufactured products which we have to import and which have been inflated on the world market in recent years. At the celebrations in Rio de Janeiro of the 40th anniversary of ECLA, I said that the countries of the European Economic Community have stockpiles of millions of tons of milk and cereal products. It would be a crime against humanity to destroy these, as some suggested, but if they were thrown on the market they would ruin Latin America to an even greater extent, because their prices would become even less profitable.

This kind of realistic analysis should not, of course, lead us to suicidal inaction. The struggle to raise the prices for our basic products, the efforts to prevent the developed capitalist countries from unloading on the world markets foodstuffs whose production they subsidize from revenues received from the export of expensive manufactured products are a part of the struggle for the new international economic order. It is a struggle that must not be halted, but it can yield results only over the long term, which is so far away that the peoples can no longer afford to wait and hope.

Until the countries of the South work out the required solutions, until we arrive at Latin America's economic integration, and until new commercial relations are established between the countries of the South (and here only the first few steps are being taken), we must concentrate on removing the most formidable obstacle in the way of development today, and it is the external debt problem. The first thing that we must do is to go on from individual attempts to collective decisions.

Refinancing Does Not Help

The first multilateral refinancing was initiated by Argentina in 1956. From 1956 to 1981, Latin America and the Caribbean carried out 12 restructurings of their debt, involving a total of $561.1 million. The gravity of the situation will be seen from the fact that from 1982 to 1987, there were 20 restructurings of the debt, involving an amount of $842.8 million.

All these renegotiations helped to improve somewhat the terms, but not to the extent of matching the gravity of the problem. The margin above the London Inter-Bank Rate (LIBOR) has lowered, but in some cases it continues to be from 0.8 to 1.5 times higher. The rescheduling, with the extension of the term to 20 years, as in Mexico's case, is insufficient in every respect and for most of our countries it does not run to more than 10, 12 or 15 years. The periods of grace average 4 or 5 years.

We often hear satisfaction being expressed over these agreements. But the first flush of euphoria is always followed by reports that the country concerned cannot pay up and that it finds itself in even more dire straits. . . .

The main conclusion that should be drawn in the light of the experience of many years of futile efforts and the steadily worsening situation is, in our view, to admit that the attempts to negotiate separately are sterile and negative. It is necessary to work out a joint approach, and not only a Latin American one, but one that is common to all the debtor countries. Considering that the creditors have their own club, the debtors should, at least, have their group to elaborate joint solutions.

The situation in each country is certainly a different one. The circumstances are dissimilar. The creditors are not always the same ones. The debt terms are different, and the products constituting the basis for payments are diverse. The terms of negotiation are not identical either.

China Daily, Beijing

But these distinctions are secondary, for the problem is the same. . . .

The most important thing is to let the creditors know that we, debtors, will act together, and that we are not going to have any partial solution to the problem, which merely goes to prolong our agony.

"Third World debtors could readily meet their obligations."

Third World Debt Can Be Repaid

P.T. Bauer

The author of the following viewpoint, P.T. Bauer, believes that Third World governments should be held responsible for their debts. Third World governments can repay the loans, Bauer contends, if they increase taxes and sell their assets. Bauer is professor emeritus of economics at the London School of Economics in Great Britain.

As you read, consider the following questions:

1. Why does Bauer believe the figures quoted on Third World debt are misleading?
2. Why does the author disagree with the idea that the Third World is in debt because of external factors?
3. Why are concessions to debtors and rescheduling of debt harmful, according to Bauer?

P.T. Bauer, "Accounts Receivable," *The New Republic*, June 15, 1987. Reprinted by permission of *The New Republic*, © 1987, The New Republic, Inc.

The realities of the so-called debt crisis are often ignored, possibly because powerful political and commercial interests both in the West and in the Third World have a stake in overlooking them. Third World debtors could readily meet their obligations, but they would be foolish to do so as long as they are not being pressed. The decision by Citicorp bank to write off $3 billion in foreign loans relieves the pressure further.

The Debtors Can Pay

Third World debt is sovereign debt, owed or guaranteed by governments. The debtors can always pay, since governments can tax their citizens. They also generally have substantial marketable assets, and they can requisition the assets of their citizens. The sovereign debtor cannot be taken to courts. Payment depends on the government's willingness, which depends on the political and economic consequences of the decision. Governments try to avoid the political and economic costs until the consequences of default outweigh them. The most important adverse consequence would be the failure to secure further external finance, which could result in economic breakdown. In the current climate, such an outcome is improbable. Debtors feel little incentive to pay.

The statistics bandied about on Third World debt sound frightening. But the figures of hundreds of billions of dollars are misleading. It is rarely made clear whether the figures are gross or net—that is, whether they allow for the financial assets of the debtors, let alone for other marketable assets. And it is often left unspecified what debts are being discussed. Some statistics refer to debt to the banks; others include debts to Western governments and international organizations such as the International Development Association (IDA). These are unindexed loans of 50-year maturity with ten-year grace periods at zero interest. Although termed loans, they are effectively grants. Yet they are included in Third World debt. Debts owed to Western governments are usually subsidized loans under foreign aid programs. They are often scaled down or written off by the creditors cum donors.

The assets of the debtors are rarely mentioned in polite international society—even large liquid assets that in many cases run into billions of dollars. Petroleos de Venezuela, the Venezuelan state oil monopoly, was reported to have billions of dollars in financial assets held in the United States. The government of Peru, an intransigent debtor, refused to pay a few million dollars of interest on its external debts. Its foreign reserves are about $1.2 billion.

Marketable Assets

Liquid reserves aside, the major debtors also have large marketable assets. In 1983 Pemex, the state-owned Mexican oil monopoly, earned $5.3 billion. It is widely believed that if it were managed privately the earnings would have been much larger. But

207

even at $5.3 billion the capital value of Pemex could then be conservatively valued at between $35 billion and $40 billion. The sovereign debt of Mexico was around $80 billion. The sale or pledge of part of Pemex might well have averted the Mexican debt crisis; it would have shown the readiness of the government to meet its obligations.

It is often argued that the sale or pledging of debtors' assets in response to demands by creditors would infringe on national sovereignty. But why should the use of assets to honor obligations arising from borrowing have this effect? In both world wars the British government pledged some of its own securities and requisitioned those of its citizens for sale without this being regarded as infringement of its sovereignty.

Another issue rarely mentioned in polite society is the disposition of the many billions borrowed by the Third World debtors. Many governments have spent hugely on prestige projects, on unviable industrialization, on politically motivated subsidies, and on other undertakings designed to keep the rulers in power.

A Mistaken Assumption

The idea that debt relief would stimulate material advance in the sub-Sahara arises from a number of seriously mistaken impressions. It is a mistake, for example, to assume that the governments in question "simply can't pay back" the money they have borrowed—much less make good on the other obligations to which they have committed themselves in contract. In most countries in the sub-Sahara, key industries have been nationalized in the post-colonial period, and government owned enterprises now figure prominently in the economy. Most of these governments have other saleable assets as well.

Nicholas Eberstadt, *The National Interest*, Winter 1987/1988.

Debtor governments typically restrict the inflow of equity capital, and reserve for themselves or their nationals a large part of the equity in large parts of their economies. For instance, Brazil, Mexico, Ethiopia, Ghana, Nigeria, and Tanzania—all debtor nations—ban foreign participation in much or all of the economy. These restrictions are maintained or even extended amid rescheduling negotiations and the pleas of debtors about their inability to pay. The restrictions have promoted reliance on bank finance and official foreign aid. They also obstruct the enterprise, know-how, and skills that usually accompany the inflow of equity.

Historical Perspective

World Bank statistics suggest strongly that, as a percentage of GNP [gross national product], neither the total outstanding sovereign debt of the major borrowers nor the interest and principal payments are particularly high by historical standards. In 1983 the GNP of the major Third World debtors was more than three times their sovereign debt, without allowing for reserves. Interest on the debt was about 2.3 percent of GNP and total debt service about 3.9 percent. As a percentage of export earnings, interest payments were about 12.9 percent and total debt service about 22 percent. Most of these ratios are significantly lower than they were, say, for Canada and Argentina on the eve of World War I, when these countries were first-class debtors.

The major debtor governments often preside over some of the most prosperous Third World economies. According to World Bank statistics, the income per capita of Mexico in 1984 was over $2,000, that of Brazil over $1,700, and that of Venezuela over $3,400. In 1985, often cited as a critical year for Brazil, the largest Third World debtor, automobile sales totaled about a million units, a near all-time record. In the same year both the earnings and the dividend of Petrobras, the state controlled oil monopoly, were almost certainly all-time highs. The cost of the construction of Abuja, the new capital of Nigeria, being built from scratch, exceeds the total sovereign debt of that country. The same is almost certainly true for Brasília in Brazil and for Dodoma in Tanzania. Such countries don't have to resort to anything remotely resembling policies of austerity to pay their debts. They could simply sell state-owned or -controlled companies, reduce the more extravagant forms of public spending, lift restrictions on the inflow of equity capital, and adopt more market-oriented policies.

Changes in the World Economy

It is sometimes argued that adverse external changes warrant substantial concessions to the debtors, and even additional transfers. It is obviously improvident to assume a country will never encounter economic setbacks. But a prudent government would accumulate foreign-exchange reserves in good times to meet its commitments in bad times. Much current discussion implies that Third World governments can be expected to behave like children with no thought for tomorrow. The possibility of setting aside reserves in prosperity is rarely mentioned. The major debtors, including Mexico, Brazil, and Venezuela, among others, enjoyed sustained prosperity from 1945 through 1980. But in contrast with Hong Kong and Taiwan, for example, they did not set aside reserves for less favorable times.

The fact is, the diversity of Third World debtors makes the deterioration of the world economy a moot point. Mexico, Venezuela, and Nigeria are large oil exporters; Brazil is a large importer. A fall in oil prices damages the former and benefits the latter. By choosing particular years, commodities, and countries, it can always be suggested that the terms of trade of debtors have deteriorated. In the 1970s the rise in oil prices was used as an argument for more aid, more lending, and debt write-offs for less developed counties; in the 1980s the decline in oil prices is used to support the same argument.

A Half-Truth

When Venezuelan President Carlos Andres Perez says he cannot pay back his loans, he is telling a half-truth. The whole truth is that Venezuela's export revenue, and tax revenues, are not adequate to cover her foreign debt, her domestic investment needs, and to maintain the bloated, costly, welfare state built by President Perez in the '70s when he was running the country, and OPEC [Organization of the Petroleum Exporting Countries] was gouging the Americans and consuming loans as fast as Citibank and Chase Manhattan could send them down.

What the Latin nations are demanding . . . is a U.S. bailout of their foreign debts. . . . They are demanding nothing less than that U.S. capitalism should bail out Latin socialism.

Patrick J. Buchanan, *Human Events*, April 8, 1989.

Another frequently cited problem is the imposition of import restrictions by Western nations. Without doubt, these adversely affect many less developed nations. But they do not have a significant effect on the debtor countries. South Korea, Taiwan, and Hong Kong are far more affected by such restrictions than debtors such as Mexico, Venezuela, Brazil, and Nigeria. Yet they have grown rapidly in recent years. The truth is the West still offers huge markets for the Third World debtors. The debtors are affected far more by domestic policies (i.e., wasteful public spending and state monopolies) than by such external factors as import restrictions or changes in rates of growth in the West.

Three additional arguments are often heard favoring large concessions to debtors and the transfer of additional funds to the Third World. First, it is said that attempts to make the debtors pay would result in a political and social upheaval that would create populist or Communist governments hostile to the West. Second, it is said that without major concessions, the plight of the debtors would endanger the Western banking and financial system. Third, it is claimed that without such concessions and transfers the Third World would buy less from the West, risking our own exports and jobs. None of these carries particular weight.

The emergence of populist, Communist, or other governments hostile to the West does not depend on the level of income or its rate of change. This is evident from experience in the Far East, the Middle East, and Africa. Moreover, the notion that concessions and transfers to Third World debtors are necessary to avert political changes damaging to the West opens the door to indefinite blackmail by Third World governments abroad and by commercial banks at home.

The Banks' Solvency

If the banks' solvency is threatened by the Third World debts, how can they declare large profits and pay substantial dividends? If their capital base is insufficient, should they not strengthen it by reducing their dividends and calling for more capital instead of lending more to Third World debtors? And if it is necessary to rescue banks with taxpayers' money, why not do it directly rather than send the money through Third World governments that are unlikely to use the funds to service their debts?

Even default by Third World debtors would not threaten the Western financial system. Western governments can ensure that bank losses will not endanger the depositors (as distinct from the stockholders or the management) of any bank—let alone the financial system. The Western governments could insist that the banks build up their capital base by reducing dividends and seeking new capital. The governments could also purchase loans at market value and/or take over some of the banks and sell them as going concerns after writing down the balance sheets.

Supporting Incompetence and Dishonesty

The most influential proposals currently under discussion for solving the debt crisis involve increased lending by the World Bank and the International Monetary Fund (IMF) to the most heavily indebted countries, combined with more lending by the commercial banks. Related proposals involve more foreign aid, and outright cancellation or scaling down of Third World debts. The Baker plan, for example, envisages increased lending by the World Bank, by the IMF, and by the banks, and more market-oriented policies by the debtors. The plan provides for additional resources on favorable terms to debtors who have not met their obligations—that is, who have defaulted. This means preferential treatment of the improvident, incompetent, and dishonest governments over those more scrupulous in meeting their contractual obligations.

Such a policy does little to promote conduct helpful to economic development. Instead, it only further politicizes life in the Third World and arouses the indignation of those Third World governments, like Colombia, that do meet their obligations. Preferential treatment of Third World debtor governments will also arouse the indignation of many debtors at home. Why should foreign debtor governments be treated leniently and even receive additional funds when domestic farmers and homeowners have to surrender their assets, which may be the source of their livelihood?

It is unlikely that the beneficiaries of such concessions and transfers would alter their policies in a more market-oriented direction without direct pressure. They may make cosmetic changes, especially in macroeconomic policies. But they will not dismantle the public sector, reduce major categories of public spending, or abandon major state controls. Why should they? Their policies, which have been supported for decades by official Western aid, accord with their own interests. They will modify them only if continued pursuit promises to result in economic breakdown threatening their political survival. . . .

Pat McCarthy. Distributed by Heritage Features Syndicate.

The likely outcome is the continued rescheduling and scaling down of existing debts and the injection of more funds into the Third World, especially Third World governments. This will encourage those who disregard their obligations. It will increase the moral hazard of lending to Third World governments. It will expand the role of the World Bank and the IMF and lead to a further waste of resources.

"The developing world's debt . . . is an economic stain on the second half of the twentieth century."

Third World Debt Cannot Be Repaid

UNICEF

UNICEF, the United Nations Children's Fund, is an international relief organization that works to improve the lives of children in developing countries. It was awarded the Nobel Peace Prize in 1965. The following viewpoint is excerpted from a report written by UNICEF staff members. They write that the effects of Third World debt are falling most heavily on poverty-stricken children. To pay back bank loans, Third World governments cut their spending on domestic programs like food subsidies, health care, housing programs, and education. The authors conclude that the Third World cannot repay its debt in full without further harming the welfare of children.

As you read, consider the following questions:

1. According to the authors, how have commodity prices affected Third World debt?
2. How does UNICEF believe banks should respond to the debt crisis?
3. How has Third World debt affected children, in the authors' opinion?

Two elements have dominated the deterioration of economic prospects over so much of the developing world in recent years. They are rising debt repayments and falling commodity prices. The total debt of the developing world is now over US $1000 billion. In many countries, annual repayments of interest and capital amount to more than the total of all new aid and loans being received each year. On average, repayments now claim almost 25% of the developing world's export revenues.

Meanwhile, as outgoings have risen, income has declined. The developing world still depends on raw materials for the majority of its export earnings. But real prices for the developing world's principal commodities—including fuels, minerals, jute, rubber, coffee, cocoa, tea, oils, fats, tobacco, and timber—have fallen by approximately 30% since 1979.

The fall in new commercial lending and the inadequate and static levels of official aid complete the four walls of the financial prison in which so much of the developing world has been incarcerated during this decade.

Capital Flight

Among the public in the industrialized world, it is still widely believed that money is flowing from rich nations to poor nations to assist in the struggle against poverty. Ten years ago, that was true. In 1979, a net $40 billion flowed from the northern hemisphere to the developing nations of the south. *Today that flow has been reversed.* Taking everything into account—loans, aid, repayments of interest and capital—the southern world is now transferring at least $20 billion a year to the northern hemisphere. And if we were also to take into account the effective transfer of resources implied in the reduced prices paid by the industrialized nations for the developing world's raw materials, then the annual flow from the poor to the rich might be as much as $60 billion each year.

For much of the developing world, the economic climate has therefore darkened quite dramatically in the last decade. As a result, most of the affected nations have been forced to adopt economic *adjustment policies* in an attempt to stave off balance-of-payments crises while at the same time meeting debt obligations, maintaining essential imports, and struggling to return to economic growth.

Adjustment's Cost

The need for adjustment is not really in question. The manner of adjustment, by contrast, is an issue which is both complex and controversial. With or without support from the International Monetary Fund (IMF), adjustment policies have usually taken the form of a dampening down of demand, a devaluation of the currency, a withdrawal of subsidies on fuel and staple foodstuffs, and deep cuts in government spending. In total, over 70 developing nations are now struggling to adjust their economies by such methods. And the effects, after decades of steady progress, have often been devastating to achievements of the past and to confidence in the future. All participants involved—governments, international financial organizations, private banks, and development agencies—have had to become involved in analysing the consequences, learning the lessons, and adjusting their policies to this new and unwelcome factor in the development equation.

Africa, afflicted by wars and drought and environmental deterioration as well as by debt and recession, has undoubtedly been hardest hit. ''Adjustment programmes,'' said representatives of 30 African countries meeting in Khartoum early in 1988, ''are rending the fabric of African society.'' In the process, what safety nets existed for many of Africa's poor have been torn away. Of the estimated half a million child deaths in 1988 which can be related to the reversal or slowing down of development, approximately two thirds were in Africa.

Backderf/Rothco Cartoons

The plight of Latin America, where average incomes are often 5 to 10 times higher than in Africa, may not at first seem as severe. But higher expectations, a more monetarized economy, and the grossest inequalities of any continent, have brought miseries which average incomes can conceal. . . .

215

Inter-American Development Bank President Enrique Iglesias has commented (September 1988) that:

> The per capita income of the average Latin American is 9 per cent lower today than it was in 1980. This is the average. In some countries the standard of living has slipped back to what it was 20 years ago. It does not take much imagination to realize that behind this statistic are plummeting real wage levels, soaring unemployment (some of it open, some hidden), increased levels of marginality and acute poverty—in short, an erosion of every measure of social well-being. Today, one third of Latin America's population—130 million people—live in dire poverty.

As the social effects of adjustment processes become more obvious, it can also be seen that the heaviest burden is falling on the shoulders of those who are least able to sustain it. It is the poor and the vulnerable who are suffering the most, and for two main reasons.

Two Main Reasons for Suffering

The first is that the poor have the least economic 'fat' with which to absorb the blow of recession. Often, three quarters of the income of the very poor is spent on food and much of what remains is needed for fuel and water, housing and clothes, bus fares and medical treatment. In such circumstances, a 25% cut in real incomes obviously means going without basic necessities.

The second reason is that the poor also have the least political 'muscle' to ward off that blow. Services which are of concern to the richer and more powerful sections of society—such as the major hospitals, universities, national airlines, prestige development projects, and the military—have not borne a proportionate share of the cuts in public spending. With some honourable exceptions, the services which have been most radically pruned are health services, free primary education, and food and fuel subsidies—the services on which the poor are most dependent and which they have least opportunity to replace by any other, private, means.

Since 1979, for example, the proportion of government expenditure devoted to health has fallen in most countries of sub-Saharan Africa, in more than half the countries of Latin America and the Caribbean, and in one third of the nations of Asia. And the cuts have not been marginal. In the 37 poorest nations of the world, spending per head on education has fallen by nearly 50% and on health care by nearly 25% since 1979. . . .

Growth and Debts

The adjustment strategies pursued, especially in relation to the middle-income developing countries, have achieved three important goals; they have prevented the collapse of the international banking and financial system; they have allowed the indebted developing countries to stay within the international economic system; and they have given the commercial banks five years to build reserves and prepare for the inevitable day when the ability of the borrowers to repay their loans was called into question. But there is equally little doubt that adjustment strategies are failing in two major ways. First, as has already been discussed, they have placed a disproportionate burden on the poorest and most vulnerable—of whom children are the most vulnerable of all. Second, they have not succeeded in their principal aim of allowing indebted economies to escape from debt through a return to healthy economic growth. . . .

Moral Tragedy

Third World debt presents a different kind of policy challenge. Failure to provide disinterested *aid* will mean economic tragedy for the poor of the South and a moral tragedy for the North. But failure to address the *debt* of the South threatens the economic stability of the North. The debt is not about humanitarian politics but hard economics. In spite of its potential for economic disruption for both the North and the South, the debt crisis has been treated as a banking problem, not a human emergency or a geopolitical crisis.

J. Bryan Hehir, *Los Angeles Times*, March 14, 1988.

Per capita GDP [gross domestic product] in sub-Saharan Africa *declined* by 3.6% in 1980-85, by 0.5% in 1986, and by 5.1% in 1987. And the future looks equally bleak. Latest World Bank projections to the year 1995, for example, show zero per capita growth in sub-Saharan Africa and only a weak rallying in most of Latin America. Similarly, the *World Economic Survey 1988* from the United Nations points out that per capita incomes in Latin America and Africa have fallen again this year (1988) and are expected to fall still further. In many nations, average incomes in 1995 are expected to be below the levels of 1980 and in some countries even below the levels of 1970.

A Chronicle of Despair

For sub-Saharan Africa, in particular, the agonies of economic adjustment are self-evidently not the birth pangs of a new economic growth. With reference to the "brutal and mindless 1980s", Stephen Lewis, Special Adviser to the Secretary-General on the UN Programme of Action for African Economic Recovery and Development, has spoken in 1988 of:

the litany of economic indices which haunt and shape the human condition of Africa. It matters not what you choose: GDP, GDP per capita, consumption per capita, export growth, import

217

growth, change in terms of trade, commodity prices, debt-service ratios, foreign aid—it is, with few exceptions, a chronicle of despair.

For most of Latin America, where unemployment, inflation, low investment, and deficiencies in economic policies have wreaked havoc with the livelihoods of not only the poor but also of a lower middle class which has been practically destroyed in some nations, there is also little sign of a return to vigorous economic growth. By cutting its imports and expanding its exports, Latin America has been able to squeeze out a surplus sufficient to make external debt repayments of $150 billion in the last five years (1983-88). But the direct consequence has been economic stagnation. As more than one Latin American spokesman has said, "we have adjusted, but we have not grown".

Sooner or later the fact will have to be faced that, in many countries, attempts to pay interest and capital on the full amount of present debts is fundamentally incompatible with return to economic development. Debt repayments at present levels mean not only reduced consumption, and all the human hardship that implies, but also a reduction in investment and in future economic progress. . . .

Debt Relief

It is becoming increasingly clear that major new moves are in prospect for dealing with the developing world's debt. One significant step has already been taken by the Toronto summit at which the major industrialized nations agreed in principle on a degree of debt cancellation for some of the most affected nations in sub-Saharan Africa (on this initiative, the question now is *when* the new measures will take effect and *how* they will be translated into benefits for the poorest groups in the nations concerned).

But the basis of the consensus now beginning to take shape is that the burden of debt servicing must be lifted not only to the point where the developing countries can *cope* with debt repayment but to the point where their economies can *grow* out of their overwhelming indebtedness.

The Banks Must Accept Losses

A second and more controversial element is that the commercial banks—which hold approximately 60% of the developing world's debt—must now brace themselves to bear a significant part of the losses involved in debt reduction. It is not necessary—nor would it be acceptable to the public in most industrialized nations—for large amounts of government money to be used to repay the banks or to subsidize their losses. Having had several years to prepare themselves, most European banks are now in a position to accept an immediate and significant reduction in the value of the developing world's commercial debt (the figure of a 30% reduction in the commercial bank debts of the 15 most indebted countries has been suggested by the UN Conference on Trade and Development). The North American banks, many of which have lower legally required ratios of assets to loans and some of which have recently sustained considerable losses in the domestic market, are perhaps not as firmly placed as their European counterparts to take such significant losses without flinching. But when lending policy turns out to have been unsound—often because of the comfortable assumption that 'countries can't go bankrupt'—then losses must be taken.

The Poor Bear the Brunt

There has been a frisson of drama as the banks felt the wash of vulnerability when their Third World investments hit the rocks. But the drama for the bankers is first and foremost their balance sheets, their corporate competitiveness, and what likelihood there is of an export surplus in the client countries to enable them to meet the banks' repayment schedules. Only a minority of bankers dig into the debts of what's going on in the heartland of the debtor countries, where the poor disproportionately bear the brunt of adjustments forced by lenders. . . .

Education has been badly affected. In Sri Lanka school attendance fell; in Jamaica the percentage of children passing examinations dropped sharply. Education expenditure declined in one-third of the African countries and in 60% of the Latin American countries.

Diseases that seemed to have been eliminated have reappeared—yaws and yellow fever in Ghana, for example, and malaria in Peru. At the same time, expenditure on health services fell by 50% in Africa—by 80% in Ghana—and by 60% in Latin America—by 80% in Bolivia, 30% in El Salvador.

Jonathan Power, *Los Angeles Times*, September 30, 1987.

The third element in this incipient consensus is that the vital role of the industrialized world's governments in tackling this crisis should be to assist the essential process of promoting *growth* in the developing world by significantly increasing flows of official development assistance.

This combination of a degree of debt relief by commercial banks and increased official aid from governments, along with measures to stabilize commodity prices and resist protectionism, is now essential to unlock the doors to growth. Without such action, today's adjustment policies will amount to little more than a rearranging of the furniture inside the debtors' prison. . . .

It is necessary to try to give some voice, however inadequate, to the children of the developing world who have no other say in international economic dealings but who are so profoundly and permanently affected by them.

What has been happening to the economies of so many developing nations in recent years, and the effect that this has had on so many of their most vulnerable citizens, is not just a regrettable fluctuation in the normal process of economic development. It is a tragedy which should never have happened and must never be repeated.

In 1986, former Tanzanian President Julius Nyerere asked the question "Must we starve our children to pay our debts?" That question has now been answered in practice. And the answer has been 'Yes'. Hundreds of thousands of the developing world's children have given their lives to pay their countries' debts, and many millions more are still paying the interest with their malnourished minds and bodies. In Brazil's impoverished northeast alone, infant death rates increased by almost 25% in the course of 1983 and 1984 as a result of economic recession.

That is why the debt crisis should not be discussed too politely. For polite discussion can imply a tacit acceptance of the unacceptable. And what has happened to large areas of the developing world in the 1980s is truly unacceptable.

The fact that so much of today's staggering debt was irresponsibly lent and irresponsibly borrowed would matter less if the consequences of such folly were falling on its perpetrators. Yet now, when the party is over and the bills are coming in, it is the *poor* who are being asked to pay. . . .

An Outrage Against Humanity

And when the impact becomes visible in rising death rates among children, rising percentages of low-birth-weight babies, falling figures for the average weight-for-height of the under-fives, and lower school enrolment ratios among 6-to-11 year olds, then it is essential to strip away the niceties of economic parlance and say that what has happened is simply an outrage against a large section of humanity. The developing world's debt, both in the manner in which it was incurred and in the manner in which it is being 'adjusted to', is an economic stain on the second half of the twentieth century. Allowing world economic problems to be taken out on the growing minds and bodies of young children is the antithesis of all civilized behaviour. Nothing can justify it. And it shames and diminishes us all.

"[International Monetary] Fund doctrine intensifies the sufferings of ordinary people."

IMF Policies Perpetuate Third World Debt

Susan George

When an indebted government can no longer make payments on its bank loans, it can turn to the International Monetary Fund, an organization established in 1944 to maintain stability in the international monetary system. The IMF loans money to desperate Third World nations. In return for its loans, the IMF requires borrowing countries to reform their domestic economic policies. These reforms, called adjustment programs, are criticized by Susan George in the following viewpoint. George argues that IMF-imposed adjustment harms poor people and depresses standards of living. A well-known consultant on hunger and Third World development, George is a senior fellow at the research organization Transnational Institute. Her books include *How the Other Half Dies* and *A Fate Worse Than Debt*.

As you read, consider the following questions:

1. How do the banks profit from IMF policies, according to George?
2. Why does George criticize the Fund's belief that promoting exports will reduce Third World debt?
3. In the author's opinion, how do IMF policies actually make it more difficult for Third World nations to pay their debts?

Although the International Monetary Fund has been an important factor in some nations for a decade or more—the Philippines, Jamaica, Kenya and Zaïre among them—its rise to stardom on the international scene is a recent phenomenon. The 1970s were the heady days of bank euphoria, with borrower governments succumbing to the charms of apparently endless easy money. In those days nobody wanted the IMF around—the lenders because they were self-congratulatory about their efficient recycling of petro-dollars, the borrowers because they had no desire to submit to the Fund's stringent conditions. Thus little was heard about the IMF in the Third World until the early 1980s, since the banks were playing the lending game to everyone's satisfaction. . . .

Banks and the IMF

Suddenly, in the wake of global recession, the heedless nature of the banks' lending policies became evident to all. The borrowers woke up to the nasty reality that a lot of their debt was short-term and at 'variable' (market-determined) interest rates that were climbing dangerously. Each increase in interest automatically added billions to their debt-service bill. Borrowers also found interest payments devouring a larger and more unpredictable share of their export earnings just as these earnings were doing a nosedive.

Although their Third World loans remained enormously profitable, the bankers also began to shed their former insouciance and to recognize that even if countries did not 'fail to exist', they could still very well have serious repayment problems. The banks were already over-exposed, yet knew they would have to loan even more just to make sure that they got their interest back, that loans continued to 'perform'. The neo-conservatives' hope for bank 'self-regulation' turned out to be a fantasy.

As the Third World's capacity to pay diminished, jittery bankers realized that, alone or even together, they were unable singlehandedly to force the debtors to make loan servicing their highest priority. Faced with the grim prospect of cascading defaults, they had to have a nominally neutral institution with both the clout to force repayment and the capacity to mobilize enough financial resources to make repayment possible.

The banks, naturally, did not want to contribute all, or even most, of these resources themselves. An international agency like the IMF could use its own money (states' quotas and other contributions). It could also make its member governments see reason and urge them to put funds into the common pot. The Mexican rescue fund was typical: the IMF's share was $1.3 billion; governments paid in $2 billion; the banks put up $5 billion in 'involuntary loans'.

Note, however, that in the Mexican case public money (yours

and mine) made up 40 per cent of the total package, compared with the banks' contribution of 60 per cent. Between 75 and 80 per cent of Mexico's debt is, however, owed to banks, which collect a proportionate amount of the interest. The IMF thus works as a *channel for funneling public money to private banks*—it matters little that these funds transit through the national accounts of Mexico. In this sense the Fund enforces taxation without representation on the citizens of the industrialized countries.

The banks get another bonus by working with the Fund—an IMF adjustment programme is the best available guarantee that countries will continue to have the means to pay. Adjustment puts export earnings above every other goal, and export earnings head straight for the banks. . . .

Juan Valdez's Government owes $20 Billion. The I.M.F has imposed austerity, forcing cheap exports, high taxes and tight credit.

WE'LL TAKE THE MULE TOO..

John William's Government owes $300 Billion. John thinks the I M F is a new English rock band.

LOOK BUFFY— MORE CREDIT CARD APPLICATIONS

GOOD / THINK WE NEED A NEW GERMAN-TURBO CHARGED GOLD PLATE CAPUCCINO MAKER

HOW SERIOUS IS NATIONAL DEBT? JUST ASK JUAN AND JOHN

Matt Wuerker, Reprinted with permission.

The basic goal of adjustment, and indeed that of many families, is simple enough: increase revenues, reduce expenditures. Third World countries in debt often do not have enough foreign currency to finance even their most basic necessities, and soon suppliers refuse further credit. To remedy this foreign-exchange shortage, the debtor must, in practice, reduce domestic consumption and increase exports.

The most frequently imposed elements of an adjustment programme include devaluation of the currency (to discourage imports and encourage exports); drastic reduction of government expenditure, particularly social spending and elimination of food and other consumption subsidies; privatization of government enterprises and/or increases in prices charged by them (electricity, water, transportation, etc.) and the abolition of price controls; 'demand management' (meaning reduction of consumption) through caps on wages, along with restriction of credit, and higher taxes and interest rates in an effort to reduce inflation.

All this may sound eminently reasonable. Countries cannot live for ever beyond their means, any more than families can. The question remains, however: who is living beyond whose means? It was LDC [less-developed countries] elites, often the military, who were responsible for incurring the heavy debts to begin with. Their development schemes benefited themselves; the majority of their people were left out. We shall shortly see how the indiscriminate application of Fund doctrine intensifies the sufferings of ordinary people.

The Chief Culprit

The IMF knows that it is being singled out as chief culprit for all kinds of social horrors in the Third World. Its defence is to affirm its 'non-political character', indeed its political impotence. The Fund's former managing director, Jacques de Larosière, thus exonerates his institution from any responsibility for social injustice:

> It is often said that Fund programs attack the most disadvantaged segments of the population, but people forget that how the required effort is distributed among the various social groups and among the various public expenditure categories (arms spending or social outlays, productive investment or current operations, direct or indirect taxes) is a question decided by governments. Generally, people refrain from drawing attention to the choices made in this respect, and instead allow the Fund to come under attack and describe its activities as inimical to the least favored segments of the population.
>
> A question that may be raised in this connection is whether the Fund should exert pressure in the determination of government priorities and even make the granting of its assistance contingent on measures that would better protect the most disadvantaged population groups. *An international institution such as the Fund cannot take upon itself the role of dictating social and political objectives to sovereign governments* [my emphasis].

This, politely put, is rubbish. . . . The IMF *could* have an enormous influence on the economic (which is to say, political) choices of its heavily indebted clients if it chose to do so, for the simple reason that money talks. If the Fund believed, which it patently does not, that economic growth can also result from greater social equality, access to education, health care and other basic services, fairer income distribution, etc., it could perfectly well make such objectives part of its programmes. On the contrary, exactly those countries that have most insisted on maintaining social objectives (for example, Tanzania and Jamaica under the People's National Party) have had the greatest difficulties in coming to terms with the IMF. . . .

A Toxic Cocktail

Almost all of South America has been destabilized because of the IMF formula: Tax increases to wring inflation out of the economy and currency devaluation to spur export growth. In small doses, this formula, concocted by Keynesian economists in the 1950s, produced the British disease of the 1960s and the U.S. stagflation of the 1970s. The IMF has been mixing this toxic cocktail for most of Latin America for at least a dozen years.

Jude Wanniski, *The Wall Street Journal*, March 20, 1989.

Those who believe that the Fund is, or ought to be, 'non-political' should also scrutinize its curious and unfailing identity of views with those of its most powerful members, particularly the United States. Some of the countries whose governments contracted the highest debts were/are also the most repressive: Brazil and Argentina under military rule, the Philippines under Ferdinand Marcos, Indonesia, Chile, etc. They are also countries in which the United States takes a keen strategic interest. Was the Fund acting frivolously when it made a sizeable loan to the Somoza regime only weeks before the Sandinista victory in 1979? Or was it gently but firmly encouraged to do so? As the then Treasury Secretary Donald Regan put it, 'The IMF is essentially a non-political institution. . . . But this does not mean that United States' political and security interests are not served by the IMF.' . . .

If the IMF were consistent, it would listen to people like Felix Rohatyn, the highly respected financier who saved New York City from bankruptcy. He notes:

The continuing deficit requires the [US] government to borrow between $180 and $240 billion each year. . . . The situation of the US too closely resembles that of . . . Argentina, Brazil and Mexico between 1975-82.

Rohatyn also warns:

The [US] government's borrowing requirements, a major factor in maintaining interest rates at very high levels, increase the risk to our banking system of large-scale failure by Third World countries to pay their debts. We are purchasing short-term prosperity by starving the rest of the world of badly needed capital and destabilizing the international monetary system. Since we live in a world market whether we like it or not, we cannot continue much longer. . . .

Nor does the Fund appear to recognize that poor countries (and even more the poor people who end up paying the debts) have no power whatever over several important factors affecting their balance of payments. Among these factors are *international inflation*, which boosts the prices of imported manufactures, services, oil and food, *high interest rates* and *weak export prices*. When one asks, as I did at Fund headquarters in Washington, how it is possible to encourage *all* countries at once to pursue policies favouring exports, the reply is that the Fund was created 'to increase world trade', so 'the more goods on the market the better'.

Lost in Never-Never-Land

But who will pay for these goods? The Fund seems mindless in its pushing of the *same* policies on everyone but finds justification in its claim that countries are 'free' to change the composition of their exports. IMF officials cited to me the so-called NICs (newly industrializing countries of Southeast Asia) as good examples of countries 'adapting'. This is wishful thinking on a par with the song in *My Fair Lady*, 'Why can't a woman be more like a man?' IMF economists seem to believe that Latin America and Africa could be more like Taiwan and South Korea if they would just put their minds to it. But where are Latin America and Africa to find enough capital to diversify, especially now that they have to pay back such a huge proportion of their earnings in debt service? And even if they could scrape together the capital, to whom would they then export?

The Fund lives in a never-never-land of perfect competition and perfect trading opportunities, where dwell no monopolies, no transnational corporations with captive markets, no protectionism, no powerful nations getting their own first. . . .

The IMF and Jamaica

To test the efficacy of the IMF prescriptions we will look first at the Jamaican economy as a whole, then at how ordinary Jamaicans are faring. For the first issue I rely heavily on a thorough and scholarly examination provided by Cameron Duncan in his doctoral dissertation in economics for the American University in Washington, DC. As for the welfare of Jamaicans themselves, I've been blessed with excellent first-hand reports. . . .

During the 1970s Jamaica suffered all the shocks common to Third World countries—quadrupling of oil prices, lower demand for its exports, declining investment in a climate of international recession. The very openness of its economy made it especially vulnerable to this sort of buffeting. A major political change further complicated the country's life when the people, sick and tired of corruption, mismanagement and police brutality, elected a democratic socialist (or social democrat, if you prefer) government in 1972. The People's National Party (PNP), headed by Michael

Manley, set out to implement bold policies benefiting the majority—rent control, a minimum wage, improved health services, equal pay for women, free secondary education, a literacy campaign, partial land reform and the like.

To finance these reforms (particularly in the wake of the 1973 oil-price rise) the government tried to gain more control over its own bauxite. It imposed a production tax on the industry and was the leading actor in forming the International Bauxite Association, a producers' organization modelled on OPEC [Organization of Petroleum Exporting Countries]. The transnational aluminum corporations were not amused. They also had more options than did Manley and his PNP. To register disapproval, they simply moved production out of Jamaica and into Australia and Africa. Tourism also fell victim to anti-PNP propaganda. Duncan says, 'Tourist agents reportedly tarnished Jamaica's image as a tourist paradise by advising clients to visit others parts of the Caribbean.'

The IMF in Zambia

The IMF program has been with us for close to 12 years now and we began to see nothing but a contraction of the economy, contracting, contracting. In the end, we were living to pay the IMF, nothing else! And we were not developing, the economy was not expanding, it was contracting. Therefore, it got to the stage where nothing was going to happen, except the death of our economy. I don't think that the IMF itself wanted that. They want us to pay our debts within a year—now this was not possible.

Kenneth Kaunda, *Africa Report*, November/December 1987.

For a time, extra borrowing slowed the vicious downward spiral induced by falling revenues and rising costs. Jamaica's foreign debt rose from $150 million to $813 million between 1971 and 1976. Meanwhile, capital flowed out in torrents as Jamaican businessmen and wealthy families stashed their assets abroad and transnational corporations disinvested and stepped up remittances to their home offices. The PNP was re-elected in 1976 with a huge majority but could no longer stave off the inevitable hard landing. Foreign-currency reserves were zero. On the heels of the electoral victory, the Bank of Jamaica was forced to suspend all foreign-exchange payments. The stage was set for the IMF. . . .

[Duncan writes,] 'It [The Fund] demanded a massive $US300 million expenditure cut in 1980, equivalent to 26 per cent of the previous year's budget. Measures included the layoff of 11,000 public-sector workers.' The Fund also obliged the government to reverse completely its policies of redistribution of wealth, with the predictable (and undoubtedly desired) result that Manley's party lost popular support. The PNP faced huge internal and external pressures; still, the party was not exactly a model of prudent economic management and political acumen.

Duncan's figures show a drop in real incomes of 25 per cent and inflation up by 320 per cent during the PNP's tenure between 1972 and 1980. Helped along by disinvestment and capital flight, joblessness hit a record 31 per cent in 1979, while factories were operating at less than a third of their real capacity. Debt soared to $1.7 billion. It is not altogether surprising that the PNP was crushed in the 1980 elections by Edward Seaga's rightist Jamaica Labour Party. . . .

As is customary in countries undergoing adjustment, Jamaicans have been bedevilled by price increases, cancelled subsidies, job losses and other measures that squeeze poor people. On 14 January 1985 the government announced a 20 per cent increase in prices for gasoline, diesel fuel, kerosene and cooking gas. This meant higher prices for public as well as private transportation, plus an unbearable tax on the poor's only source of energy. A cartoon shows a dilapidated shack at night, with a darkened window. Issuing from the window: 'Hey, mama, we can't see the food.' Mama replies, 'Take your choice. Raw food with the light on or cooked food in the dark.' . . .

Erna and Her Children

Oxfam employee Belinda Coote introduces us to some women who are trying to survive. One is Erna. She is lucky, in a sense, because she has a job and one-room lodgings which she shares with her two children. Coote met her on the makeshift barricade she and her neighbours built on their street the day of the 'kerosene riots'. Erna told her, 'I've never been a member of any political party and probably never will be, but this government is too much. We've had enough.'

'Enough' means that her electricity has been cut off for a year. When it quadrupled in price, she could no longer pay the bill. She works as a cleaner in a Kingston hospital, but she's afraid of losing her job since the government announced plans to cut a further 1,500 workers from the public-health-sector payroll. 'If somebody leaves, they don't get replaced these days, and yet we are already overworked. The hospital is dirty, crowded and short of basic items such as cleaning materials. I'm just waiting for them to say, "Erna, we don't need you any more," and then I don't know what I'll do.'

Understandably, Erna already has trouble making ends meet on her salary of $US9 a week. She well remembers when rice cost two and a half times less than it does today—yet her wages have not gone up at all. Having some chicken necks or salt fish to put in the rice is a dim memory. Erna worries about the effects of a poor diet on her children. Since she cooks on a kerosene stove, she will now have to cook less, or eat less, in order to afford kerosene.

Erna is rich compared with Sandra, who has two children aged 6 years and 7 months. The father of her children had a job, and they were happy for the first few years; 'then he lost his job and we had to make do on my earnings. I used to sell fish and bammy [cassava cake] in the market, but the fish got too expensive and no one could afford to buy it, so I had to give that up. We had nothing then, but a boy to support and another on the way. It was too much for him. He left and I haven't heard from him since.' Now Sandra keeps herself and her children alive by begging. 'When I have to go out to get food, I leave the baby with the boy. I have to keep him off school, but what else can I do? Sometimes I send him out to find scraps on the street with the other kids. It's the only way.' . . .

Sheer Stupidity

The sheer stupidity of IMF-imposed measures ought to be obvious, and doubtless is, to anyone except the blinkered economists who make up the Fund's staff and draw up its adjustment programmes. No mosquito control today will mean malaria tomorrow. Missed vaccinations will translate into epidemics. Dead mothers, birth-damaged, malnourished babies and unschooled children will necessarily weigh heavily upon the community at large tomorrow. People simply do not produce efficiently when they are faint with hunger. The IMF cannot seem to understand that investing in the kind of healthy, well-fed, literate population that Jamaica once had is the most intelligent economic choice a country can make. For the Fund it's creditors first, and Jamaica owes $3.2 billion. . . .

The tragic irony is that all the hunger, misery and deaths *will not even help the country to pay back its debts*—ostensibly the reason why so many sacrifices are being demanded. Without high, guaranteed prices on world markets for bauxite and sugar, the country's major exports, and an unending flow of rich tourists, Jamaica doesn't stand a chance. Neither, alas, do Jamaicans.

"Adjustment is a pragmatic necessity."

IMF Policies Reduce Third World Debt

Jahangir Amuzegar

Jahangir Amuzegar is an international consultant who was formerly the executive director of the International Monetary Fund. In the following viewpoint, he argues that the IMF is unfairly criticized. The IMF's adjustment programs increase economic growth, he argues. By encouraging non-inflationary growth, the IMF helps the Third World pay its debts.

As you read, consider the following questions:

1. What policies does the IMF recommend to reduce debt, according to the author?
2. How does Amuzegar respond to critics who contend that the Fund's prescriptions to ease debt are always the same?
3. Why does Amuzegar disagree with people who argue that IMF austerity programs incite riots in Third World countries?

Jahangir Amuzegar, "The IMF Under Fire." Reprinted with permission from FOREIGN POLICY 64 (Fall 1986). Copyright 1986 by the Carnegie Endowment for International Peace.

The global economic challenges of the 1980s—the colossal debt overhang, wild swings in exchange rates, and continued imbalances in external payments—have presented the International Monetary Fund (IMF) with the immense task of devising orderly and effective solutions. And they have focused unprecedented attention on the organization. Thrown suddenly and inadvertently into the epicenter of the world economic crises after the 1973-1974 oil price shocks, the IMF has gradually, and erroneously, come to be seen as the world's master economic trouble-shooter. A limited-purpose organization, conceived in 1944 to deal with 1930s-style exchange and payments problems, the Fund has recently been pushed by circumstances into becoming a superagency in charge of the global debt and development problems of the 1970s and 1980s—tasks for which it has neither adequate expertise nor sufficient resources.

The IMF still enjoys the support and respect of many multinational economic organizations, bankers, business leaders, government officials, and academics in both industrialized and developing countries. But misconceptions and unrealistic expectations have prompted harsh and often distorted criticisms from other quarters, especially the media.

The IMF's Critics

Initially confined to some left-leaning fringe elements in the Third World, recent attacks on the Fund have been echoed by a curious coalition—including some U.N. agencies—that defies both North-South and Left-Right divides.

Critics from the less developed countries (LDCs) and their supporters paint the IMF as a highly rigid, single-minded, biased institution dominated by a cabal of industrial countries. These critics accuse the Fund of following a narrow, free-market approach to external imbalances and contend that the Fund shows little or no concern that its adjustment policies often cripple economic growth and further skew income distribution in Third World countries. They also think that the IMF is cruelly indifferent to the social and political consequences of its stabilization programs.

Fund detractors in industrialized countries criticize the IMF for being insufficiently market-oriented; for helping noncapitalist and anti-Western countries; and for progressively evolving into a softheaded foreign-aid agency. . . .

The Fund's argument is that, within the Bretton Woods framework for postwar stability and development, its global task has been to serve as a monetary and financial agency, dealing with short-term gaps in external payments, exchange fluctuations, and capital flows. Its added responsibility for economic expansion and larger productive capacity in the Third World, the IMF emphasizes, must be achieved by encouraging balanced growth in international trade and by evening out short-term capital movements, not by dispensing aid. Economic stabilization under the IMF's standard "monetarist" model sees short-term external balance as a precondition for long-term growth. But many liberal critics insist that IMF programs must speed up economic growth and thereby achieve a viable balance of payments by stimulating supply instead of reducing demand. They believe that growth is a condition for adjustment. According to these critics, the Fund's model subverts LDCs' development strategy in many ways. Essentially, they claim that the IMF view blames inflation on excess aggregate demand while the real culprits are structural bottlenecks in the agricultural, foreign trade, and public sectors; supply shortages due to unused capacity; and other nonmonetary problems common in developing countries. Thus combating inflation and external imbalances by choking off demand—by devaluing currency, reducing credit subsidies and imports, and raising taxes—results in depressing the economy instead. Economic stability requires removing supply bottlenecks by reallocating investment, cutting taxes, and somehow restraining prices and wages.

Debtor Policies

The failure of growth and investment to recover adequately in most countries with debt-servicing difficulties suggests that these countries need to intensify their efforts to raise domestic saving, encourage investment, promote efficiency, control inflation, and encourage the repatriation of flight capital. For their part, creditors need to ensure that determined reform efforts are met with appropriate and timely financial support.

Communique of the Interim Committee of the Board of Governors of the International Monetary Fund, April 4, 1989.

But the record of the IMF shows that as the nature and causes of the initial problems differ widely in different countries, so do the Fund's policy recommendations. A 1986 Fund staff study, *Fund-Supported Adjustment Programs and Economic Growth*, by Mohsin S. Kahn and Malcolm D. Knight, reiterates that Fund-supported adjustment programs comprise three distinct features: demand-side policies aimed at cooling an overheated economy, supply-side measures designed to expand domestic output, and exchange-rate incentives to improve a country's external competitiveness. For example, IMF programs in Gabon, Panama, Peru, and South Korea during the late 1970s and early 1980s did emphasize demand restraint. But similar programs in Burma and Sri Lanka encouraged an increase in the rate of public investment and the liberalization of imports. In Gabon, Panama, Peru, South

Korea, and Sri Lanka, the objective was to increase supply by using excess capacity, improving external competitiveness, or boosting private or public investment. . . .

A review of some 94 Fund-supported programs in 64 countries during the 1980-1984 period, prepared by Charles A. Sisson and published in the March 1986 issue of *Finance and Development*, shows a distinct variety of approaches to the adjustment problem and a wide range of policy measures. Although nearly all programs contained limits on credit expansion and government current expenditures, only 55 per cent included measures related to currency values and external trade liberalization; 41 per cent required a cap on or reduction in consumer subsidies; and a mere 28 per cent dealt with budgetary transfers to nonfinancial public enterprises. Even some of the Fund's more knowledgeable critics, such as the economist Graham Bird, clearly admit that "it is far too simplistic and inaccurate to claim that the Fund is a doctrinaire monetarist institution."

The Fund and Causes of Debt

Critics who concede that the Fund's primary objective is restoring short-term external balance still assail its approach to adjustment. They maintain that the Fund perceives LDC balance-of-payments deficits, foreign-exchange shortages, budgetary gaps, supply crunches, declining rates of productivity, inflation, and black markets to be largely of domestic origin—the result of economic mismanagement, overspending, exorbitant social welfare programs, and price controls. Domestic inflation and balance-of-payments deficits, in turn, are allegedly traced by the Fund to excessive consumption, insufficient investment, excessive import levels reflecting increased aggregate demand and caused by large budget gaps and loose credit, and anemic export earnings due to domestic inflation and overvalued currencies.

These critics maintain that LDC external imbalances are in fact frequently caused by a host of other external factors beyond LDC control that have nothing to do with domestic waste or inflation: oil prices, artificially stimulated rapid growth through easy credit, worldwide inflation, declining demand for commodities, deteriorating terms of trade and protectionism, rising real rates of interest on foreign debt, and poor harvests. The Fund is thus blamed for believing that deficits—no matter how they are caused—call for adjustment, and that adjustment must focus on the deficits, whether temporary or persistent. . . .

The Fund's critics are right in claiming that it always insists on adjustment regardless of the nature or origin of the external balance. But the Fund also has an equally valid position in arguing that the need for adjustment is a pragmatic necessity, not the reflection of any dogma. In the March 1986 issue of *Finance and Development*, IMF Managing Director Jacques de Larosière

233

observes that countries with soaring inflation, enormous fiscal deficits, huge and wasteful public sectors, money-losing public enterprises, distorted exchange rates, and low interest rates are unlikely to mobilize domestic savings or attract foreign investment, and are bound to crowd out domestic resources in a way that will hurt growth. Without adjustment, writes Fund staff member Wanda Tseng, external and internal imbalances eventually will deplete the country's international reserves, erode its international creditworthiness, dry up access to foreign funds, and result in the stoppage of needed imports.

Adjustment and the Poor

While the poorest have in some cases been the hardest hit by adjustment, there is little reason to think that this is inevitable. For example, devaluation of the currency and removal of food subsidies may be conducted in such a way that the poorest benefit by increases in the prices of what they sell, at the expense of relatively wealthy urban consumers of food and imports. Reorganizing government-run industries may provide an opportunity to increase employment of the poor, improve their access to basic services, and increase their wealth by promoting their ownership of the privatized industry.

Kurt Schaefer, *Eternity*, June 1988.

With regard to the origin of external deficits, Fund critics seem bent on constructing a general thesis out of isolated cases. Some, but not all, balance-of-payments gaps are clearly caused by factors outside a country's control. In the case of Jamaica, for example, even one of the Fund's most astute critics admits that during the 1972-1980 period domestic policies and structural factors were the prime culprits behind the excess demand and the worsening payments position. Nor was imported inflation found to be a "major cause" of the island's deteriorating economy. In general, the authorities declined to adopt unpopular adjustment measures necessitated by their own profligate fiscal and monetary policies. Another IMF critic attributed Indonesia's 1965-1966 crisis mainly to hyperinflation between 1962 and 1966 resulting from government deficit financing. Even in Kenya between 1974 and 1982, where major external factors—mainly the two oil shocks—were at work, domestic monetary forces and the mismanagement of the coffee and tea boom had to bear their share of responsibility. . . .

A much stronger and more vituperative attack is aimed at the Fund's conditions for making its resources available. . . .

Fund-prescribed microeconomic remedies are considered by the critics particularly ill-conceived, if not downright harmful. Devaluation is regarded as inherently regressive because it raises the costs of essential imports, leaves untouched exports subject to extremely low supply elasticities, and adds to domestic inflation. Higher interest rates are judged irrelevant in the context of Third World economies because so much credit goes to the public sector, because private savers are usually few and insignificant, and because capital flight has little to do with interest-rate differentials. Reduced real wages, lower subsidies for the poor, and cutbacks on other social welfare programs are regarded as the nemeses of sociopolitical stability. Credit restrictions are thought to reduce employment rather than inflation.

The IMF responds by arguing that conditions are neither rigid nor inflexible and that they are designed jointly with the member country. IMF conditions are applied flexibly as well, with varying socioeconomic circumstances taken into account. The periodic review of Fund programs confirms the agency's interest in ensuring sufficient flexibility. Further, the IMF's approach to balance of payments does not work only through demand deflation and real-income reduction. The relationship between monetary factors and external imbalances is important, but the IMF approach embraces all aspects of economic policies, bearing on both demand and supply conditions. Finally, although restoring the external balance is admittedly a Fund objective, it is not the sole purpose of adjustment. The IMF believes that adjustment ultimately encourages high employment and long-term growth by balancing aggregate demand and supply better.

Fund programs are also often blamed for their allegedly high social and economic costs. The critics argue that, despite its best efforts, the IMF can hardly avoid politics. National strikes, riots, political upheavals, and social unrest in Argentina, Bolivia, Brazil, the Dominican Republic, Ecuador, Egypt, Haiti, Liberia, Peru, Sudan, and elsewhere have been attributed directly or indirectly to the implementation of austerity measures advocated by the IMF. . . .

Critics frequently argue that the heaviest and most immediate burdens of adjustment are likely to be passed by the upper and middle classes to the poor. The Fund's alleged insistence on reducing or eliminating food and other consumer subsidies is further attacked on the ground that these policies are in fact a rational means of internal income redistribution in countries lacking an effectively progressive tax system or adequate social security schemes.

Political Unrest

Fund supporters argue that blaming the IMF for fomenting political unrest merely confuses cause and effect. Many countries do not come to the IMF until the seeds of political turmoil are firmly rooted in their soil. Indeed, economics-related civil disturbances are hardly unknown in countries without Fund programs—witness Iran, Nigeria, South Africa, and Tunisia. And scores of countries adjusting with the IMF's assistance have been remarkably stable. Of the 67 countries that carried a stabilization program at some period between 1980 and 1983, critics can single out only the 10 mentioned previously as having experienced serious turmoil—not all of it Fund-related. Nevertheless, the unrest that can be blamed on the IMF must be considered a minus for adjustment policies. . . .

A Lack of Evidence

The critics' ardent contention that the cost of adjustment is always borne disproportionately by the poor has seldom been supported by any statistical evidence. Rather, there is usually an a priori presumption that Fund programs aggravate income inequities because the rich and the strong see to it that they avoid the effects of the stabilization measures. The arguments have been at best theoretical, and usually anecdotal. The countless books, articles, speeches, and statements critical of the Fund contain not a single piece of empirical information or statistical data showing that Fund-supported programs have, in a clear and convincing manner, aggravated internal income-distribution patterns.

Moreover, the impact of IMF programs on income distribution essentially depends on how the program is implemented by national authorities. In the Fund's view, any other approach would entangle the IMF directly in microeconomic policy measures closely related to a country's social and political choices. Such involvement probably would be vehemently resisted by most countries, and would also violate the Fund's own mandate and guidelines.

Market-Based Initiatives

The International Monetary Fund and the World Bank, in the exercise of their catalytic roles, must continue to support market-based initiatives involving debtors and creditors that are aimed at transferring the advantages of market reductions of debt to the debtor countries.

Communique of the Group of Twenty-Four on International Monetary Affairs, April 2, 1989.

In addition, the Fund believes that changes in income distribution as such cannot be performance criteria in adjustment programs because this area is so difficult to quantify. The numbers can be affected by methods of classifying income recipients. Further, few programs last long enough to allow a comprehensive study of their distributional implications, particularly where necessary information on consumption, government transfers, nonmonetary sources of income, and personal income levels is inadequate or unreliable—as is generally the case in developing countries. Finally, the Fund maintains that any given domestic distributional system is the product of deep-rooted economic, social, political, and cultural phenomena going back decades, if not centuries. Fund programs, being of relatively limited scope and duration, cannot be expected to make much of a dent in the system.

In the absence of clear-cut evidence and good data, theoretical arguments do assume importance. In the short run, stabilization programs can worsen income distribution. But the story scarcely ends there. The distributional outcome of a cut in government outlays, for example, depends on where the specific reductions are made. A reduction of food subsidies to urban workers could help the rural poor by raising farm prices. A tax on urban services and amenities could likewise redistribute income from workers in modern industries—a minority in the labor force—to the rural poor. Moreover, a reduction in inflation itself tends to favor poorer groups because they can rarely adjust their incomes to rising prices.

The Fund and the Poor

An IMF study, *Fund-Supported Programs, Fiscal Policy, and Income Distribution*, concludes, after presenting some case studies, that Fund programs have not been directed against the poor; often, in fact, policies have been designed to protect low-income groups as much as possible. Even when total consumption has been reduced through prudent demand-management policies, high-income groups probably have been hit hardest. The elimination of large general subsidy programs has inflicted some hardships on the population as a whole, including the poor. But the study calls such programs "inefficient and ineffective" mechanisms for redistributing incomes.

"The debt crisis has temporarily opened a 'window of opportunity' for some conservation measures."

Debt-for-Nature Swaps Are Beneficial

John Cartwright

Concern about the destruction of rainforests in Third World countries has led to a new conservation tactic called debt swapping. In a debt swap, the bank that owns the debt lessens the amount that is owed. An environmental or development group buys the discounted debt, and then negotiates an agreement with the indebted Third World government. The government agrees to set aside land for conservation. The author of the following viewpoint, John Cartwright, believes these debt-for-nature swaps can reduce the seriousness of two major problems facing the Third World: environmental destruction and rising debt. Cartwright is a political science professor at the University of Western Ontario in Canada.

As you read, consider the following questions:

1. How do Third World countries benefit from protecting their environments, according to Cartwright?
2. Why does the author disagree with the argument that the Third World must exploit its resources to industrialize and develop?
3. How does the author respond to those who criticize participation in debt-for-nature swaps?

John Cartwright, "Conserving Nature, Decreasing Debt," *Third World Quarterly*, Volume 10 (4), 1988. Reprinted with permission.

Two crises haunt the Third World today: the debt burden and environmental degradation. The debts arising from the borrowing which took place in the 1970s in order to produce economic growth, and which failed to cover its costs have brought to Third World countries a legacy of run-down infrastructure and reduced social services, a situation compounded by the insistence of Western lenders that they curtail expenses still further in order to keep paying. At the same time, and in part because of these pressures, many Third World countries are rapidly running down their stock of natural resources—forests, fisheries, minerals and grazing lands—with the result that they suffer frequent droughts and floods, erosion, landslides and other 'natural' disasters, and face the loss of a patrimony which could provide their future generations indefinitely with a comfortable and secure means of living.

While there are no simple or easy solutions to either of these crises, the industrialised countries are beginning to realise that Third World environmental degradation will adversely affect their own long-term well-being, and that they should therefore be contributing to Third World environmental protection or restoration out of self-interest. Herein lies an opportunity for the Third World to achieve a measure of debt relief, while protecting key natural ecosystems and moving towards more environmentally sustainable modes of economic activity. This article will focus on one widely discussed approach: the reduction of debts owed to Western lenders in exchange for the conservation of natural ecosystems. . . .

Benefits to the Third World

There are several good reasons why the protection of ecosystems would be more beneficial to Third World countries than their destruction. First, the non-economic benefits of conservation are significant to many indigenous peoples, who find sacred or spiritual qualities in their natural surroundings. Although these people generally hold only marginal political power within their states, their desire to conserve these areas will continue to gain more and more support, even if for more aesthetic and recreational reasons, from an increasingly numerous and prosperous urban middle class, as one can already see happening in such newly-industrialising countries as Malaysia. Nigel Collar has argued persuasively that to wipe out these ecosystems and the species in them is to curtail the freedom of individuals, by denying them the opportunity to enjoy the existence of such species in the future; and on a more materialistic level, a loss of ecosystems cuts down future options for all human activities, economic as well as social.

Second, while volcanic and floodplain soils are capable of sustaining agriculture for centuries, the majority of tropical soils are not. Most forest clearing in Amazonia and in Africa can provide only a few years of cleared-land farming before the farmers are forced to move on. Sustainable farming in single locations involves getting farmers to adopt often labour-intensive methods, such as the 'matengo pit' system of alternating pits to catch water and heaped-up soil in order to grow plants on dry hillsides, or the 'chinampas' system of agroforestry in tropical moist forests, whose benefits may not be apparent until there is no new land to clear.

Finally, the economic argument that exploiting one's natural resources to the full will provide the wealth to finance more technological development depends on some rather shaky assumptions. First, it assumes that somewhere there are the raw materials available to support this industrialisation, and in particular, adequate food supplies that a country can import. Second, it assumes either that the country will be able to sell its industrial products on world markets, or else that it has a big enough domestic market to absorb the increasing range of products from its industrialisation. Third, it assumes that the money it can get from its present exploitation of natural resources is in fact sufficient to finance this industrialisation. . . .

Reducing Two Problems

Debt-for-nature swaps and other innovative financial tools should be encouraged. The sum of Latin America's external debt plus "blocked funds"—money belonging to multinational corporations being held in foreign countries in local currencies—probably approaches $500 billion. Obviously, not all of this money can be used for conservation. But the more that can be swapped for land or local currency to underwrite better land management, the more the twin problems of Latin debt and environmental degradation will be reduced.

Spencer B. Beebe and Peter W. Stroh, *The New York Times,* July 28, 1987.

The debt crisis has temporarily opened a 'window of opportunity' for some conservation measures. While such measures can only make a small dent in the total debt problem (even I. Rubinoff's grand scheme of compensation for a world-wide system of tropical forest reserves involved only some $3 billion a year, less than one-fiftieth of the total annual debt service bill), they do offer a mutually face-saving compromise on the debt issue, while providing a substantial benefit in terms of conservation. Some purists will object that since the debts themselves were illegitimately foisted on the Third World, any action which legitimates them ought to be repudiated (just as hard-liners among the banking fraternity dismiss any action which appears to 'forgive' debtors), but it seems to me unrealistic to expect that creditor governments and private institutions will ever accept a total repudiation of these debts, and thus it would be sensible to seek a myriad of modest actions that could be undertaken relatively quickly, and that could contribute to an overall reduction of the debt burden.

Among conservation non-governmental organisations (NGOs) in the West, 'debt-for-conservation' swaps have attracted wide attention. The sale by creditor banks of debts at a discount in the secondary market has allowed Western conservation NGOs to buy up some of the debts, and then arrange to write off the debt in exchange for the debtor country putting some local currency (and effort) into conservation. Three widely publicised agreements were reached in 1987. In Bolivia, the government had created the Beni Biological Reserve of 134,000 hectares in 1982, but lacked the funds to develop and safeguard it effectively. Seeking the resources to make the reserve effective, a US foundation, Conservation International, in 1987 acquired a Bolivian debt of $650,000, discounted to $100,000, from a Swiss bank. Conservation International then cancelled the $650,000 debt, and in exchange the Bolivian government set up a zone of 1.4 million hectares around the reserve and a $250,000 endowment, to be managed by a Bolivian foundation, and asked Conservation International to advise on the management of the reserve for the next five years. Steps are under way to draw up a management plan which will involve the local people in the buffer zone around the reserve. In Costa Rica and Ecuador somewhat different arrangements were made with World Wildlife Fund-US and the Nature Conservancy. These NGOs acquired debts at a heavy discount, and cancelled them in return for long-term local currency bonds issued by the governments concerned, in order to finance conservation activities. In each of these cases, the specific scheme arose out of a broad commitment by the national government to protect the area concerned, and the implementation arrangements are under the control of a locally based foundation: this has so far succeeded in deflecting the charge that foreigners are forcing the country to do what they want. Other similar arrangements are under negotiation, aided by a US Internal Revenue Service ruling which allows US banks to claim as a tax deduction the value given by the debtor country in its own currency to the conservation NGO for the debt instrument, even though it had sold the instrument to the NGO for a good deal less.

No Foreign Domination

Limited in scope though they are, these arrangements have enabled governments to protect critical areas to which they might not otherwise have been able to allocate resources. The fact that such areas have been operated through national conservation foundations and have been fitted within the context of overall government conservation objectives has reduced the perception that foreigners are dictating the government's priorities. Unlike debt-for-equity swaps, they do not give ownership of a country's resources to a foreign entity. However, it remains to be seen whether such schemes could be worked in a situation where powerful business interests or other government departments have different goals, such as, for example, Peru's Manu Park or parts of Sumatra or Irian Jaya in Indonesia. It is also cause for concern that so far the emphasis has been on the immediate task of setting aside and protecting specific areas; yet if these areas are to avoid biological isolation and continual encroachment, the people living around them must be provided with access to alternative land, fuelwood and other resources. This could be achieved through some kind of sustainable agroforestry on lands already altered by human activity, but would be both costly and time-consuming. . . .

Environmental Protection Is Essential

Debt-for-nature swaps will not be the primary answer to the Third World debt problem. Debtor nations don't like any sort of debt-equity swaps, which they see as a giveaway of real national wealth. But it's time for Brazil, the World Bank and rich industrialized nations to wake up to this reality: In the Third or First World, it's no longer a matter of economic development versus environmental protection. We can't have one without the other.

Hobart Rowen, *The Washington Post National Weekly Edition*, April 10/16, 1989.

Despite these cautions, Third World countries concerned about their long-term self-interest would do well to examine such arrangements with institutions from the North, both private NGOs and also government agencies. The value of biological reserves—particularly tropical rainforests—can only increase as our need for, and our ability to use, genetic materials grows. There is a sharpening awareness, among the public and even among politicians in the West, of the importance of these genetic reservoirs as well as of the potential climatic impact resulting from the destruction of tropical forests. Such awareness gives Third World states an opportunity to obtain wealth from these areas without necessarily cutting them down and selling them to the industrialised states. Provided that they also bargain for the financing to establish alternative ways of living on the land for their people, Third World states *can* have their forests and live off them too, for a price a good deal lower than they will have to pay once they have exhausted them by present methods of exploitation.

It can be objected that debt swaps of any sort tacitly grant the legitimacy of the Third World's debts, and therefore should be totally shunned. I suggested above that such a view is unrealistic, and in any case, even if there were some eventual possibility of achieving a full repudiation of these debts, the threat to natural ecosystems is severe enough that action needs to be taken even at the cost of principles. (I could draw a parallel here to the readiness of African front-line states to buy food from South Africa when faced with famine.)

Improving the Environment and the Economy

Many people in both the North and the South now recognise that the contribution of tropical ecosystems to the welfare of mankind is so great that everyone ought to contribute to their survival. With sufficient prodding from their own NGOs, Third World governments can press for financial support, in order to help them to protect major ecosystems from further damage; and they can certainly expect support in this demand from Northern NGOs. Since most states can be moved to act when their own well-being is threatened, the present situation provides a promising opportunity for Third World governments to seek an improvement on both their environmental and economic front.

"Debt swapping should not be regarded as an acceptable response to the debt problem."

Debt-for-Nature Swaps Are Harmful

Carol Barton

In the following viewpoint, Carol Barton opposes schemes to reduce debt by requiring Third World governments to adopt conservation measures. According to Barton, these debt swaps deny Third World governments a voice in how their land will be developed. She believes the Third World should not be required to make payments on unjust debts and argues that the moral solution to the debt crisis is to forgive the debts. A former Methodist missionary in Peru, Barton is a member of the Debt Crisis Network, an activist organization that is a forum for discussion and action on global debt.

As you read, consider the following questions:

1. Why does the author argue that debt-for-nature swaps benefit banks?
2. How does debt swapping infringe on Third World sovereignty, in Barton's opinion?
3. What policies does Barton believe activist organizations should advocate?

Carol Barton, "Debt Swaps: New Game in Town," *Christianity and Crisis*, March 7, 1988. Reprinted with permission. Copyright 1988, Christianity and Crisis, 537 West 121st Street, New York, NY 10027.

Imagine a response to the Third World debt crisis where everybody wins. Imagine a deal where the banks, private investors, and Third World governments all have something to gain, or a deal where U.S. churches and private voluntary organizations can multiply their funds for Third World development and at the same time help to erase some of the burdensome Third World debt.

Sounds like a great idea, right? Yet when this idea, called a "debt swap," is actively promoted by the biggest U.S. private banks, when the U.S. government rushes to change banking regulations to allow banks involved in swaps to take big tax writes-offs, when the *Wall Street Journal* and *Business Week* praise particular swap arrangements, and when many grassroots voices in the Third World question its implications, we need to take a second look. The issue is critical for U.S. churches and organizations concerned about the impact of debt, and about just development in the less-developed world—"the South," in terms of a North/South world-view. Already a number of mission agencies have been approached about getting involved in swaps. In responding, our churches are faced with major moral, ethical, and political decisions.

A Moral Issue

Nations of the South now owe Northern banks, governments, and multilateral agencies over $1 trillion. Private banks are owed about $350 billion. The debt, which has mushroomed due to factors beyond the control of Third World governments (high interest rates, low prices for raw materials, high costs of imported goods), cannot be paid. What little is paid is being squeezed out of the poorest sectors of society through inflation, cuts in services and unemployment. For churches in both the North and South, the debt has become a moral issue as well: A debt that is unjustly contracted, that takes the lives of the poor to reward the rich, that guarantees a net flow of "aid" from the South to the North, and that denies dignity and life for God's people, is a sin.

Private banks have begun to acknowledge that most of their Third World loans will never be repaid, and have sought ways to recoup a portion of their bad loans. Enter debt-for-equity swaps. The idea is to sell this bad debt at a tremendous discount to a third party—usually a transnational corporation (TNC) interested in investing in Latin America. The TNC, now the new creditor, accepts repayment of the debt in local currency instead of costly dollars. The TNC then uses the local currency to purchase or expand operations in a country, while the bank and the debtor nation write the corresponding amount of dollar debt off their books. . . .

However, the swaps do not cancel any debt; they merely transfer ownership. The debtor nation still has to pay. What's more, loan debt is exchanged for equity debt—that is, ownership of assets that will continue to provide profits for foreign investors long after this "debt crisis" is settled. A flow of interest payments to the North is replaced by a flow of profits.

Repo Man

What we have here is a classic case of the "repo man." Just as banks repossess the car when payments are overdue, U.S. banks and TNCs are appropriating pieces of Third World nations. These swaps simply guarantee new forms of domination, while getting private banks off the hook. For church people concerned about justice, it is relatively easy to critique such operations. But alternate "debt-for-development" or "debt-for-nature" swaps seem to some to hold the potential for constructive change. Unfortunately, this isn't the case.

A Delicate Matter

The Treasury's debt-for-development idea was in part inspired by recent debt-for-nature swaps. In these arrangements U.S. environmental organizations purchase heavily discounted debt in exchange for a commitment by a developing country to set aside lands for parks. . . .

From a Third World country's point of view, however, the matter is highly delicate. As one official put it, "How would you like it if the Japanese used your trade deficit to buy the Grand Canyon?"

U.S. development groups should ponder deeply how much they want to exploit Third World financial weakness, and how badly they want to strike business deals with the governments and banks that they generally blame for the debt crisis.

Patti Petesch and Sheldon Annis, *Los Angeles Times*, December 9, 1987.

Some development agencies are considering swaps as a way to help debtor nations retire debt and "develop" at the same time. In this version, a nonprofit group would buy discounted debt at perhaps 15 percent of full value, sell it to the Third World government in local currency at perhaps 50 percent or more of its full value, and use the additional money for local aid or development projects they administer. The Christian Children's Fund is already involved in swaps at the rate of $1 million per month (since May 1987) in Brazil, and $500,000 per month in the Philippines. They see this as a way to multiply their resources to aid those most hurt by the debt—children.

Environmentalists' Involvement

Debt-for-nature swaps attract environmental groups. Their concern is that the "development model" pushed by the World Bank and International Monetary Fund on debtor nations in order to service debts is one that is destroying natural resources. This model encourages agricultural and industrial exports with little regard for the devastation of vital rain forests and other resources. Some environmentalists hope to use debt-for-nature swaps to lessen the debt burden and to create nature reserves in Third World countries. They are buying discounted debt and offering to cancel it completely if the debtor agrees to set aside nature preserves.

In Bolivia, Conservation International bought $650,000 worth of debt for only $100,000 (15 cents on the dollar), and agreed to cancel the debt when Bolivia established a buffer zone around the Beni rain-forest reserve and set aside $250,000 in local currency for its maintenance. However, the buffer zone is not a wilderness preserve, as it has been presented in the U.S. press, but an area where cattle production (for export) and lumbering are being promoted—part of the very export-oriented development model that many environmentalists reject. The $250,000 in local currency supplied by the government of Bolivia, moreover, represents a large part of the budget for its national park system. Thus an outside agency set the priority for Bolivian budget allocation, rather than the Bolivian government or people—to say nothing of the 500 indigenous people who live on reserve lands and never were consulted by any party to the swap. The U.S. Agency for International Development (AID), actively promoting export-led development, participated in the Bolivia deal and is courting private voluntary organizations (PVOs) to do similar swaps.

Footing the Bill

While nonprofit debt swaps seem to offer some real benefits, they pose serious problems. First and foremost, participation in debt swaps means participation in the inequitable system that created the debt crisis—one where Western banks and governments control the resources and set the terms, where nations of the South cannot get fair prices for their goods, and where Third World elites are rewarded by the North for pillaging their countries and repressing their people. Swap arrangements avoid the question of how the debt was originally contracted and the "rules of the game" by which it has escalated. It assumes that the debt is legitimate, that debtor nations are responsible, and that they must find a way to repay.

In a January, 1988 Conference of North/South nongovernmental organizations (NGOs) in Lima, Peru to discuss common action on the debt, labor leaders and grassroots representatives stated clearly that the debt has already been repaid many times, and should no longer be serviced. The payment of record high interest rates, capital flight, undervalued Third World exports, and repatriation of profits add up to a net flow of money from South to North that is larger than the Marshall Plan, in real terms. While we imagine that we are sending development aid southward, the reality is the reverse. Participation in debt swaps legitimizes the "rules of the game" and the unjust debt itself.

Dan Wasserman. © 1986, Boston Globe. Reprinted by permission of LATS.

It is important to note the precise moment that banks and the U.S. government have chosen to court development groups to get involved in swaps. Private banks and even the U.S. Treasury have been forced to acknowledge that the Third World debt will not be fully repaid. In December 1987, First Boston and Riggs Bank wrote off major portions of their Third World debt (while continuing to charge debtors for the full amount!), and the U.S. Treasury backed a deal with Mexico admitting the debt is worth only half its face value. Thus they have stepped up the search for mechanisms to recoup some of their losses while maintaining control over Third World economies. . . .

There is another key element to understand about the timing. U.S. churches and development organizations—many of them involved in the Debt Crisis Network—have emerged as an important moral voice challenging the practices of the powerful actors in the debt crisis. . . .

As the impact of this movement begins to be felt, these very organizations are approached by the banks about getting involved in swaps. According to Jesuit priest and economist Xabier Gorostiaga of the Nicaraguan think-tank CRIES, addressing the Lima N/S NGO meeting, debt swaps mean the cooptation of NGOs. "What is the logic behind this?" asked Gorostiaga. "That of the banks' internal crisis. They hope to clean up their portfolios, reduce their taxes, and clean up their image—they want to legitimize their activities by working with the NGOs who now challenge them. We need to explore the new mechanisms of cooptation that are emerging, and understand how they work."

While we may see *some* debt swaps as beneficial, because they go to assist real grassroots development projects in the South, NGOs' very participation undermines the potential for broader changes by justifying the debt through the swap process. Legitimizing the mechanism, it opens the door for the more insidious debt-equity swaps that may undermine our own efforts. It might even open the door for swaps by Moonies or right-wing fundamentalist groups to expand their work. Once we buy in, it cuts both ways. It also silences the prophetic voice of churches and other organizations in both North and South who speak out on the debt crisis. When groups are involved in such deals with the banks, they lose the moral authority to speak out against the debt upon which the deals are based.

The swaps beg the question of sovereignty as well. While we may be outraged at the idea of U.S. banks repossessing parts of another country, why should Northern NGOs be deciding on appropriate development paths for the South instead of the local people themselves? Be it TNCs or church agencies, debt swaps enable outsiders to set the agenda and decide how resources will be spent and who will spend them. . . .

Through debt-for-development swaps, *less* development aid is flowing from North to South—instead, Third World governments are being asked to cough up their own resources for development projects defined by outsiders.

The Real Issue

Debt swapping should not be regarded as an acceptable response to the debt problem. Our involvement in debt swaps compromises our efforts and diverts our attention from the real issue—the need for a just solution to the debt crisis that does not place the burden on the poor, and for new international arrangements in finance and trade that benefit the nations of the South and allow them to define their own development. Rather than putting our money and our energy into debt swaps we need to be working in the U.S. to create a political space for Third World nations to define their *own* future without U.S. economic or military intervention.

Understanding Words in Context

Readers occasionally come across words which they do not recognize. And frequently, because they do not know a word or words, they will not fully understand the passage being read. Obviously, the reader can look up an unfamiliar word in a dictionary. However, by carefully examining the word in the context in which it is used, the word's meaning can often be determined. A careful reader may find clues to the meaning of the word in surrounding words, ideas, and attitudes.

Below are excerpts from the viewpoints in this chapter. One word is printed in italics. Try to determine the meaning of each word by reading the excerpt. Under each excerpt you will find four definitions for the italicized word. Choose the one that is closest to your understanding of the word.

Finally, use a dictionary to see how well you have understood the words in context. It will be helpful to discuss with others the clues which helped you decide on each word's meaning.

1. The government of Peru is an *INTRANSIGENT* debtor. It refuses to pay a few million dollars of interest, yet it has reserves of $1.2 billion.

   INTRANSIGENT means:
   a) stubborn   c) kind
   b) economic   d) careless

2. Critics of the IMF paint it as a rigid, biased organization dominated by a *CABAL* of wealthy countries whose secret manipulations hurt the Third World.

   CABAL means:
   a) conspiracy   c) church group
   b) liberal organization d) circus

3. *DIVERSIFIED* forms of financial aid—from banks, private businesses, governments, and international organizations—must increase to help Third World debtors.

DIVERSIFIED means:
a) identical
b) varied
c) monotonous
d) forgetful

4. Allowing world economic problems to be taken out on the growing minds and bodies of young children is the *ANTITHESIS* of civilized behavior. It shames us all.

ANTITHESIS means:
a) mathematical equation
b) group concern
c) statement of fact
d) exact opposite

5. As Third World nations deplete their natural resources, they face the loss of a *PATRIMONY* which could provide future generations with a comfortable means of living.

PATRIMONY means:
a) male relative
b) inheritance
c) forest
d) ruler

6. Just as banks take back the car when the buyer defaults on the loan, so US banks are *APPROPRIATING* pieces of the Third World as part of a solution to debt.

APPROPRIATING means:
a) taking
b) loaning
c) giving
d) selecting

7. As Third World debt has risen, bankers have shed their former *INSOUCIANCE* and recognized that the debt may not be repaid, thus hurting their profits. Now they are finally beginning to panic.

INSOUCIANCE means:
a) financial accounts
b) sadness
c) nonchalance
d) humor

8. The Fund's director defends the organization and *EXONERATES* it from any responsibility or social justice.

EXONERATES means:
a) to accuse
b) to ignore
c) to relieve of blame
d) to carefully plan

Periodical Bibliography

The following articles have been selected to supplement the diverse views presented in this chapter.

Jahangir Amuzegar — "Dealing with Debt," *Foreign Policy*, Fall 1987.

Pat Aufderheide and Bruce Rich — "Environmental Reform and the Multilateral Banks," *World Policy Journal*, Spring 1988.

Doug Bandow — "What's Still Wrong with the World Bank?" *Orbis*, Winter 1989.

Carol Barton — "Debt: New Plan, Old Ideas," *Christianity and Crisis*, May 22, 1989.

Tom Bethell — "Third World Hydraulics," *The American Spectator*, June 1989.

Fantu Cheru — "Development, Debt, and Dependency," *Multinational Monitor*, July/August 1988.

Barber Conable — "To Make the Baker Initiative Work, Fine-Tuning Is in Order," *Los Angeles Times*, January 3, 1989.

Antonio-Gabriel M. Cunha — "African Debt: A Light at the End of the Tunnel?" *Africa Report*, May/June 1987.

Kevin Danaher — "Debt Is Enslaving Africa to Global Economic Forces," *Los Angeles Times*, May 5, 1987.

Juan de Onis — "Don't Blame It on Debt," *Los Angeles Times*, June 4, 1989.

Hernando de Soto — "A Latin American View of the Brady Plan," *The Wall Street Journal*, May 19, 1989.

Ray Ekpu, interviewed by Barry Shelby — "Africa's Struggle Against Debts and Dictators," *World Press Review*, July 1988.

Malcolm S. Forbes Jr. — "Self-Made Crisis," *Forbes*, February 20, 1989.

Susan George — "Financing Ecocide in the Third World," *The Nation*, April 30, 1988.

Susan George — "Several Pounds of Flesh," *New Internationalist*, November 1988.

Robert T. Grieves

"Poverty as Pollution," *Forbes*, November 14, 1988.

Susanna Hecht and Alexander Cockburn

"Defenders of the Amazon," *The Nation*, May 22, 1989.

Fran Hosken

"Austerity's Human Toll," *The Humanist*, January/February 1989.

Cheddi Jagan

"Poverty: Causes and Cures," *World Marxist Review*, August 1988. Available from Imported Publications, 320 W. Ohio St., Chicago, IL 60610.

Peter T. Kilborn

"Debt Reduction: Ways To Do It," *The New York Times*, April 6, 1989.

Penny Lernoux

"Beggaring Our Latin Neighbors," *The Nation*, December 12, 1987.

George Marotta

"A Serious Global Problem," *The World & I*, February 1989.

William R. Milam

"Strategies for an LDC Debt Workout: A US Perspective," *Department of State Bulletin*, October 1988.

Bernard D. Nossiter

"Loan Sharks," *The Nation*, May 15, 1989.

Richard Rothstein

"The Human Cost of Misguided Policy," *Los Angeles Times*, October 5, 1987.

James L. Rowe Jr.

"Latin America's Cash Famine," *The Washington Post National Weekly Edition*, August 31, 1987.

Barbara Rudolph

"Enter the Brady Plan," *Time*, March 20, 1989.

Jeffrey Sachs

"Robbin' Hoods," *The New Republic*, March 13, 1989.

Irwin M. Stelzer

"Third World Deadbeats," *The American Spectator*, April 1989.

Roger D. Stone

"Why Save Tropical Forests?" *The New York Times*, November 8, 1986.

Roger Thurow

"Development Bank in Africa Transcends the Region's Despair," *The Wall Street Journal*, May 16, 1989.

Alvaro Umana

"Costa Rica's Debt-for-Nature Swaps Come of Age," *The Wall Street Journal*, May 26, 1989.

John Williamson

"A Few Kind Words About the IMF," *The Wall Street Journal*, April 3, 1989.

Organizations To Contact

The editors have compiled the following list of organizations which are concerned with the issues debated in this book. All of them have publications available for interested readers. The descriptions are derived from materials provided by the organizations. This list was compiled upon the date of publication. Names and phone numbers of organizations are subject to change.

Agri-Energy Roundtable
2550 M St. NW, Suite 300
Washington, DC 20037
(202) 887-0528

The Roundtable is an association whose members include oil company executives and international agribusiness leaders. It works to improve cooperation between developing nations and industrialized nations on food and energy issues. It publishes a quarterly newsletter, *Agri-Energy Report*, and numerous books such as *Managing Agro-Economic Peacekeeping: Trade and Development Realities for Food Security*.

The American Enterprise Institute for Public Policy Research (AEI)
1150 17th St. NW
Washington, DC 20036
(202) 862-5800

AEI is a conservative think tank that analyzes national and international economic, political, and social issues. It publishes the monthly *AEI Economist* and bimonthly *Public Opinion*, as well as numerous papers and books including *The International Monetary System: A Time of Turbulence*.

The Brookings Institution
1775 Massachusetts Ave. NW
Washington, DC 20036
(202) 797-6105

The Brookings Institution is a liberal think tank engaged in research, education, and publishing on important issues of foreign and domestic policy. It publishes the quarterly *Brookings Review* as well as a catalog of its books and other publications.

Cato Institute
224 2nd St. SE
Washington, DC 20003
(202) 546-0200

The Institute is a libertarian public policy research organization. It recommends minimal government interference in domestic affairs and noninterventionism in foreign affairs. Its publications include papers, books, the bimonthly *Policy Report*, and the triennial *Cato Journal*.

Center of Concern
3700 13th St. NE
Washington, DC 20017
(202) 635-2757

Center of Concern engages in social analysis, theological reflection, policy advocacy, and public education on issues of peace and justice. It advocates self-determination and economic independence for developing nations. Subjects of its workshops and writings include international development, women's roles, economic alternatives, and a theology based on justice for all peoples. It publishes a bimonthly newsletter, *Center Focus*, and books including *Dialogue on Debt: Alternative Analyses and Solutions*.

Committee for Production Sharing
1629 K St. NW
Washington, DC 20006
(202) 296-3232

The organization's members include manufacturers, customs personnel, banks, and civic groups. Its goal is to enhance US economic competitiveness by encouraging US multinational corporations to establish factories in the Third World. It publishes the monthly *Washington Bulletin* and a book, *Production Sharing: A Viable Alternative*.

Council on Foreign Relations
58 E. 68th St.
New York, NY 10021
(212) 734-0400

The Council studies the international aspects and impacts of American political, economic, and strategic problems. It publishes the *Foreign Affairs* journal five times a year.

Environmental Project on Central America
Earth Island International Center
13 Columbus Ave.
San Francisco, CA 94111
(415) 788-3666

The Project works to stop ecological devastation in Central America. It monitors US policy towards Central America from an environmental standpoint. It also works to educate the public about deforestation, pesticide use, and US-funded militarization in the Third World. It publishes regular *Green Papers* on these issues.

Exxon Corporation
Corporate and Public Affairs Department
PO Box 101
Florham Park, NJ 07932
(201) 765-7000

Exxon Corporation is a multinational petroleum business with worldwide commercial interests. Its search for untapped oil reserves leads it into many Third World countries where it conducts oil explorations. Exxon publishes a quarterly magazine, *The Lamp*, for its shareholders that is also available to others upon request.

The Heritage Foundation
214 Massachusetts Ave. NE
Washington, DC 20002
(202) 546-4400

The Foundation is a conservative public policy research institute. It supports competitive free enterprise as the basis for a viable world economy. One of its divisions, The Center for International Economic Growth, specializes in research on the Third World. In addition to hundreds of books and papers, the Foundation publishes a quarterly journal, *Policy Review*, the periodic *Backgrounder*, and the *Heritage Lectures* series.

The Hunger Project
1 Madison Ave., 8A
New York, NY 10010
(212) 532-4255

The Project is an educational organization committed to eliminating world hunger by the year 2000. It educates the public about the worldwide problem of hunger and starvation. Its semimonthly report of facts, trends, and opinion on international development, *World Development Forum*, is free.

Institute for Food and Development Policy (Food First)
145 9th St.
San Francisco, CA 94103
(415) 864-8555

The Institute provides research and education on world hunger issues. It believes that foreign aid is counterproductive and contends that world hunger can be eliminated if First World countries like the US allow Third World countries to take control of their own food production. The Institute publishes books, pamphlets, study guides and the quarterly *Food First News*.

Inter-Hemispheric Education Resource Center
Box 4506
Albuquerque, NM 87196
(505) 842-8288

The Center provides educational materials on issues such as human rights and oil and uranium exploration in underdeveloped areas. It opposes US policies in Central America and the Caribbean and informs the public about these. It publishes *Central American Factbook* and other books as well as a quarterly newsletter, *Resource Center Bulletin*.

International Monetary Fund (IMF)
700 19th St. NW
Washington, DC 20431
(202) 623-7000

The IMF's purpose is to promote international economic cooperation, to help keep a balance of trade among nations so that all benefit from the expansion of trade, and to lend its member nations money when necessary. It publishes the semimonthly *IMF Survey* and brochures including, "Ten Common Misperceptions About the IMF," "Helping the Poor: The IMF's New Facilities for Structural Adjustment," and "What Is the International Monetary Fund?"

Maryknoll Mission Center of New England
50 Dunster Road
Chestnut Hill, MA 02167
(617) 232-8050

The Center was established to increase awareness about the Third World. It provides educational materials on world hunger, the harmful effects of multinational corporations in the Third World, and US involvement in Central America. It publishes *Maryknoll* magazine monthly.

National Clearinghouse on Development Education (NCODE)
c/o American Forum for Education in a Global Age
45 John St., Suite 1200
New York, NY 10038
(212) 732-8606

NCODE provides the latest information on programs, materials, and practices in teaching about developing nations. Its goal is to ensure that American schools achieve and maintain a global perspective in education so that students become responsible citizens in a global age. NCODE publishes the *Global Resource Book*, *Global Yellow Pages*, and the monthly bulletin, *Access*.

Oxfam America
115 Broadway
Boston, MA 02116
(617) 482-1211

Oxfam America is part of a global network of organizations known as Oxfam that funds self-help projects in the Third World. The goal of these projects is that the recipients achieve economic self-reliance, particularly in food production. Oxfam publishes a triannual newsletter, factsheets on several topics related to development called *Facts for Action*, and numerous brochures, pamphlets and audiovisual materials.

Population Council
1 Dag Hammarskjold Plaza
New York, NY 10017
(212) 644-1300

The Council conducts research and provides technical support and services around the world in contraception technology, family planning, and population-related policymaking. It publishes the bimonthly *Studies in Family Planning*, and the quarterly *Population Development Review*.

Population Renewal Office
36 W. 59th St.
Kansas City, MO 64113
(816) 363-6980

The organization advocates world population growth and opposes population control. It believes a declining world population is more dangerous to human survival than overpopulation. It publishes brochures and articles on a variety of topics specific to population, such as, "Out of Africa: Some Population Truths."

Third World Women's Project
c/o Institute for Policy Studies
1601 Connecticut Ave. NW
Washington, DC 20009
(202) 234-9382, ext. 234

The Third World Women's Project is a program of the Institute for Policy Studies. It works toward global education on such issues as women in Third World development and human rights. The Project also provides policymakers and concerned citizens with a critical examination of US policies toward the Third World and offers alternative strategies for policymaking. The Project publishes the quarterly *Letelier-Moffitt Update* on its human rights project and a book, *A Dialogue on Third World Women: Learning Through the Humanities*.

Bibliography of Books

Kwamena Arquaah — *International Regulation and Transnational Corporations.* New York: Praeger, 1986.

Robert J. Berg and Jennifer Seymour — *Strategies for African Development.* Berkeley: University of California Press, 1986.

Peter L. Berger — *The Capitalist Revolution.* New York: Basic Books, 1986.

Peter L. Berger and Michael Novak — *Speaking to the Third World: Essays on Democracy and Development.* Washington, DC: American Enterprise Institute, 1987.

Phillip Berryman — *Liberation Theology.* Philadelphia: Temple University Press, 1987.

Jeanne Bisilliat and Michèle Fiéloux — *Women of the Third World.* Cranbury, NJ: Associated University Presses, 1987.

Willy Brandt — *Arms and Hunger.* New York: Pantheon Books, 1986.

Sue Branford and Bernardo Kucinski — *The Debt Squads: The US, the Banks, and Latin America.* London: Zed Books, 1988.

Pascal Bruckner — *The Tears of the White Man.* New York: The Free Press, 1986.

Fidel Castro — *The World Crisis.* London: Zed Books, 1984.

Bernard Chidzero and Altaf Gauhar — *Linking the South.* London: Third World Foundation, 1986.

Kathleen Corbett and Karl Borgin — *The Destruction of a Continent.* New York: Harcourt Brace Jovanovich, 1982.

Miranda Davies — *Third World, Second Sex.* Vol. 2. London: Zed Books, 1987.

Samuel Decalo — *Psychoses of Power: African Personal Dictatorships.* Boulder, CO: Westview Press, 1989.

Javier Perez de Cuellar — *External Debt Crisis and Development.* New York: United Nations, 1988.

Hernando de Soto — *The Other Path.* New York: Harper & Row, 1989.

Margaret Garritsen de Vries — *Balance of Payments Adjustment, 1945 to 1986: The IMF Experience.* Washington, DC: International Monetary Fund, 1987.

Frederic D. Deyo, ed. — *The Political Economy of the New Asian Industrialism.* Ithaca, NY: Cornell University Press, 1987.

René Dumont — *Stranglehold on Africa.* London: Andre Deutsch, 1983.

Nicholas Eberstadt — *Foreign Aid and American Purpose.* Washington, DC: American Enterprise Institute, 1988.

Nicholas Eberstadt — *The Poverty of Communism.* New Brunswick, NJ: Transaction Books, 1987.

258

Paul R. Ehrlich and John P. Holdren	*The Cassandra Conference: Resources and the Human Predicament.* College Station, TX: Texas A&M University Press, 1988.
Richard Fagan, et al., eds.	*Transition and Development: Problems of Third World Socialism.* New York: Monthly Review Press, 1986.
Richard E. Feinberg and Valeriana Kallab, eds.	*Environment and the Poor.* New Brunswick, NJ: Transaction Books, 1989.
Deane William Ferm	*Third World Liberation Theologies.* Maryknoll, NY: Orbis Books, 1986.
Lewis Feuer	*Imperialism and the Anti-Imperialist Mind.* Buffalo, NY: Prometheus Books, 1986.
Galia Golan	*The Soviet Union and National Liberation Movements in the Third World.* Boston: Unwin & Hyman, 1988.
Gustavo Gutiérrez	*A Theology of Liberation.* Maryknoll, NY: Orbis Books, 1988.
Peter C.W. Gutkind and Immanuel Wallerstein	*Political Economy of Contemporary Africa.* Beverly Hills, CA: Sage Publications, 1985.
Steve H. Hanke, ed.	*Privatization and Development.* San Francisco: Institute for Contemporary Studies, 1987.
Lawrence E. Harrison	*Underdevelopment Is a State of Mind.* Lanham, MD: University Press of America, 1985.
Jerry F. Hough	*The Struggle for the Third World: Soviet Debates and American Options.* Washington, DC: The Brookings Institution, 1986.
Jacqueline R. Kasun	*The War Against Population.* San Francisco: Ignatius Press, 1988.
S.K. Kaushik, ed.	*International Banking and World Economic Growth.* New York: Praeger, 1987.
Michael Klare and Peter Kornbluh	*Low Intensity Warfare.* New York: Pantheon Books, 1988.
Melvyn B. Krauss	*Development Without Aid.* New York: McGraw-Hill, 1982.
Gerald J. Kruijer	*Development Through Liberation.* Atlantic Highlands, NJ: Humanities Press, 1987.
Frances Moore Lappé and Joseph Collins	*World Hunger: Ten Myths.* San Francisco: Institute for Food and Development Policy, 1982.
John P. Lewis and Valeriana Kallab, eds.	*Development Strategies Reconsidered.* New Brunswick, NJ: Transaction Books, 1986.
John P. Lewis, et al.	*Strengthening the Poor: What Have We Learned?* New Brunswick, NJ: Transaction Books, 1988.
Ellen L. Lutz, Hurst Hannum, and Kathryn J. Burke, eds.	*New Directions in Human Rights.* Philadelphia: University of Pennsylvania Press, 1989.
Charles K. Mann and Barbara Huddleston	*Food Policy.* Bloomington, IN: Indiana University Press, 1986.
Philip Mattera	*Off the Books.* London: Pluto Press, 1985.
James H. Mittelman	*Out from Underdevelopment.* London: Macmillan Press, 1988.

Paul Mosley	*Foreign Aid: Its Defense and Reform.* Lexington, KY: The University Press of Kentucky, 1987.
Ashis Nandy	*The Intimate Enemy: Loss and Recovery of Self Under Colonialism.* Oxford: Oxford University Press, 1983.
Bernard D. Nossiter	*The Global Struggle for More.* New York: Harper & Row, 1987.
Michael Novak	*Liberation Theology and the Liberal Society.* Washington, DC: American Enterprise Institute, 1987.
Nzongola-Ntalaja	*Revolution and Counter-Revolution in Africa.* London: Zed Books, 1987.
Emilio A. Núñez	*Liberation Theology.* Chicago: Moody Press, 1985.
Michael Parenti	*The Sword and the Dollar: Imperialism, Revolution, and the Arms Race.* New York: St. Martin's Press, 1989.
Charles S. Pearson, ed.	*Multinational Corporations, Environment, and the Third World.* Durham, NC: Duke University Press, 1987.
Alejandro Portes, Manuel Castells, and Lauren A. Benton, eds.	*The Informal Economy: Studies in Advanced and Less Developed Countries.* Baltimore, MD: The Johns Hopkins University Press, 1989.
John P. Powelson and Richard Stock	*The Peasant Betrayed: Agriculture and Land Reform in the Third World.* Boston: Oelgeschlager, Gunn & Hain, 1987.
Carlos Rangel	*Third World Ideology and Western Reality.* New Brunswick, NJ: Transaction Books, 1986.
Richard D. Robinson	*The International Transfer of Technology.* Cambridge, MA: Ballinger Publishing Co., 1988.
W.W. Rostow	*Rich Countries and Poor Countries.* Boulder, CO: Westview Press, 1987.
Sam C. Sarkesian	*The New Battlefield: The United States and Unconventional Conflicts.* Westport, CT: Greenwood Press, 1986.
Scott R. Sidell	*The IMF and Third World Political Instability: Is There a Connection?* London: Macmillan Press, 1988.
Hans Singer, John Wood, and Tony Jennings	*Food Aid: The Challenge and Opportunity.* Oxford: Clarendon Press, 1987.
Douglas D. Southgate and John F. Disinger, eds.	*Sustainable Resource Development in the Third World.* Boulder, CO: Westview Press, 1987.
Jennifer Seymour Whitaker	*How Can Africa Survive?* New York: Harper & Row, 1988.
Alan Woods	*Development and the National Interest: US Economic Assistance into the 21st Century.* Washington, DC: Agency for International Development, 1989.
Aguibou Y. Yansané, ed.	*Decolonization and Dependency.* Westport, CT: Greenwood Press, 1980.

Index